FINGERPRINTS
OF GOD

Evidences from Near-Death Studies, Scientific Research on Creation, and Mormon Theology

ARVIN S. GIBSON

Foreword by KENNETH RING

First Printing: October 1999

International Standard Book Number:
0-88290-674-7

Horizon Publishers' Catalog and Order Number:
1258

Printed and distributed
in the United States of America by

& Distributors, Incorporated

Mailing Address:
P.O. Box 490
Bountiful, Utah 84011-0490

Street Address:
50 South 500 West
Bountiful, Utah 84010

Local Phone: (801) 295-9451
WATS (toll free): 1 (800) 453-0812
FAX: (801) 295-0196

E-mail: horizonp@burgoyne.com
Internet: http://www.horizonpublishers.com

The complexities of the creation of the universe are summarized from the "beginning" to the present. The methodical application of proven scientific facts and logic leaves a vanishingly small window for skeptics to proffer a credible alternative to Gibson's premise of a God-centered universe.

—Philip R. Pluta, Ph.D., Nuclear Engineer.

This book offers a profoundly exciting approach to the consideration of a divine creation of life and the universe. It is solidified with scientific, physical and spiritual support.

—Fred L. Beckett, Utah State Mycobacteriologist.

A fascinating and powerfully grounded work. Arvin Gibson has combined his understanding of science with his tireless investigations of the near-death experience. The result will captivate and educate you.

—Lynn D. Johnson, Ph. D., Psychologist.

Arvin Gibson teaches us that God's fingerprints are pressed into the physical creations of the cosmos. He clarifies that science and religion are just different hands of a whole body of truth.

—B. Grant Bishop,
Physician and Author of *The LDS Gospel of Light.*

The science versus religion debate is taken to a new level, posing some challenges to science-oriented skeptics that cannot easily be explained away. And the logical transition from NDEs to the everlasting gospel of Jesus Christ is fascinating. It gives us a peek into eternity.

—Jon M. Taylor, Ph.D.,
Businessman and Author of *The Network Marketing Game.*

Arvin Gibson shares with us the benefits of his own search for truth, and he shows how apparent conflicts between science and religion disappear in the growing light of truth. Ultimately, as he explains, truth embraces all legitimate science and religion.

—Craig R. Lundahl, Ph.D.,
Sociologist, Near-Death Researcher; Co-author of *The Eternal Journey* and Author of *The Nature of Humanity* and the *State of America,* and *The End of Time* and *The Millennium of Peace.*

Front and back cover pictures: Each photograph was taken by the Hubble Space Telescope orbiting the earth. Spiral galaxy NGC 4414 is 60 million light-years away. The bright center contains older yellow and red stars. The outer regions show young blue stars and clouds of interstellar dust. Nebula NGC 3603 shows star birth and death. The bright star clusters in the black field are young blue stars. The single bright star to their upper right is a blue giant near the end of life. The yellow-orange gases are cast off dust from dying stars and supernova.

Contents

Dedicated to the memory of
Donald L. Wood (DeLynn),
a fabulous and courageous man
whose life was an example
to all who knew him.

Acknowledgments

This book would not exist save for the efforts and encouragement of many people. First among those is that exquisite lady, Carol Gibson, whom I somehow was wise enough to marry forty-nine years ago in Berkeley, California. Carol assisted me in many aspects of this book. She acted as a research assistant in helping with references and with the original interviews of those people who had near-death experiences.

Upon completion of the publication of my last book, a novel, Duane Crowther of Horizon Publishers and Distributors asked me when I was going to write a really serious book. At the time I was tired from writing three other books that he published so I declined. Four years and much introspection later I decided that Duane was right, hence this book. Much of those portions of the book which deal with near-death experiences draws from the material published in the earlier books. Horizon Publishers and Distributors, Inc., of Bountiful, Utah, graciously granted permission to use that material.

Craig R. Lundahl was co-author with me on an earlier paper submitted for publication to the *Journal of Near-Death Experiences*. This is the primary technical journal of the International Association for Near-Death Studies (IANDS). The paper we submitted was entitled, *Near-Death Studies and Modern Physics*. Considerable information in this book was taken from that paper including large portions of Craig's research materials. I am indebted to Craig for his stellar effort and to Human Sciences Press, Inc., for their permission to use that material in this book. At the time that this book went to press the article was also in press for Volume 18 of the *Journal of Near-Death Studies*.

In 1994 Carol and I interviewed Theresa Holland who had an extensive near-death experience. Portions of her experience are included in this book by reason of her gracious permission and that of her publisher. A more complete version of her story is included in her book *Only Your Heart Will Know*, published by Temple Publishing of Ohio.

Also, in 1996, Jake was interviewed in our home after calling me from Colorado and expressing an interest in telling of his NDE. Jake's story was especially interesting since it is the only recorded NDE that I am aware of where an entire group of people had a simultaneous NDE—as a result of fighting an out-of-control forest fire. Jake kindly granted permission to print portions of his NDE.

Most recently, in 1999, Carol and I interviewed Dan, George Thompson and Sylvia. They were chosen as a diverse group specifically for this book, and we are indebted for their substantial assistance.

Several individuals read earlier drafts of the book and offered helpful comments. Included in that group were: Phil Pluta, Craig Lundahl, B. Grant Bishop, Aaron Gibson, Martin Tanner, Tim Hunt, David Conklin, Rose Mari Finter, Marian Bergin, Harold Widdison, Leanne Mayo, Jon Taylor, Steve Tomsik, Lynn Johnson, Aldene Preston, Janis Gibson and J. Rand Thurgood. Many others also read early versions of the book and offered encouragement to the author.

Melvin Morse, who has contributed substantially to NDE research by his work with children, also helped me in several areas in the book. In particular he suggested a restructuring of the book from an earlier version. Dr. Morse also contributed with his thoughts on the function of the right temporal lobe of the brain during an NDE.

A special debt of gratitude is extended to Kenneth Ring for his continued encouragement and very helpful comments advanced during the evolution of this book. He offered a unique perspective which was extremely helpful to the author. And, of course, I am grateful for the kind Foreword which Dr. Ring provided.

The local chapter of The International Association for Near-Death Studies (IANDS of Utah) continues to provide assistance to Carol and me in numerous ways. In particular, Bill English and Sandra Cherry gave help in key areas important to the production of this book.

This book could not have been written without the decades of work by the many scientists, researchers and writers who labored in the fields of cosmology, physics, astronomy, mathematics, chemistry, anthropology, geology, biology and biochemistry. Information in much of this book was gleaned from their magnificent effort. They have made possible an understanding—although ever changing—of our universe and our world which provides significant insight into how we came to be.

Similarly, physicians, psychiatrists, psychologists, sociologists, other researchers, and above all, those who have had near-death experiences, have given us an appreciation of this unique phenomenon which was largely unknown fifty years ago. George Ritchie, Raymond Moody, and Kenneth Ring in their pioneering work gave me the impetus to launch my own research effort on NDEs. I am indebted to all of these people.

Above all, though, I must acknowledge the Word produced under revelation from God by prophets through the centuries. That Word has come down to us as scriptures and other prophetic utterances which represent pure Light and Truth.

Although the data included in this book comes from many sources—as witnessed by the Notes and Bibliography Sections—the thoughts which tie them together are my own. If there are errors of judgment or overstatements based on the facts presented, please, dear reader, accept my apology. It is my hope, however, that you will sense, as I did in gathering the information, the awesome import of the evolving story derived from such different sources.

Birth and Death of Stars

This photograph, taken from the orbiting Hubble Telescope, shows Nebula NGC 3603 where stars are dying and being created. The bright cluster of stars in the upper-left-center are new, blue stars. The gasses and star dust are from exploding supernova. The bright spots in the gasees are new stars being born.

Foreword

by Kenneth Ring, Ph.D.,

*(Kenneth Ring is Professor Emeritus of Psychology at the University of Connecticut and Co-Founder and Past President of the International Association for Near-Death Studies. Doctor Ring has done extensive research in the field of near-death studies and has written numerous books and articles on the subject. His writings include **Life at Death, Heading Toward Omega, The Omega Project,** and **Mindsight**. He is recognized world-wide as an authority on NDEs, and his latest book, **Lessons from the Light**, is a defining work for researchers and lay-persons alike.)*

The author of this book and the author of this foreword constitute an unlikely pair. Arvin Gibson is by temperament a man of science, by training a mechanical engineer who devoted much of his career to research and development in the field of nuclear energy, and by family tradition, a lifetime Mormon deeply committed to his faith. I, on the other hand, grew up a deracinated Jew, with no interest in religion of any kind, who, lacking any gift for the hard sciences or mathematics, drifted into psychology as an undergraduate and eventually became a university professor with a speciality in the social psychology of interpersonal relations. Nevertheless, after we each followed the trail of our very divergent talents and interests into lives that, apart from their professional callings, could scarcely have been more different, we ultimately discovered that we were long-lost brothers.

How we came to this improbable but undeniable realization is a story that can briefly be told. Since Arvin tells his in this book, which is essentially an account of his own intellectual and spiritual journey the fruits of whose wisdom he is understandably eager to share, I will take just a moment here to describe the path I followed that led to our linkage. In 1977, while in my early 40s, I became interested in the study of near-death experiences (NDEs), and have spent much of the twenty-plus years since exploring and writing about them. In the course of doing so, I found that the atheism of my younger years was insupportable and, *mirabile dictu*, I no longer had any doubt about God's existence and in fact came to believe that God was intimately involved in the orchestration of NDEs. Indeed, over the years, I have sometimes found myself standing in the pulpit of Christian churches where I have been asked to talk about NDEs and reflecting on the ironies, given my own origins and still vivid recollections of how such settings were long utterly alien to me, that I should now be seemingly so at ease in these houses of God. I especially remember the aftermath of one such talk when a member of the congregation came up and told me in a loud voice what an "inspiring Christian message" I had just delivered. You can imagine how I chuckled to myself at that one!

About a dozen years after I had started my work on NDEs, Arvin, now retired from his professional career, began his. As he mentions in this book, to some extent he based the research he carried out with his wife, Carol, on my earlier studies, but at any rate over the next few years Arvin produced several books on NDEs and quickly established himself as one of the new important investigators of the phenomenon. Sometime during the mid-'90s, I became aware of his work, admired it, quoted from it in my own writings and lectures, and regularly read his articles in The Journal of Near-Death Studies. When I was invited to give some talks on NDEs at Brigham Young University in the fall of 1997, we finally met briefly, but about a year later, at the annual conference of the International Association for Near-Death Studies in Salt Lake City, we had a chance to have an in depth conversation and that was where we really connected in a deeply personal way.

At that time, we found that we had more in common than we had imagined—quite apart from our interests in NDEs. For example, it turned out that we both graduated from the University of California at Berkeley in the 1950s (I later learned that we even lived on the same street), and the area where I was now living was one that Arvin knew very well. We also had had quite a few similar health concerns in recent years that had threatened to interfere with or even terminate our work on NDEs, and as we shared the stories of those challenges with each other, that seemed to create still another bond between us. At that same meeting, Arvin mentioned to me the work that he was then engaged with—the writing of the book you now hold in your hands—and made it clear that he regarded it as the final distillation of what he felt he had learned from his years of research, study and reflection, not only in regard to the NDE, but drawing on his scientific and religious training and experiences as well. As I had just published a book that had attempted to sum up what I felt were the essential lessons of the NDE, based on my two-decade-long involvement in the field of NDE research, which was to be my final contribution to this domain, once again it appeared that Arvin and I were involved in a similar undertaking, indicative of still another commonality between us.

Naturally, he was keen to have me read the draft of his book, and eventually, in the course of some very warm e-mail correspondence that followed our meeting in Salt Lake, he did me the very great honor of asking me to write the foreword to it. By then, of course, I could scarcely do otherwise; we had become great buddies, and I had grown very fond of Arvin personally in addition to the respect that I already had for his work. Thus it was that this life-long Mormon hooked up with an irreligious Jew who will now turn to the proper subject of this foreword, Arvin's book itself.

To begin with, it needs to be said that this is a book that weaves together the three major strands of Arvin's own search for meaning in life—science, which came first; the study of near-death experiences, which came last; and Mormonism, which was there throughout but which Arvin came to appreciate anew after his immersion in near-death studies. Although these three strands are obviously independent realms of knowledge, it is Arvin's gift and special task in this book to show their intimate interrelationships so that they can be seen, in effect, as three shining jewels in the crown of God. For it is God that is at the center of this book whose traces (or "fingerprints," to use Arvin's metaphor) are to be found, once one knows where and how to look, in the story that modern science now tells about how the universe came into being and how life emerged on this planet, in the evidence of a spiritual world provided by NDEs, and in the revelations issuing from Mormonism's prophet, Joseph Smith, which Arvin shows to be broadly congruent with both the scientific story of creation and the findings of contemporary NDE research.

Because of the particular combination of his interests, talents and background, Arvin is a man who is uniquely fitted to know where and how to look for these traces, for he is equipped to see what others, especially the young in quest of life's meaning, might easily overlook or fail to recognize. Arvin is in fact a marvelous pattern-analyzer who, because he is so at home in the worlds of science, near-death studies and Mormonism, can show us unmistakably that only the invisible hand of God could have produced the traces in the patterns Arvin helps us to discern. But—and please mark this—it is not just the patterns within these domains, but those that bridge them that Arvin is at pains to make clear in this book. Science and religion, far from being in conflict, reflect the same underlying patterns and, in a certain sense, one crucial link between them is to be found in the same subject that unites Arvin and me, the NDE.

And indeed in this domain, Arvin and I do share a lot of common ground, particularly in regard to our skepticism that anyone will be able to frame a convincing reductive, purely physical or biological explanation of the NDE and in our viewpoint that God's fingerprints are all over this phenomenon. In any event, both the research that Arvin cites in this connection and the many case histories from his own investigations he offers in this book certainly make a powerful and, to me, compelling brief for his thesis.

Nevertheless, as you might very well expect, Arvin and I do not see eye-to-eye on all matters related to NDEs. For example, in one of his appendices, he casts a very cold glance on some of the data that suggest reincarnation might be a part of the NDE story and takes several pages to counter that position by laying out some objections that almost everyone, including partisans of this hypothesis, would not take exception to. Frankly, this section troubled me, not because of the stance that Arvin takes on this matter, but because there was in his tone here something uncharacteristic—an element of derision, snideness and even harsh dismissal that seemed unnecessary.

It is not my purpose here to enter into this debate (although I do not have any particular stake in this hypothesis, one way or the other), since countless words have already been expended on this issue over the centuries without its being resolved, but I think it is nevertheless instructive to look at it from another angle altogether.

Obviously, Arvin is an unlikely candidate to carry the banner of reincarnation into the NDE fray because of his commitment to Mormonism, and even if the evidence for the NDE-reincarnation link were strong and undeniable, it would be a problem for him since his faith would not permit him to endorse such a doctrine. However, unlike some other Mormon NDE writers and near-death experiencers, Arvin is completely upfront about his allegiance to Mormonism and his conviction that its tenets are true; likewise, he acknowledges that, like anyone, he comes to the NDE with his own biases, which need to be factored into any assessment of his conclusions.

This is no picayune matter, and, frankly, I think it would be a disservice to Arvin and the value of his book to gloss over it. The reason I want to bring this to the fore is precisely because I want Arvin's work to gain a broad audience and not, as I believe has been largely true for his previous books, to appeal to and be read predominantly by persons already affiliated with LDS who will, by and large, find in it what they know from their own faith to be true. The danger, however, is that because of Arvin's open avowal of Mormonism and its use in the subtitle of his book, he will be dismissed by a larger public as "just another Mormon writer with an axe to grind."

Let's face it: There are many books and articles already published on NDEs that seem to bear the mark of such religious axes, and that clearly reflect the convictions of their authors that their particular religious faith or spiritual tradition has a privileged purchase on the NDE. Persons writing from various Christian perspectives, from mainstream denominations to smaller sects, have made these claims; some Tibetan Buddhists have done likewise; and then there are the Theosophists, the followers of A Course in Miracles, and New Agers of various stripes and shadings, and so on—people representing the most diverse beliefs have all wanted to hitch a ride on the NDE wagon and take over its reins. How can this motley collection of contenders all be so ardent and insistent that their claim should be honored, and how can we know which one of them is in the right?

Readers who are members of LDS or are familiar with the history of its founder, Joseph Smith, will appreciate the irony here because this was precisely the question that initiated his quest for the truth. He was confused by the welter of claims and counterclaims that were to be found among the competing Christian sects of his day and, realizing that they could not all be true, sought in the most earnest way to find out which one was. The reader of this book must in effect ask the same question.

Of course, I will not presume to answer this question for others, but I would like at least to share the answer that has been provided to me by my twenty-plus years of exploring the NDE. In my view, the reason that so many diverse groups can latch onto the NDE and seek to adopt it as their own is that the NDE has certain universal features that are found in many of the world great religions and spiritual traditions, including, as Arvin makes pellucid in this book, Mormonism. The Light, the separation of the spirit from the body at death, the life review, and so many of the other familiar components of the NDE are not the unique property of any one of these faiths or spiritual systems but present in many of them, and therefore the NDE does not necessarily compel an allegiance to any one church, teaching or doctrine.

Any careful reader of Arvin's book will find that, far from its being doctrinaire, it argues precisely for this understanding and Arvin illustrates this in a most beautiful way.

At the same conference where Arvin and I met, one of the keynote speakers was a man named Howard Storm. Howard has become quite celebrated in NDE circles because of having had a most unusual NDE, the result of which was that he ceased being an atheistic art professor and became in time a very dedicated and effective pastor of the United Church of Christ. What is especially important for us in this context—and this is the story Arvin himself tells in full in his book, to striking effect—is that Howard, too, during his NDE was led to ask his spiritual guides the same question that prompted Joseph Smith to initiate his religious quest in 1820: What was the true religion?

Howard of course was not destined to be a prophet, but "only" a pastor; still, it is very instructive to consider the answer he received, which was, "The best religion is the religion that brings you closest to God." This, to me, also sums up the real treasure that is to be found in Arvin's book—it is not a disguised call to Mormonism at all, much less an attempt to convert readers to it. Rather it is a book that leads us back to God by helping us to see God's hand in all the domains that Arvin's own life and unique talents have enabled him to explore so deeply and thus fashion him into the expert guide for any reader who would take this journey with him.

Now, with this larger context and purpose in mind, we can come back to the particular contribution Arvin does make in regard to his own faith, Mormonism, which receives an extensive treatment, in the light of the NDE, in this book. Clearly, as is well known, there are many teachings in LDS that are very consonant with the implications of NDEs, and, furthermore, Arvin gives a few examples of NDErs, some of whom I also know, who found these congruencies so impressive and spiritually authoritative that they converted to LDS. I have no doubt that some readers of this book, whether they are affiliated with LDS or not, after noting the many parallels that Arvin points out between the doctrines of his church and the NDE, will have cause to think deeply about their significance and be grateful to Arvin for his exegesis on these matters.

But to me, what Arvin's work makes plain is just why so many Mormons have already been attracted to the NDE, and that is this: Mormonism, by virtue of its very origins and traditions, is a religion of direct personal revelation, and one's own testimony concerning one's spiritual experiences are given high value. The same thing, obviously, is true of NDEs. Both Mormonism and the NDE are really expressions of the same gnostic impulse that is the source of religious renewal that helps to break down encrusted and fossilized forms of religion worship. The Mormon experience was a breakthrough, by the gnostic revelation of an inspired prophet, that gave rise to an entirely new expression and understanding of Christianity. The NDE, too, has given fresh impetus and new life to perennial religious ideas in need of revitalization. Thus, because of what is universal in Mormonism and NDEs and common between them, members of LDS and near-death-experiencers are bound to have a natural sympathy for each other, and certain Mormon NDE researchers and their irreligious Jewish counterparts can discover that they are brethren after all.

Kenneth Ring, Ph.D.

Millennial Thoughts

The first printing of this book occurs as the millennial clock begins its turn into the twenty-first century. Much has been written of an introspective nature concerning the passing from the old into a new thousand-year period.

Although this book is not about history, as such, it is about a search for truth. In the process of describing the paths the author followed in trying to find the truth, inevitably those paths led to a study of certain key historic individuals and of their contributions to the cause of truth.

Two individuals loom inordinately large in the pages of this book. One of them made his initial contribution in the nineteenth century and the other marked the pages of history with his accomplishments beginning in the early part of the twentieth century. The deeds of both of these giants of history will continue to ricochet through time, building a majestic legacy that is still only dimly appreciated.

Joseph Smith, Jr., the young American prophet, born in humble circumstances in 1805, in his short life of 38½ years set in motion a religious movement that was and is unique in its foundations and theology. By any measure, his contribution to religious thought and action is prodigious.

Albert Einstein, the Swiss patent clerk, was twenty-six years old when he developed the special theory of relativity in 1905. He published the general theory of relativity in 1916. Those two theories changed our very concept of the universe, how it came to be, and how it worked. From the smallest particles of matter to the limitless cosmos, all were shown to be subject to the laws of relativity, and the way we and future generations lived were changed forever.

As you follow my paths to truth, therefore, be aware of these two individuals who stand as giants astride their own millennia. Perhaps the new millennium will usher in another of their caliber. Let us pray that it be so.

Introduction

From Skeptic to Believer

Why This Book?

The title of this book is *Fingerprints of God*, and the subtitle illustrates three such fingerprints. They are fingerprints which provide evidence of God's intimate association with his earthly children, of his handiwork in the architecture of the universe and the world, and of his continuing communication with prophets. During my lifetime I have been privileged to work and be closely associated with people involved in near-death studies, in the physical sciences, and in The Church of Jesus Christ of Latter-day Saints (Mormons).

This book, therefore, is my attempt to show what I have found to be true; namely, that near-death studies, scientific research on creation, and Mormon theology all serve as evidence for the existence of a living and a loving God.

Beginnings

Although my roots were founded in Mormonism—both my parents were practicing members of The Church of Jesus Christ of Latter-day Saints—my year during World War II spent on Iwo Jima, and my graduation from the University of California in Berkeley had made a skeptic of me. Berkeley taught me the value of a structured approach to the search for truth with a strong reliance on the scientific method. To me, the self-correcting techniques of modern science, with their accumulation of evidence through trial and error, were superior means for finding truth compared with the spiritual approach demanded by most religions—including my own.

It took me some years to recognize that there are other types of evidence than the physical forms of evidence so appealing to most scientists, and these other forms could be just as compelling in their persuasive power as were the more material forms of evidence. In particular, although derided by many if not most of the scientific community, certain spiritual sensations and feelings appeared to have the power to persuade and to change the lives of those who became practitioners of the techniques. At first this troubled me, but thanks to an understanding wife I initially suspended judgment concerning spiritually derived truths, and ultimately I came to embrace such truths. How this came to be and what forms of evidence changed my mind are the subject of this book.

Early Work in Nuclear Energy

My first job after graduation from college was with Bechtel Corporation, the giant construction and engineering firm headquartered in San Francisco. One of their projects was a government sponsored classified effort to study the peaceful application of nuclear energy. It was at Bechtel that I developed my first love affair with nuclear energy. It was, to me, obviously the answer to the world's appetite and need for an almost limitless energy—with few of the adverse pollutants so common from oil- and coal-fired energy sources.

Bechtel was sufficient to kindle my interest, but it was not sufficient to satisfy my desire for direct participation in the development of nuclear energy. As a result I worked successively for Advanced Technology Laboratories, Atomics International and General Electric Company. All of these companies had government contracts involved in the research and development of nuclear energy, and I quickly became deeply enmeshed in that research effort.

A Troubling Experience

When just a youth my parents described to me an experience my father had before I was born where he had two massive heart attacks, the second of which they claimed killed him. He passed, they said, into another world of peace and beauty. My mother, a person of great faith, sent for a local Mormon Bishop who gave my father a blessing and he returned to life.

Following is a partial accounting of the experience as related to me by my father, Marshall Stuart Gibson, when I was a young man. He only told the experience a few times in his lifetime; each time was a spiritual event. The account is taken from the book *In Search of Angels* which provides a more complete description of the incident.

. . . I found myself walking . . . in a completely different sphere. It was beautiful beyond description and we were walking on a path. . . . It was a different world than this one. . . . As we walked along the path I noticed a profusion of flowers and trees. They were of a wider variety, and they had many more colors than on earth—or maybe it was that I could see more colors than on earth, I'm not sure.

. . . I noticed someone on the path ahead of us. As we got closer to the individual I could see and feel that he was a magnificent person. I felt overwhelmed as I looked at him. He was bathed in light. [My guide] asked if I knew who that was, and I answered yes. It was Jesus Christ.

When we got close to the Savior, I felt a tremendous love emanating from him. It's hard to describe, but you could feel it all around him. And I felt a similar enormous love for him. I fell at his feet—not because I thought about it, but I couldn't stand. I felt an overpowering urge to fall at his feet and worship him.

. . . As I knelt there at the feet of this marvelous being I became conscious of my past life being reviewed for me. It seemed to occur in a short period, and I felt the Savior's love during the entire process. That love was . . . well, it was everywhere. And it was as if we could communicate with each other without speaking. After a period the Savior reached down and I knew I should stand. As soon as I stood, he left.

[My guide] next led me to a city. It was a city of light. It was similar to cities on earth in that there were buildings and paths, but the buildings and paths appeared to be built of materials which we consider precious on earth. They looked like marble, and gold, and silver, and other bright materials, only they were different. The buildings and streets seemed to have a sheen and to glow. The entire scene was one of indescribable beauty.

. . . There was a feeling of love and peace. On earth there always seems to be something . . . you know how things bother you here. There's always some problem troubling you—either it's health, or money, or people, or war—or something. That was missing there. I felt completely at peace, as if there were no problems which were of concern. It wasn't that there were no challenges. It's just that everything seemed to be under control. It was such a wonderful feeling that I never wanted to lose it.

And there was the feeling of love. Love from . . . from Jesus Christ. It emanated from him, and it was all around; it was everywhere. . . .

The event described by my father occurred in 1922 while he was working in Bingham, Utah for Western Union, and was the result of a massive heart attack. My mother, my grandmother, and my aunt were present during the attack. My father ultimately recovered and lived a full life, passing away in 1963.

For many years I was troubled by what my father and mother told me about his experience. I knew that they never lied, and they insisted that it was real, but I wondered whether what he described could not have happened by some other means. Perhaps he had a bad meal and hallucinated, I wondered; but whenever I spoke of it to my parents they insisted that it was real. As my mother expressed it: "Your father was as cold and dead as a mackerel from the fish market when I tried to wake him."

For some years I put this troubling incident concerning my father in the back of my mind and vigorously pursued what was by then a major interest in my life, nuclear energy and its development. Science and its accomplishments seemed a fruitful path to follow, both from a pragmatic point of view—I could make a good living at it—and from the intellectual satisfaction that it offered in my, as yet, unrecognized search for truth.

Probabilistic Analysis

From my work in nuclear energy it became clear that the basic designs of nuclear cores depended upon predictions of how neutrons would behave in an uncertain stew of moving neutrons colliding and reacting with the atoms of the reactor cauldron. A new vocabulary was developed to help describe what, at first, seemed almost indescribable.

Nuclear analysis, by its very nature, required the use of probabilistic techniques. There was no way to predict the action of any one neutron in a reactor core. Instead, probabilities were used to make predictions of how, *on average*, a large group of neutrons would behave.

During this period of intense nuclear activity I gained immense respect for the scientific method—and especially for the tools of probabilistic analysis. It was clear from the nuclear field that although precise deterministic predictions of all natural phenomena could not yield useful results, the mathematics of probability could often accomplish what otherwise would have been impossible.

And it was clear from reading and studying the research from other fields, including those of astrophysics and biology, that similar results were being achieved. Probabilistic analyses coupled with the power of modern computers were producing data with predictable and repeatable outcomes in areas previously impossible even to consider.

It was inevitable, therefore, that scientists would attempt to determine, by means of these same tools, whether life could have appeared spontaneously on the earth. One of the first, and one of the most impressive, books I read on the subject was Human Destiny by Lecomte du Noüy.[1] Dr. du Noüy was an internationally known French Scientist, born in Paris in 1883 and educated at the Sorbonne. From 1927 to 1937 he served as head of the Bio-Physics division of the Pasteur Institute. He escaped Nazi occupation of France in 1942 and served out the rest of his life in the United States.

In *Human Destiny*, published in 1947, Lecomte du Noüy used the mathematics of probability to address two questions: What is the probability that life could have come into being spontaneously? and, was there sufficient time after the earth cooled for life to have appeared by accidental means?

For the first question du Noüy showed that the probability that a configuration of a degree of disymmetry 0.9 (90 percent unsymmetrical) would appear spontaneously was 2.02×10^{-321}, or two chances out of 10^{321}. Most mathematicians consider 1 chance in 10^{50} to be impossible. Dr. du Noüy further explained that a single living cell would be significantly more complex than the simplified example he used and would, therefore, have an even greater improbability of occurring.[2]

To the second question du Noüy took a single molecule of high dissymmetry and assumed chemical reactions forced by a tumbler being shaken at 500 trillion shakings per second (corresponding to the magnitude of light frequencies). He calculated that the time to form one molecule would be 10^{243} billion years.[3] But since this time, which staggers the imagination, is impossibly longer than the age of the universe, it is impossible.

It is important to note that Dr. du Noüy did not take issue with the basic principles of evolution. Indeed, he gave numerous examples of how evolution worked *once life was found to exist on the earth*. His primary effort was to illustrate the impossibly low probability that life could ever have accidentally occurred on earth. A summarizing conclusion of his book was: "From the very beginning, life has evolved as if there were a goal to attain, and as if this goal were the advent of the human conscience."[4]

Although knowledge concerning biology, micro-biology, astrophysics and theoretical physics has increased tremendously since Dr. du Noüy's time, the basic principles that he used are still valid.

Near-Death Experiences (NDEs)

In 1978 I read Dr. Raymond Moody's book *Life After Life*.[5] Later I read Dr. George Ritchie's *Return from Tomorrow*.[6] Both books detailed experiences of people who had supposedly died, left their bodies, and later returned to life. Some of the accounts were remarkably similar to what my father had, years before, told me.

In 1982 Kenneth Ring's book *Life at Death* was published,[7] and in 1984 his seminal work *Heading Toward Omega* was published.[8] Dr. Ring was a professor of psychology at the University of Connecticut and a founder of the International Association for Near-Death Studies (IANDS). As a direct result of his effort researchers all over the world began to do work in the field of NDEs and to report on their effort.

In *Life at Death*, Dr. Ring described how, beginning in 1977, he spent thirteen months tracking down and interviewing scores of people who had come close to death. He sought out and found people who had actually nearly died. In some cases his research subjects had suffered "clinical" death, that is, they had lost all vital signs, such as heartbeat and respiration. In most cases, however, the men and women he interviewed had found themselves on the brink of medical death but had not, biologically speaking, quite slipped over. His aim in conducting the interviews was to find out what people experience when they are on the verge of apparent imminent death. His findings led to the identification of a series of events which most commonly might be expected in an

NDE. Those findings are still used as a gauge on how complete or how typical the particular NDE being studied might be.

These books on near-death experiences and the related research work were fascinating to me. They tended to confirm the reality of what my father, mother, grandmother and aunt claimed had happened when my father "died and visited the other side." In the meantime, however, events were changing in the scientific arena, and those events were also shaping my thinking.

Anthropic Universe

In 1974 the British Cosmologist Brandon Carter coined the term *Anthropic Principle* when he produced a paper entitled: "Large Number Coincidences and the Anthropic Principle in Cosmology."[9] Anthropic came from the name, "man," and he defined two versions of his principle, a *Weak* and a *Strong* form. The Weak Principle says "that our location in the universe is *necessarily* privileged to the extent of being compatible with our existence as observers." The Strong says that our universe "must be such as to admit the creation of observers within it at some stage."

Carter's paper, in lay terms, contended that the many supposed arbitrary constants in nature used by physicists to compute the characteristics of our universe have the remarkable tendency of being precisely the values needed for a universe capable of sustaining life. The constants which physicists speak of are such things as the force of gravity, the electromagnetic force and the strong nuclear force. These forces have values which are fixed (constant) according to certain observed laws of physics. The apparent compulsion of the fundamental constants found in nature to arrange themselves for a life sustaining universe suggests an even more astonishing fact. It is that all the myriad laws of physics seem to have been fine-tuned from the beginning of the big bang to have been expressly designed for the emergence of human beings.

An obvious connotation of Carter's paper was that some type of Creator or Creative Force must have provided the design necessary for the universe—or at least that portion of the universe which we can observe—to have arrived in the anthropic form that we find it. This recognition was a powerful catalyst to set physicists and cosmologists scrambling to find alternative answers to how the universe came to be.

And, being the clever people that they are, they combined their fertile imaginations with the tools of probability analysis to derive several ways that our universe could have accidentally arrived on the scene of reality—a reality defined by living and thinking observers.

One of the most common arguments against some of the implications of the anthropic principle is that "the universe simply must be this way *because* we are here; Had the universe been otherwise, we would not be here to observe ourselves, and that is that."[10] Of that argument, John Leslie, in his book *Universes* says: "Too many philosophers construct such arguments as that if the universe were hostile to Life then we shouldn't be here to see it, and that therefore there is nothing in fine tuning for anyone to get excited about. . . . Too many have confused being rigorous with rejecting everything not directly observable."[11]

It is fascinating, today, to compare the summary conclusion of Lecomte du Noüy with a summary of Carter's Anthropic Principles. From du Noüy is the statement: "From the very beginning, life has evolved as if there were a goal to attain, and as if this goal were the advent of the human conscience." And from the discussion above of Anthropic Principles, "all the myriad laws of physics seem to have been fine-tuned from the beginning of the big bang to have been expressly designed for the emergence of human beings." It should be noted, of course, that those two statements came from different propositions. Lecomte du Noüy examined the probability of life spontaneously erupting on a pristine earth, and Carter examined the probability of a universe being expressly designed for life. In succeeding material I shall consider both of these propositions in light of current knowledge.

NDEs and My Search for Truth

By late 1989 my curiosity concerning my father's experience got the best of me and I decided to find out for myself what was going on in these kinds of experiences. My earlier work in research and development in the field of nuclear energy had shown me the value of careful preparation, planning and documentation in any research effort expected to stand the later scrutiny of peers.

In consultation with my wife we developed a pattern for the work which was similar, in some respects, to what Kenneth Ring had done at the University of Connecticut. To find suitable candidates we used two methods: referrals from friends, relatives, and associates; and advertisements in local papers and publications. Both methods were fruitful. Indeed, the respondents could have been multiplied many times simply by continuing the effort for a longer period.

During the period from December 1990 through June 1991 we interviewed 45 respondents, of whom 38 first-hand experiences were included in the book *Glimpses of Eternity*.[12] There were also four second-party experiences which were incorporated. Two first-hand experiences from other sources were included, bringing the total of first-hand accounts to 40. Numerous others were rejected because they didn't meet certain criteria having to do with the types of experiences that we had previously established.

In soliciting candidates to interview, no attempt was made to screen for religious or non-religious beliefs. The only criterion that had to be met was that the candidate had undergone some type of NDE, or other incident, which led to an out-of-body or related spiritual event. By reason of the location of the interviews, in the greater Salt Lake City region, most of those interviewed (71%) professed allegiance to the Church of Jesus Christ of Latter-day Saints (Mormon Church).

The interviews were conducted in my home or in the home of the respondent, except for one which was conducted by telephone. Where women were involved, my wife, Carol Gibson, was usually present and she assisted in the interviews.

All the interviews were taped, later typed, and forwarded in draft form to the respondent. The respondents then made changes that they felt were appropriate to correspond more closely to their memory of what happened.

Some of those interviewed preferred to be recognized with their true identity; others preferred a pseudonym. For those desiring complete identification we used their full names; others desiring anonymity were assigned a pseudonym for a given name, with no surname.

To assure complete coverage of the subject those interviewed were first asked to give background information about themselves and the incident. Then they were asked to tell, as completely as possible, what had happened to them. We had previously prepared a check sheet with pertinent questions that were to be covered before the interview was complete. By reviewing the check sheet as the interview proceeded we were able to ascertain where desired topics had not been covered. We then asked questions, in as open-ended a manner as possible, to cover the desired issues.

The results of this effort were so productive that it was difficult to stop interviewing people. So, encouraged by our publisher, beginning in the summer of 1992 and extending through the spring of 1993 we interviewed twenty-nine candidates whose firsthand stories were detailed in the book *Echoes From Eternity*.[13]

During this period of intense study concerning NDEs, my wife Carol and I, together with Dr. Lynn Johnson, Martin Tanner and Fred Beckett founded a local chapter of IANDS (IANDS of Utah). We established monthly meetings in which various individuals who had experienced an NDE or who were involved in research—or who needed support—could meet and trade information. Gradually that effort expanded until today (1999), from 50 to 90 individuals meet monthly in formal meetings. A newsletter is published which has approximately 500 subscribers. Our local group also assisted Brigham Young University establish, in 1997, an honors class in near-death studies.

In the process of this and succeeding effort Carol and I have heard the stories of scores of individuals. A major conclusion that we came to as a result of this exposure was that those stories we were familiar with did, indeed, represent real experiences for the people involved in them. Moreover, in the near-death research community attempts to arrive at some scientifically rational explanation which accounts for all of the events known to occur with those having an NDE, and which avoids other-world explanations, are nearing exhaustion. This is forcing a recognition of the strong probability that humans have a dual nature, and upon death individual consciousness continues in some other-world dimension.

Mormonism

As my search broadened, studies in the science area convinced me that there was substantial evidence for providential intervention in the creation of the universe and our world. I also became convinced that the scientific world would soon have to acknowledge the probability of a duality of human life. It was natural, therefore, that I reexamined some of the beliefs of my own religious heritage in light of these scientifically deduced findings. In commenting on some of the teachings and scriptures of The Church of Jesus Christ of Latter-day Saints I hasten to add that I cannot represent myself as an official spokesperson for the Church. That privilege is reserved for the Prophet and other General Authorities. Rather, I speak as a person who has spent most of my adult life as an active participant of the Church, and I speak as one who is convinced that the LDS Church is true and is led by a modern prophet.

Near the end of this book I will examine some of the historical events, teachings, and doctrines of the LDS Church as they correlated with my findings in the scientific arena. From my expanding search it became ever more evident—to my surprise—that these correlations were pronounced. Comparisons will be made, therefore, in areas where LDS doctrine may shed additional knowledge on observed scientific findings. Admittedly, these will be biased comparisons since they will reflect conclusions I have already reached. It is hoped that the reader will forgive my biases and look beyond them to the fundamental facts being presented.

Finally, I shall present the evidence which changed my perspective from that of skeptic to believer. Perhaps it would be better to say that I changed from being an avid skeptic—one that challenged most sacred beliefs—to a more open minded position. Some of the skepticism that stood me so well in my search for truth is still a part of my nature, but I am less likely to reject the sacred in favor of the profane. My skepticism has led me, for example, to accept the scientific world's claim that the universe and the world are of immense age—15 billion years for the universe[14] and 4.5 billion years for the earth.[15] The evidence for an extended age seems to me to be overwhelming. Nevertheless, I have also become convinced that many of the so-called conflicts between religion and science do not exist. Often religion, and particularly the LDS religion, is in a position to answer questions which contemporary science cannot answer. And those answers are just as efficacious as any answers generated in the laboratories and the computers of scientists. In many cases the answers obtained from the religious perspective not only provide a sure way for finding a measure of the truth, but they also create an atmosphere for a vastly improved society.

Unfortunately, in recent decades religion has fallen into disrepute amongst many of the "Intelligentsia." The reasons are varied and complex, often stemming from a mistaken belief that science and religion are incompatible. The result of this disparagement of religion and its values is a society increasingly adrift in a sea of relativism. As Gregg Easterbrook observes in his book *Beside Still Waters—Searching for Meaning in an Age of Doubt:*[16]

> Yet there is no reason science and spirituality must stand as opposing superpowers, each wishing the other's destruction. Both, after all, are truth-seeking disciplines. . . .
>
> Rising up from the findings of modern research is a strange kind of homage to meaninglessness. The new view depicts absence of meaning as a legitimate, even welcome, interpretation of human prospect. That human existence lacks purpose is now thought comforting; that it may bear meaning is what discomfits.
>
> . . . Reflecting this new conventional wisdom, Jessica Mathews, head of the Carnegie Endowment in Washington, D.C., declared in 1996 that men and women should accept that "human life is a cosmic accident with no purpose."

Religion gives hope for a universe of meaning, one designed expressly for the development and growth of man. Without religion one falls into the abyss of relative humanism or some other similar philosophy. Truman Madsen, in his book *Eternal Man* expressed it this way:

> Man, on this view, is a temporary event, a fleeting figure in the blind careenings of the cosmos. . . . His identity is soon to be obliterated, and with it all of his expressions of beauty, goodness, knowledge, and love. All will be swallowed up in what Russell calls "the vast death of the solar system." . . . As Montague has it, the things that matter most will ultimately be at the mercy of the things that matter least.[17]

Who This Book is For

My purpose in writing this book was to reach out to individuals, like myself in my youth, who find themselves perplexed by life's journey. I wanted to respond to those who wondered about the mysteries of existence and were searching for answers. Obviously no single book nor any one person can provide comprehensive answers to all of the questions arising from life's mysteries. Nevertheless, my particular journey convinced me that by confining the search to a few key areas substantial progress could be made.

In particular, during the early part of the search, I wondered about the apparent conflict between science and religion concerning certain subjects. And I wondered how one could obtain a real yard-stick for measuring truth. As noted above, I confined my investigation to the creation as understood by science, near-death studies, and Mormonism. As my intellectual and spiritual journey expanded I began to see patterns that pointed toward an inescapable conclusion: that God was the author of much that I saw and studied. Many of the issues which I initially saw as insurmountable conflicts between science and religion melted in the sunlight of my new found knowledge. Some problems remained—and still do to this day—but they were swallowed up by the assurances I obtained from the scientific and religious fields which I did study. I found, for example, that the science of the physical world, and the theology of the religious-spiritual world, tended to be bridged by the developing science of near-death studies.

Another lesson learned in my journey was that patience is a valuable commodity, especially in certain disciplines of science. When I started my search in the early 1950s Jonas Salk had not yet solved the riddle of polio (my sister died of it in 1954), radiometric dating for determining the age of fossils was in its infancy, the space program was still a dream, giant atom smashers such as the Fermilab Collider had yet to be built, J.C. Kendrow was on the verge of succeeding in the use of X-ray crystallography for getting a detailed picture of the protein myoglobin structure, the monstrous IBM 650 Computer was less powerful than today's laptop computer, nuclear power plants were in the early research stage, the Hubble space telescope wasn't even a dream, most fossils dating into the Cambrian period had not been found, James Watson had yet to win his Nobel Prize for defining the details of DNA, the term near-death-experience would not be coined by Raymond Moody for another twenty years, and the big bang was in its infancy as a model for understanding how the universe developed. In short, there has been an explosion of knowledge during my lifetime concerning issues which I was seeking information about. The same will be true—to an exaggerated extent—during the lifetimes of you younger readers. So be patient, dear reader, if all that you wish to know is not immediately forthcoming.

Have faith in what you do know, and lean upon me and others of my generation who may have something of worth to tell you.

The evidence which persuaded me to come to the conclusions that I did is given in the following chapters. As this Introduction illustrates, my search led me through a study of the creation as understood and as described by science, near-death experiences and their evolving science, and my own religion. Be advised, therefore, that as you proceed some of the material may be in terminology not completely familiar to you. By necessity I used the language of the disciplines that I was illustrating. Where possible I tried to explain different concepts in lay terms, but I may not have been completely successful—at least according to my wife. Where that is true please proceed to succeeding areas and see if the subject does not become more clear. A Glossary is provided near the end of the book to assist readers with definitions of many of the words and technical terms used in the book.

Appendix A includes supportive material concerning near-death research. For those readers who are interested in a rather complete understanding of the physics, mathematics, geology, biology and cosmology underlying the creation and development of life, several appendices are also devoted to those subjects. For all others the chapters are arranged for a concise and yet complete story of my intellectual journey.

Because of the importance of near-death studies and because of the impact they had on my own journey I shall commence with that subject. As the story unfolds I believe that you will find, as I did, the bridging that occurs between science and religion by the evolving science of NDEs. For that reason, also, I shall frequently intermix pertinent near-death stories with the cosmological, physiological and religious ideas.

As you proceed please look for the fingerprints of God in the unfolding evidence. My prayer is that you will find this necessarily abbreviated account of my journey both understandable and as exciting as I did.

Large and Small Numbers

In much of this book we will be discussing concepts which require a grasp of very large and very small numbers. To deal with large and small numbers mathematicians have developed a system of using powers of ten. A power of ten is simply a number with a base of 10 and a logarithm or exponent given to the base. In simpler terms, the number 4,000 is represented in powers of ten as: 4×10^3. It is determined by noting that the value starts with 4 and then counting the zeros (or decimal points) after the four, or three zeros. 10^4 is shorthand for $10 \times 10 \times 10 \times 10$ or 10,000. The number of seconds in a year is $60 \times 60 \times 24 \times 365 = 31,536,000$, or more simply, 3.15×10^7. One million, 1,000,000, would be 1×10^6, or simply 10^6. One billion would be 1,000,000,000 or 10^9.

Mathematicians consider impossibility to be expressed by a probability number: one chance in 10^{50}. 10^{50} may also be written as $10^5 \times 10^{45}$. Recognizing that one billion includes nine zeros and that 45 zeros divided by 9 zeros is five, we can conclude that 10^{45} corresponds to a billion, billion, billion, billion, billion. Thus impossibility, as defined by mathematicians, is equal to one chance in 100,000 billion, billion, billion, billion, billion tries.

Small numbers can also be expressed in powers of ten. 10^{-4} is the same as $1/10^4$ which is the same as $1/(10 \times 10 \times 10 \times 10)$ which is the same as .0001 which is the same as 1×10^{-4}. Physicists speak of Planck time as the first moment in the creation of the universe when normal laws apply. This occurs at 10^{-43} seconds. 10^{-43} seconds may also be written as $10^{-45} \times 10^2$ seconds. Recognizing, as above, that a billion includes nine zeros, which divides into 45 zeros five times, Planck time corresponds to 100 billionths, billionths, billionths, billionths, billionths of a second.

Ann's Angel

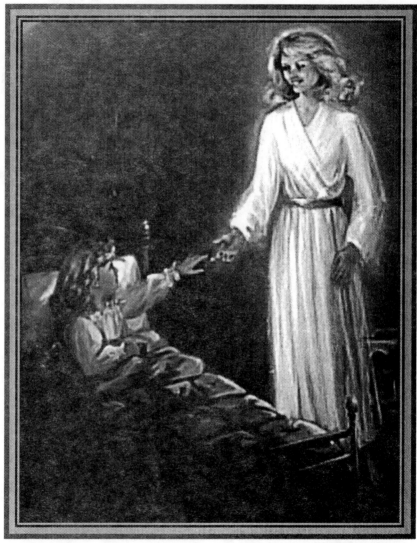

This picture, taken from a painting by Florence Susan Comish, and used on the cover of the book *Glimpses of Eternity*,represents a near-death experience of a four-year-old child, Ann, who was dying of leukemia. Portions of her story are told commencing on page 109.

1
Near-Death Experiences—
A Different Reality

What is a Near-Death Experience (NDE)?

In the modern era—1970s to the present—near-death experiences reached public awareness by means of Raymond Moody's book, *Life After Life*, George Ritchie's *Return from Tomorrow*, and Kenneth Ring's *Heading Toward Omega*. In these books the authors gave examples of people who apparently died, left their bodies, visited some other realm, had a variety of experiences and returned to life as we know it.

In the process of conveying and analyzing the different stories, these three authors illustrated certain patterns which appeared to constitute the majority of events in a "typical" NDE. Some of the events included: a sense of ineffability by the person having the NDE, leaving his or her physical body, loss of pain, hearing the news of their own death, hearing or sensing a noise or music, passing through a dark tunnel at great speed, seeing and being enveloped in light, having feelings of great peace and love, meeting others—often deceased relatives, seeing or sensing a being of light and love, having a life review, making a choice to stay or return, coming back to life. The authors established that not all of these events happened in every NDE, and some NDEs had other characteristics, but there was sufficient repeatability to allow a structured approach to the growing volume of such stories. More will be said about some of the early research methods and results in the next chapter.

For the purposes of this book NDEs are defined as those which have a majority of the elements listed above. In addition, experiences are included where there is no imminent threat of death but many of the other events listed are present. Instead of physical trauma, some of these experiences appear to be triggered by emotional trauma, fear, prayer, meditation or in some cases appearance of other-worldly beings for the purpose of teaching or warning the recipient.

Why the Emphasis on NDEs?

In the Introduction I explained how my father's NDE caused me to investigate them in detail in later years. But my interest goes beyond what happened to my father. The research I did convinced me that there was a universal message being generated in the research and stories of those who visited, but briefly, eternity. And because an increasingly aware group of psychologists, medical practitioners, sociologists and educators were devoting much of their careers to the study of this burgeoning phenomenon, the growing information base had the potential to make major changes in the philosophy of life and death.

Simultaneous with the growth of interest in NDEs by this group of scientists an army of physicists, astronomers, cosmologists, mathematicians, chemists, biologists, microbiologists, geologists and paleontologists were gaining a greater appreciation that the creation of the universe and life could no longer readily be explained as a purely mechanical-physical series of events. Scientists in these latter fields were continuously being faced by conundrums which confounded what were previously almost sacred theories and beliefs. The very nature of investigation in the so-called "hard" sciences demanded a fierce skepticism about anything not readily measurable in a physical sense, yet physical measurements of many fundamental processes of nature no longer worked as they should—witness "quantum weirdness" (to be explained in later chapters).

Into this scene of growing uncertainty amongst those working in the hard sciences are beginning to march the newly more confident and aggressive psychologists, medical practitioners and others studying NDEs. Their intrusion into the sacrosanct halls of the hard scientists, in my view, is inevitable. There is too much evidence being generated which buttresses the arguments for the existence of another and a different realm than the one we live and die in. And that intrusion by a growing number of scientifically educated professionals— albeit in different disciplines than the hard sciences—has the capability of shifting attitudes in what does or does not constitute reality. Equally important, near-death studies, by their very nature, offer a bridge to the world of religion. What may have seemed to be a conflict between science and religion could dissolve or be mitigated by the increased knowledge growing from a marriage of NDE scientists and others working in the hard sciences.

Paul Davies is a theoretical physicist living and working in England. He has written over twenty works on various aspects of physics and cosmology. In a recent book, *The Fifth Miracle—The Search for the Origin and Meaning of Life*, he addresses the question of how life came to be in our universe. He explains how he used to believe that simple organic building blocks could have spontaneously been created and then, by Darwinian evolution, replicated themselves into an abundance of life. He says of that former belief:

> . . . I am now much more skeptical. It seems to me very unlikely that all that is necessary is for the right chemical reaction or the right molecule to turn up. Real progress with the mystery of biogenesis will be made, I believe, not through exotic chemistry, *but from something conceptually new* (italics mine).[1]

I couldn't agree more. Davies then proceeds to speculate on what new concepts might better explain the origin of life, none of which relate to NDEs, but that will change. The burden of examining the mounting evidence coming from NDE research cannot forever be dodged by those claiming to seek the truth from whatever quarter.

It is for these reasons that NDE plays such an important role in this book. This chapter and the next two are devoted almost exclusively to that subject. Furthermore I have intermixed NDE information in other portions of the book where the interrelationships with different scientific or religious disciplines seem pertinent.

Some Initial Examples

Throughout this book portions of different individual's NDEs will be given as those experiences pertain to the particular subject being discussed. To gain a perspective, however, of the spontaneity, sense of awe, and in some cases profound thoughts produced by those describing their experiences it is useful to read a complete version of the interview between the researcher and the candidate. To that end the following three experiences are given. They are each previously non-published stories. The candidates were recently (1999) interviewed by my wife, Carol, and me in accordance with the procedures outlined in the Introduction. They are not particularly unusual in terms of the many such experiences we have heard and researched. At the end of the three stories I shall provide a brief analysis in which I shall point out certain patterns and/or unusual aspects.

Dan—A Child's Experience

Dan's Background

Dan and his lovely wife Anna met with me and my wife, Carol, at my home on April 17, 1999. Dan was a large man with a broad smile, dark hair, a neatly trimmed beard and a deep voice. After a brief get-acquainted period Dan explained a little of his background. He was born in Utah in 1948 and graduated from high school there.

In his youth Dan's parents joined a particular religious group and became quite active in it. This affected Dan during his youth, and when he graduated from high school for some time he pursued a religious vocation. Ultimately he became disenchanted, and he and his wife terminated their affiliation with that religious body.

Dan's experience happened when he was three years old. Our interview follows:

A Candy Treat

"My mother and father had six children, so there was a lot to cope with. One of my older sisters, who is now deceased from multiple sclerosis, sort of became a surrogate mother to us twins—I have a twin brother. Jean was always watching out for my brother and me . . . she was very loving towards us. She was six years older than us and she was more of a mother than a sister.

"On a particular day, I remember Jean asking my mother for some coins so that she could buy some candy for my brother and me. Back in those years we didn't have stores that were close by. What we called the "Store Truck" was in our neighborhood. It carried many commodities for every-day use, such as canned goods, bread, vegetables and an array of candy. You could walk into the truck and pick what you needed just like you would in a store.

"The truck pulled up and blew its horn and we came outdoors. My sister told my brother and me to stay in the front yard behind the picket fence while she went in the truck to get some candy for us. She left . . . and this is strange since I can remember it so well even though I was so young . . . she left and I can remember thinking: *When she disappears around the front of that truck I'm going to run over so I can look into the truck.*

"So I waited purposely for her to cross the road and disappear around the nose of the truck. As soon as she did I ran into the middle of the street. I don't know whether I heard the squealing of brakes or what . . . I don't know why I stopped in the middle of the street.

"For whatever reason, I did stop, and I remember looking at the front of a car coming at me. It had a large chrome bumper and I can almost give you the number of the license plate. It's still that clear in my memory.

Hit by a Car—The Light

"The car hit me and threw me into the air. According to my parents it was traveling pretty fast. After being thrown through the air I hit face down on the asphalt road. At that point—at least as I remember it—I picked myself up and walked to my neighbor's parked truck in front of their house and sat on the running board and put my head between my knees. I don't remember any pain, but I felt awful.

"I raised my head up and saw my father run out of the house, through the yard, past the fence into the middle of the road. He reached down—and I can remember wondering: *Why isn't he coming to get me?* Since I was sitting on the running board of our neighbor's car, I couldn't understand what he was doing in the middle of the road.

"When my Dad reached down, then I saw me. He picked me up from the middle of the road. And I remember thinking: *I'm over here. What are you doing?* And I could see the anguish on his face as he rushed hurriedly across the road.

"I got off from the running board and followed my father, while thinking: *Wait for me—I'm here!* When I got to the middle of the road, that was when there was just light, everywhere. It was just wonderful light. It was in me, around me, . . . it was granular. That's the only term I can think of, like little beads of light.

"At that point I didn't feel awful anymore. There was just a fantastic sense of peace and tranquility. There was an undeniable loving and fulfilled feeling associated with the light. It seemed to embody everything that I was. There was a warm feeling that seemed to flow through me and all around me like the arms of a loving parent. It took away the fear, confusion and somehow answered all my questions.

"When I was in the light and thinking how terrific this felt—and no longer worried or even thinking about my father—I had a sense that somebody was standing on my right side. And I wasn't afraid, it was more like they were supposed to be there . . . or, I expected them to be there.

A Choice to Stay or Return

"That being, or person, or whatever, asked me: 'Do you want to go or to stay?'

"For a brief moment I thought: This is nice, I'll stay. But that was only for the briefest moment. And while I was thinking how nice it was I became aware that I was making that assessment as an adult. I was no longer a child. My thought processes and everything that was happening to me was as a mature being. Then I thought: *No, if I stay here it will kill my mother.* Within the snap of a finger I looked around and my mother was hovering over me as she cleaned my cuts and bruises."

At this point in the interview I asked Dan, "Do you know the extent of your injuries?"

"My mother later told me they were from the tip of my toes to the top of my head—there wasn't an inch that wasn't cut, bruised or bleeding. The bumper apparently hit me in the face so all of my baby teeth were knocked out, the doctor said I had a skull fracture, my lip was torn and swelled so that it was above my eye. My pain was intense, but in addition, as I looked at my mother I felt terrible that she felt so bad. But I knew that I wasn't going to die."

Return and Recovery

"What happened after you became aware that your mother was helping you?"

"I was sitting on the toilet and she was cleaning me. And I could hear my father chastising my sister Jean. He was saying, 'Why didn't you watch these babies?' She really had watched us and it wasn't her fault. She blamed herself for the rest of her life. In fact, shortly before she died I told her again that it was not her fault.

"Our neighbor, Joyce, came over to help my mother. When they finished cleaning me up they took me into one of my parent's rooms and placed me on a bed. Joyce was afraid that I might have a concussion and she repeatedly said, 'Don't let this boy go to sleep.' I kept drifting off and they kept waking me. Dr. Strand came shortly after that and he stayed for a long time.

"To keep me awake until they were sure I was okay, the doctor kept putting coins under my pillow for me to find. He did that for a dual purpose, I think. It kept me involved in finding the coins, and it helped my parents because they didn't have any money and the doctor knew it. Later I gave the coins to my father to help the family."

"For weeks after that the doctor would come to the house to see how I was doing. Usually I lay on a couch and I drank everything through a straw. My teeth were knocked out so I couldn't chew. And I couldn't speak for some time because of the injuries to my jaw and face."

Recalling the Event

"How is it, Dan, that you are able to remember so much detail about what happened to you at that very young age?"

"My wife has lived with me for thirty-one years. Has my story changed or varied over those years, Anna?" Dan asked his wife.

"No, it has not," she answered.

Dan continued, "I'm not sure why I am able to remember it so well, I just am."

"Did it seem real, or was it more like a dream?"

"It was as real as anything . . . that's maybe the reason that I remember. It wasn't like a dream."

"Could it have been an hallucination?"

"No, not even close. I've been in an industrial accident where I had amnesia for a period, and this was not anything like that. It was clear, and . . . it was probably one of the most deeply entrenched experiences and mental images that I've ever had in the fifty years I've lived."

"Did you tell others, when you were young, of your experience?"

"Yes, I tried to, but because of their religious beliefs they dismissed it. They told me that I was dreaming. As a little boy I didn't want to cause any trouble so I just kept my mouth shut. And I actually kept my mouth shut until I was about forty-five or so."

Anna interjected: "You started talking about it when you read some books on near-death experiences. You then told me and others that that was what happened to you."

Challenges to Dan's Belief System

"What were the religious beliefs that caused people in your youth to disbelieve you?"

"My father and mother were active in their church, and they did not believe that you lived immediately after death. They believed that you are in the memory of God, but not alive, until the resurrection at some future date."

"Did this belief bother you?"

"When I got old enough to understand, yes it did. While I was young I accepted the teaching that you are non-existent after death. Yet I knew what I had experienced, and it was real."

"What significant impact has the experience had on you?"

"There are many ways that it has impacted my life, including having increased sensitivity about the feelings of others, but the one thing that has always been with me since the accident was the feeling that I had something special to do."

Thoughts About Life and Death

"What is your feeling about death, now?"

"Death is a natural progression to another reality, just like walking through a door."

"Are you afraid of it?"

"Not at all. I actually look forward to it—as long as I have done, in this life, what I need to do."

"Do you know what it is you need to do?"

"I wish I did. There is a feeling in me that somehow I am to help others."

"Are there any special messages you would like to leave with others who might read your story?"

"As a youngster and young man I lived with the belief that most of mankind would suffer at the hands of God in a future war over wickedness. Only a select few would escape through the blessings of God's kingdom. I taught that as part of my religion. But down deep inside of me I knew that no matter what happened in the world everything was all right, everything would be okay. Whatever we go through individually—or collectively as a nation and a world—it all is for a common . . . goal. That goal is to learn and improve so as to move closer to the source of the light of love. In fact, in your research you point out people who have had near-death experiences in which they want to move toward the light. I think that there is maybe a genetic . . . or an innate desire in all of us, at this level, on this plane, to do this—to move closer to the light. We are evolving to a higher awareness and a deeper concept of what it is all about. It's like a preschool preparing you for another school—and that's what life is. I don't know when those schools end, maybe never. And that's exciting to me."

"So you think that life is a school?"

"Yes, the experience of life is so profound and has so much more to offer than we normally think. Pain and suffering for example are an important part of life. One day of life is worth all the pain and suffering that we might have to go through. My death experience—if that's what it was—doesn't hold a candle to how I now value and get joy from each day. When we cross over that reality will become so clear."

"What is your feeling now about religion?"

"I honestly don't see any religion being closer to God or any better than another. They are all part of the school of life. All religion is man's best effort to understand God. At least that's the way I feel now; I could not endorse one over another."

"Do you feel that you are a religious person?"

"I feel that I am a spiritual person."

George Thompson—
A Senior Citizen's Experience

An Englishman's Beginning

It was a sunny spring day in 1999 when George Thompson came to my home to be interviewed. Appearing at my door was a handsome, white-haired man with a distinct British accent. His obvious sense of humor and twinkling eyes quickly put both of us at ease. He had driven from his home some fifteen miles south of mine through the heavy traffic of Salt Lake City. Ordinarily this would not have attracted my attention, except that George was ninety-one years old. Our interview was scheduled for the noon hour by George since he had arranged a fishing engagement later in the day with a friend.

As is usually the case with such interviews I explained to George that I first wanted background information on him, and we would then discuss his near-death experience. Our interview follows:

"I was born in 1908 in a place called Middlesbrough in the northeast corner of Yorkshire in England. It was before the first world war. My mother was a member of the Church of Jesus Christ of Latter-day Saints, and all of us children were raised as Mormons. There were seven of us children, three boys and four girls. One of my brothers was killed in the first world war in Gallipoli. My other siblings married and stayed in England except for my elder sister who emigrated to the United States with her son and daughter in 1953.

"Often, during those early years, we had LDS missionaries living with us in our home. My father was not a member of the Church. He claimed to be a Methodist but he never went to church."

"Where did you go to school, George?" I asked.

"In Middlesbrough, it was just Elementary School."

"Did you find your wife in England?"

"Yes, I met her at a cycling club. It was a party to celebrate the start of the cycling season and I was attracted by her beautiful big brown eyes. I was twenty years old at the time. Later, the lady she was living with told me: 'George, Doris has got a crush on you.' That gave me courage, and on one of our cycling expeditions when we were alone I reached to give her a kiss. She jumped up and took off." George laughed at the thought.

"So you married Doris?"

"Yes, we courted for about three years and then we married. We had two children, a boy and a girl, and we were married for 63 years until she died."

"Was she a member of the LDS Church?"

"No. She was a member of the Church of England, but just before she died she told me that she believed the LDS Church was true."

The War Years

"Where did you work?"

"I worked as a molder in a foundry for nineteen years until the second world war broke out. During the war I worked in a factory producing battle tanks. Also, I worked as a first-aid helper where I had some terrible experiences."

"Were you bombed?"

"Often. On one occasion I was outside trying to get the people into the shelters when three bombs landed, one after another. It was a moonlit night and I saw a policeman running towards where a bomb had dropped. I joined him straightaway. A lady that I knew was pleading: 'Somebody please come and see my poor husband.' He had apparently brought his little boy to a shelter and had returned to his upstairs room for some reason when the bomb hit and blew the windows out. The bomb had blown both of his arms off and he bled to death. There were other similar awful events that I witnessed during the war."

America and a Heart Attack

"When and why did you come to America?"

"My sister was already here with her children, and I decided to join her with my family in 1954."

"Where did you work when you came here."

"I went to work for the Kennecott Copper Company. I worked there for twenty years before I retired."

"Now, George, if you would describe the events that led up to your near-death experience, and tell me what happened during the experience."

"It was about five years after I retired, and I was seventy years old. I was going to get some tires for the car, and as I went outside to start the car I suddenly started to get pains in my chest which I had never had before. This seemed strange since I was in pretty good health and had not experienced anything like this.

"So I went back into the house and I told my wife that I was getting terrible pains in my chest. She immediately told me that she was going to call the ambulance so it could take me to the hospital.

"Kennecott had a doctor's office in Salt Lake City, so I called it and told them about my chest pains. The nurse who answered told me to come to the office so that they could take an electrocardiogram. So I got Doris—she didn't drive—and I drove us through town to the doctor's office. By the time I got there I was in such pain and distress that I could hardly function. My limbs were shaking badly, and I could barely manage to get into the office.

"The doctor was not there so the nurse put me on a bed and began to hook up the electrocardiograph leads. By then my limbs were jumping all over the place. I could not control them. After a time the doctor returned. As soon as he saw me he said, 'Good heavens, get the ambulance. We've got to get him to the hospital.'

"The ambulance arrived in a few minutes, and they took me out on a stretcher. The paramedics came and joined us in the ambulance while it traveled. Doris got in the front, and they took off with the siren sounding.

A Beautiful, Peaceful Light

"All of a sudden I wasn't in the ambulance any more. There was this beautiful scene. I was looking into this light . . . it was straightaway, and I was looking into this big light. At the time I thought, *Good heavens, I have never seen anything like this before.*

"It's hard to explain what it was like since I had never experienced anything like that before. The light was brighter than daylight, and it was a peaceful light. It's hard to describe. When I looked down instead of up I saw all these beautiful colors—colors that were completely new to me.

"While I was studying the colors, suddenly I saw people moving. They seemed to be about twenty yards away. They were off the floor and they were moving in the same direction. They weren't walking—it was more like they were gliding. They had robes on from the neck down to their ankles, with long sleeves. And the colors, I had never seen . . . they were different colors.

"It wasn't only the colors, though, it was the feeling. There was such a peaceful feeling. All of my pain was gone and there was just this peace, it . . . it was different. After all the pain, and now it was gone and there was such peace. You can imagine—and I never thought I was dead.

"And just like that, I was back in the ambulance. Only this time I was not in such pain. But I turned on my side and I vomited all over the floor. It upset me, but the attendant told me not to worry about it. He also told me that they were in communication with St. Mark's Hospital, and he said that they had lost me twice.

"Shortly thereafter I lost consciousness until I awoke later in the intensive care unit of the hospital with my wife next to the bed."

Questions About George's Experience

"Let me ask you some questions, George," I remarked. "When you saw the people, did you know who they were?"

"No."

"Were they male or female, or could you tell?"

"There were about five or six of them, all moving in the same direction, and there seemed to be both men and women."

"You kept using the word peaceful, why did you use that word?"

"Well, for the simple reason that there were no body functions or problems, such as the pain I had experienced, and it was the most indescribably peaceful feeling I had ever had."

"Did you tell anyone what had happened to you."

"Later, when I realized that I had died, I waited for the doctor. When he came to see me I asked him if the brain could function when the heart stopped. He told me that it couldn't, but he reassured me that I would be okay because my heart had not stopped that long. Then he questioned why I wanted to know about the brain. So I explained that I had been through a very unusual experience when my heart stopped. His response was: 'Oh, I have heard about those kinds of experiences.' And that was all that he said."

"Did your experience seem like a dream, or did it seem real?"

"Oh no, it was nothing like a dream. Dreams are different altogether. It was real. It was a reality, and I know that for sure."

"What is your feeling about death?"

"It's something I am looking forward to."

"Are there any messages from your experience which you would like to leave for others?"

"Yes. I know that this life is just a short part of an eternal existence, but a very important part. Everything is so organized, and if it is that organized there has to be an organizer. Also, no matter what our race, color or background, we are all sons and daughters of a loving God. We should, therefore, love our brothers and sisters, and we should not judge others."

Sylvia—A Young Atheist

Her Early Life

Carol and I had previously met Sylvia at the annual meeting of the International Association for Near-Death Studies held in Salt Lake City in October, 1998. Later we arranged to interview her, so in the late spring of 1999, we traveled to Sylvia's city. She was employed there as an Associate Professor in a leading university in one of the Western States. After a delightful Italian dinner, where she freely conversed in Italian with the restaurant personnel, we adjourned to our hotel room, and the interview took place.

Sylvia was a striking woman with beautiful brown hair and, as Carol described it, an effervescent calmness, which, coupled with her easy laugh, made her interview a most pleasant experience. The interview follows:

"Sylvia, tell me a little of your early life and background," I commenced.

"I was born in 1956 in Geneva, Switzerland. My father was an American citizen, so I was born abroad as an American citizen. In 1957, I arrived with my family in the United States where my sister was born. My father worked as an electronics engineer on missiles for the military. During an eight-year period we moved many times to be near his work at military bases throughout the United States. The majority of my childhood time was spent in Cheyenne, Wyoming, and it was there that I started school.

"In 1964 when my parents divorced, my mother was granted custody of my sister and me, so she brought us to Italy which is where she was originally from, and my father stayed in the United States."

Her Educational Background and Working Career

"Were either of your parents religious?"

"My father came from a largely non-practicing Jewish background, and my mother was a non-practicing Roman Catholic. So I grew up with little religious education, affiliation or beliefs. In fact, in my teenage years I became a very rebellious, atheistic person."

"Okay, so you moved to Italy. What happened next?"

"At the time, I was eight years old, and I had to learn Italian. The first four or five years in Italy were wonderful with the sense of music, history, and culture that was there. Later, though, as a young American living abroad, I felt increasingly like an outsider. This was true even though I finished elementary-, middle-, and high school there, and I obtained my first doctorate from the University of Rome."

"What was your first doctorate in?"

"English and American literature with a minor in medieval history from the University of La Sapienza. After getting my doctorate, and after fourteen years in Italy, I realized that if by that time I hadn't blended into the culture, I probably never would. Moreover, I was living in an abusive family situation, so I decided to come back to the United States with a stopover in Germany. I had always wanted to learn German.

"In Germany, I continued my study of languages at the Universität Konstanz where I attended for three semesters and became pretty fluent in German. My employment at that University as a linguist provided me with the resources to support myself. It was there that I decided I did not want to make my life's work in linguistics, so I applied to a couple of American universities for acceptance in their doctoral programs in Italian literature, and I was accepted at the University of Wisconsin in Madison. So I spent five years there getting my master's and doctorate. In addition to the Ph.D. in Italian literature, I received a minor from them in German literature. I graduated in 1986 and obtained a teaching position at a Jesuit liberal-arts college in Maryland."

"What did you teach there?"

"I taught Italian and German languages and culture. It was a pleasant eight-year experience, and I got tenured there; but I wanted to come out West. My heart was still in Cheyenne. There were friends and colleagues whom I got to know from my present university, so I packed everything in a big rental truck and headed west. A position had opened up in my specialty of Italian Romanticism and Holocaust studies, and I was hired. So I have been working here since 1994, and I love it."

A Motor Scooter Accident

"Okay, Sylvia, now why don't you tell us what led up to and what happened in your near-death experience."

"It was in early December of 1973, and I was seventeen years old—an angry seventeen."

"What were you angry about?"

"The world, my family, and my place in both. I was the most angry, the most uncooperative, the most arrogant, the most atheistic rebel teenager that you can imagine. "

"So what happened?"

"I had a little 50cc motor scooter." With a chuckle, Sylvia continued: "At that time in Italy not many girls had 50cc motor scooters, and I was very proud of mine. The accident happened around two o'clock in the afternoon."

"What town was it?"

"Latina, which is a town about an hour's south of Rome. I lived in Latina from 1971 through 1976; that was during my high school years and during my first year at the university. So, in 1973 I was in my third year of high school, and I was coming home on my motor scooter.

"The day was glorious, the sun was shining and it was warm. It felt like mid-October, a day with a yellowish patina to it. My route home was the normal route, so there was nothing unusual about my path or direction. As I came to an intersection, I was traveling from the right, so that if anyone were coming from the cross street, I would have had the right of way.

"As I approached the intersection, I remember looking to the left to see if anyone was coming. Way back in the distance, at the end of the block, I saw a car coming, but there was no doubt in my mind that I could clear the intersection. There was no need for me to slow down, so I didn't.

"Upon entering the intersection I again glanced to my left, and in my peripheral vision I saw a sportsy red car. This thing was going so fast that I knew it was going to hit me. At the same time, I noticed an elderly man, dressed in a brown suit, on the other side of the street, on the sidewalk. He had a cane, and he was walking haltingly in the same direction in which the car was traveling. After seeing the man, the last thought that I had was that I needed to pull up my knees and tuck them to my chest—otherwise I knew that my legs would be smashed as the scooter went under the car.

"So I pulled up my knees and went into a fetal position and, sure enough, I heard and felt the bang of the car hitting my scooter's body. In the tucked position, I flew across the intersection.

A Life's Review

"As I was flying through the air, I remember thinking that I needed to keep my head somehow protected between my hands, and tucked close to me, so that when I landed I would not hit my head."

"Did you have a helmet on, Sylvia?"

"No. It was not mandatory, and I was a wild, rebellious teenager. There is no way you could have made me use a helmet.

"Flying through the air, I landed on my derriere. My thinking during this event was that I would be okay once I hit if I controlled how I landed. It never occurred to me that I might bounce. But bounce I did, and when I flew again, I lost control of my body. I wasn't able to tuck or control how I landed the second time. It was almost in slow motion, and I was thinking that I should tuck, but I couldn't.

"So while I was in the air during this second bounce, it . . . it was almost like being in an aquarium. And while I was flying my whole life flashed in front of me—it was in an instant, because when I hit the ground again, it was gone. But it wasn't like a film in fast-forward, it was really like reliving every single month of my life.

"I understand rationally that if this happened between the first and second bounce it must have happened within just a couple of seconds. Yet, to me, it was as though I were living my entire life up to that point all over again with the same feelings, the same hurt, the same anger, the same sensations. It truly was as though I relived my whole life.

"During the second bounce while flying across the intersection, I must have turned, because when I landed I was facing the direction I had come from. There was the curb of the sidewalk behind me, and I remember hearing this awful noise as my skull hit that curb when I landed.

A Tunnel and a Light

"Then, I don't know how . . . how I got to the tunnel. There was no sense of a beginning, of an entrance to get into that tunnel. It was just immediately thereafter that I found myself floating in this . . . oh, it was amazing, it was the best moment in my entire life. And I was floating in this tunnel, and the tunnel . . . well, the tunnel . . . I don't know how big it was. The diameter was maybe seven or eight feet, because it was quite a bit larger than me. Inside it was a very, very dark gray—almost black but not quite—and it was opaque, not shiny. The tunnel was inclined upwards at about a forty-five degree angle.

"The . . . essence . . . of me was there, but my body that was floating through the tunnel in that moment was not my body as I had known it until that point in life. I was floating upward in the tunnel toward what I believed would be the other end of it, and the best analogy I can use to describe the form of my body is that I was similar to a jellyfish. My direction was head first, and my eyes seemed to be straight on top of my head, because I was looking at things from up there.

"My impression was that I had a head, and eyes on the cusp of it. Also, I seemed to have a neck and ears—I'll tell you later about the ears, because there was this music which I could hear. From the neck down, though, it was like a very gentle medusa—or a very gentle octopus. There seemed to be many appendices on me which were mellifluously floating. The manner in which I moved upward was by the shrink-and-stretch movement of these appendices and maybe partially of my neck—similar to the movement of jellyfish. There were no arms and legs, just these gently moving appendices.

"In the tunnel through which I was moving there were lots and lots of bubbles. The best way I can describe it, is with an analogy: the glass-bottled Cokes which, when opened, display myriads of bubbles rising in the bottle. In the tunnel, the movement of the bubbles rising was like in slow motion. There were bubbles of slightly different dimensions—their diameters ranging from perhaps 1/2 inch to about 1½ inches. Since I was traveling at about a forty-five degree angle, and the bubbles were traveling straight up, they must have congregated somewhere, but I don't know where. Whatever their final destination, they were beautiful.

"The bubbles were translucent, and on their surfaces I could see reflections in bright-yellow and purple. It was the absolutely most beautiful purple that I had ever seen. Never again have I seen that shade of purple in real life. Amethyst purple is close but it is not the same thing. It was deeper, it was stronger, it was . . . it was more purple.

Sylvia paused in the narration of her story as she laughed and said, "What is frustrating about recounting my NDE to you is that I am in literature, I work with words every day. And even though I have words in three languages, I need to speak in analogies when I talk about my near-death experience. I do not have the words to describe what happened, they simply don't exist. It is like reducing a beautiful experience to the words we use every day—it is frustrating.

"And so these bubbles were reflecting this beautiful purple on one side, and many of them also displayed a smaller bright-yellow reflection on their surface. And the bubbles . . . they were translucent so that I was able to see the dark of the tunnel through them. The bubbles were rising, and I was floating in this beautiful environment when I heard this music. It was . . . I'm not sure whether I heard it with my ears or by means of telepathy—I think I heard it with my ears. As I recall it, it was a tri-tonal music.

"At that time, I was not aware of electronic synthesized music, but what I heard was similar to that. Recently, maybe a year ago, I was in a music store and, by coincidence, I happened to buy a five-volume CD collection of the recordings that the space-ship 'Voyager' made when it went into outer space. The sounds of the music that I heard in the tunnel come close . . . the music . . . it's not exactly the same, but it is very close. Only in the Voyager CDs one also hears some beats, almost percussion-like sounds, and those were missing in the tunnel experience. Instead, while in the tunnel, there was this very beautiful tri-tonal music that would slightly rise or fall in pitch—always so beautifully harmonized. The music accompanied me in the tunnel as I floated upward, and I thought at the time that this was the best thing that ever happened to me.

"There was no doubt in my mind that I was experiencing the process of dying. I knew what was going on, and I was thinking, 'I am dying and, boy, this is not bad, this is cool!' The music was so soothing. It was a very solitary experience. There was nobody in the tunnel; just me, floating in this wonderful setting, the temperature being somewhat on the coolish side. I wasn't scared of anything—not even of the dark. It did not look all that dark with the bubbles. The music was so . . . it was so loving, it was so beautiful.

"About the music, somehow I connected it with a sense of mathematics or geometry. The tri-tonal sound had musical intervals that seemed to have a reason for being. It was connected to numbers—I don't know, but that was the sense that I got.

Sylvia stopped the narration of her experience to explain, "Remember, I want to emphasize to you that I was a rebellious, atheistic teenager. In addition, I was living in an abusive family situation. So, there was nothing in my background to bring me intuitively to feel comfortable, and safe, and loved, and peaceful during this kind of experience. It was really a completely new sensation for me.

"As I floated, suddenly at what seemed to be the end of the tunnel, I saw this light. It was a real light; a bright source of light. But it didn't hurt my eyes. Using another analogy, if you were to take wax paper and hold it against a light, that is the kind of sensation that I had. The light was very bright, but it was somewhat diffused, and I could look at it without its hurting my eyes at all. It was white, very bright white.

"So, with all this beautiful music I floated, and I felt so . . . to me the word is 'accepted.' There was just me there, and I was accepted. It was so good, because I had never felt so accepted before; I was not being criticized for my faults. There was a sense of belonging, of returning, a very natural movement toward the light. There was just a sense of acceptance for who I was. The entire process seemed natural and fine, and unfolding in the way it was intended to happen. Although I knew that I was the only one in the tunnel, there was a feeling that a lot of people did this—what I was doing—maybe each in his or her own time. It was cool, it was fine, I was happy, and I liked it.

A Choice and the Return

"When I got to within about two feet from the membrane of the light, this voice—a telepathic voice, not like the music which I heard with my ears, but a voice that I heard with my . . . heart . . . or my head, I'm not sure—it spoke to me. The voice seemed to be coming from the other side of the membrane of light, and it asked me if I wanted to go beyond the membrane. That's exactly the way it asked me, it communicated: 'Do you want to go beyond the membrane?'

Again, Sylvia interrupted to say, "I've asked myself many times what kind of voice it was. It seemed pretty neutral, but as to gender . . . if I have to decide what the voice was, it certainly was not a female voice. I probably would have to say that it communicated to me in a male-register. Philosophically, you need to know that claiming the voice was male-gendered bugs me.

"As I pondered the question asked to me by the voice, for some reason, I thought of my motor scooter. My first thought was, 'No, I want to continue to ride my motor scooter.' So I communicated by internal thought that, no, I did not want to go beyond the membrane. Somehow I knew that if I went beyond the membrane I would never return to life on earth." Sylvia laughed as she thought about the incident, and her reason for wanting to come back.

"The instant I said, no, my body . . . my jellyfish body . . . it resumed the shape of my usual human physical body and, in a fraction of a second, the tunnel became like the narrow tube of a vacuum cleaner. Immediately, I felt sucked very rapidly backwards. As I was being sucked, derriere first, I remember seeing my long hair being blown in the direction opposite that from which I was being sucked. My two arms and my two legs were in an outstretched position, as though reaching out, in front of me. And I remember thinking, 'Wow, what an over-reaction to my saying no.' In my estimation it took no more than about one-and-one-half seconds to be propelled from near the membrane of light back to the sidewalk.

"It felt right, though. It was as though I were empowered, since what was happening was a direct consequence of my having responded 'no.'

"As soon as I was out of the tunnel, I opened my eyes. My head was on the sidewalk with my body still partially on the road, and there was this curb under my head that hurt like crazy. The elderly man, whom I had seen before the car hit me, was standing, in a stooped manner, over me. He hardly had any teeth, and with an incredible smile, in a Southern-Italian dialect he said: 'Signurì, signurì! Ma allore . . . ma allore . . . nun sied' mort'! ('Oh, miss! Oh . . . oh . . . so . . . oh . . . you are not dead!')

"Fortuitously, the intersection where the accident happened was only a block-and-a-half from where a hospital was located. So almost immediately there were paramedics at the scene, and they tried to pick me up from my armpits.

"My reaction to their attempts to help me was to get all giggly, and I kept telling them that I was okay. When I tried to stand, though, I crashed again. Still, I giggled, and I glanced at my smashed motor scooter and continued to giggle. So they helped me walk to the hospital where they took X-rays. It turned out that I had several scratches and bruises and a head concussion. They kept me in the hospital for a short while and then sent me home that evening with instructions to be awakened every half hour. I had to stay in bed at home for about six days, so many of my high school friends came to visit me. My head and body ached for a while, and then I returned to school."

Some Questions About Sylvia's Experience

"May I, now, ask you some questions about your experience, Sylvia?"

"Of course."

"When you had your life's review, did you see it, did you feel it, did you think it, or what was it?"

"It was in front of my eyes, I saw it, and I felt it. It was like going to a movie and seeing a film. I recognized myself as the star of the movie, but I also felt all over again the same emotions I had originally felt when I lived the experiences. It didn't feel like a video in fast-forward, though. The scenes and emotions were in real time, just as I had lived them, and I can't explain it. How long does it take to bounce from one spot to another during a road accident? Yet it felt as though I relived my entire seventeen years—all the cities we lived in, all the fights I had with my sister."

"In seeing your life flash in front of you, when you fought with your sister, did you feel her emotions as well as your own?"

"No. Mine was a very self-centered NDE. My review was devoted only to me and to my feelings. I was the protagonist, and I relived my life as a carbon copy of the original, probably from the time I was about two years old until I was seventeen."

"The music, you said there was love in the music. What did you mean?"

"It was harmony, it was perfect, and it was the best sense of beauty and peace that my heart has ever been impressed with. There was also a sense of mathematics connected with it, even though I cannot explain exactly what this means. The intervals between the musical tones seemed to have a mathematical, geometrical reason for being. I came back with a sense of the importance of mathematics and geometry, and I have never been very good at mathematics and geometry, so I don't understand the connection."

"Concerning the light at the end of the tunnel, you said that it gave you a feeling of being accepted. What did you mean by that?"

"It wasn't just the light, it was the entire process of the NDE. There seemed to be a meaning which might be paraphrased as: 'You are a good girl, you are accepted and you are loved, you are a wonderful human being,' or something on that order. Remember, I was growing up in a situation where I was frequently hit, I was termed the idiot and the bad girl who was always wrong. My experience in the tunnel was exactly the opposite of that, and it was the first time in my life that I really felt validated as a human being."

"You also used the words *natural* and *normal*. Why?"

"It seemed so normal, the whole process. I thought, 'Wow, this is cool, so this is how it is to die, this is what I have been wondering about.' My intuition was that this was the natural place to be; I felt as though I was going back to where I belonged. I knew that I was dying, but it seemed that it was simultaneously a natural transition and a beginning of my next stage. One phase flowed naturally and normally into the next."

"There was no fear, then?"

"Not only was there no fear, it was the best thing I had experienced up to that time—and from that time to now. A part of it was a sense of curiosity and wow, because it was so beautiful, so balanced, so harmonious. I was flying, I was flowing, and there was a feeling of awe in a very peaceful way. Also, I had this idea that, 'I need to learn all this, to bring it along with me into whatever that light is.' There was a big sense of duty, of responsibility of learning. This feeling remained with me, notwithstanding, then, my decision not to pass through the membrane of light."

"So you were gaining knowledge as you progressed in the experience?"

"Yes. Yes, tremendously. All of a sudden it was just there, wham! I am not able now to retell and explain what I gained, but I have this memory that all of a sudden all things made perfect sense and were clear, and I understood how everything came together in the universe, the reason for things being the way they are. And somehow math and geometry were seminal to understanding all of this puzzle. It became so clear, and I wondered how I could not have understood it before—it was now so simple, so beautiful. I was absorbing this knowledge as I floated towards the light.

"This feeling of everything coming together harmoniously in the universe, for things being the way they are—for all forms of life being connected—it made perfect sense. In fact, even though I cannot now explain how it all works, remnants of that memory persist, to the extent that I have a tremendous sense of respect, compassion, and an abiding love for all forms of life, even including rocks. I have become a vegetarian. Also, I have learned never to take for granted a smile, a tear, a word, a drop of rain, or a sunset. I do not take for granted a single instant of my life."

"In the beginning of your NDE, you mentioned that you were in a sort of flowing form with many appendices, but when you announced to the voice that you didn't want to stay, from that moment you had back your human form, is that correct?"

"Yes, when I said no, instantly I had my physical human body back. My hair, and my arms and legs were visible, and my clothes were back, too. I was not naked."

"Now let's see, wasn't your physical human body lying on the sidewalk where the accident took place? If that is true, then this could not have been your human body."

"Hmmmm, you're right, my human body was on the sidewalk, so . . . that's right . . . you know, I never thought of that before. That's a good observation. My other body being sucked backwards in the tunnel must have been some kind of a duplicate of my body lying in the road. It had to be an exact . . . man, I'm starting to see things in a different way. It was an exact duplicate of my human body, and it wasn't a see-through ghost-type of body texture, it was the real thing. And then I got sucked back, and somehow these two bodies must have overlapped again, or merged together, and I opened my eyes and saw the old man."

"After your experience, did you tell your story to anyone?"

"No. My immediate family would never have believed me."

"How long was it before you told anyone?"

"In about 1985, I hesitantly approached my Dad's wife about it. After briefly outlining my experience to her, she went to her bookcase with a smile, and without a word she handed to me one of the early books on NDEs. After I read the first few pages, I thought, 'I'm not crazy. This same thing happened to me, too.' And then I told her of my experience."

"How many times have you told your story?"

"You are the fourth."

"Could your experience have been a dream or an hallucination?"

"No. There is no doubt in my mind that my NDE was a real event, and that I was experiencing it while it happened. I heard the sounds, felt the coolish temperature, saw the surprising colors. It was a harmonious, consistent and coherent development of a very complex set of elements which I could have never thought of, or made up myself. Nothing which I had experienced up to that moment in my life would have led me to even come close to being able to invent such dynamics or coherence. It was as real as when I drive to school from home, or when I shop at a supermarket. I'm sure that it was not an hallucination, a dream, or any other type of fantasy."

"What's your feeling about death?"

"I do not fear it. It was the most beautiful experience I have had in 43 years of living."

"Have you noticed any problems with watches or electrical devices since your experience?"

"Yes. Probably every two years, or so, my watch stops and won't run for a while. When I take it to a jeweler, they always tell me that the battery is okay and there is nothing wrong with the watch. It runs again, when I shake it, for awhile until the next incident. Occasionally when this happens I can correlate it with an emotional or traumatic event in my life."

"Why did you ask me about electrical problems?" Sylvia asked.

"It is not uncommon amongst those who have had NDEs to notice such effects. Are there others that you have noticed?"

"Well, yes. Sometimes when I am driving along or walking down a street at night, the street lights will turn off as I drive or walk past them. After I have passed them for some distance, then they turn themselves back on. This happens, maybe, two or three times a year, usually when I am under stress or really very tired. It can be embarrassing if someone is with me, since it is so obvious that they turn off and then on again as I pass them. It's kind of funny to watch the street lights go off and then on again as I drive along. Immediately before this phenomenon happens, I can feel a sort of force or energy in my mid-section which gradually rises until it conglomerates and reaches inside my head. Then it seems to need to explode out of me, out of my head, and that's when the lights go out, at the moment of the . . . the explosion. There often is a sequence of maybe three or four street lights and then it is gone."

"Before you had your NDE you apparently were an atheist. What is your belief now in God, do you believe in such a being?"

"A 'being,' you ask? No, probably not . . . I don't know . . . I haven't resolved this yet . . . it's a very difficult question. I came back to this earth from my near-death experience with an intuitive feeling that the concept of a 'God' is much, much more complex than just that of a 'being.' So, to your question, posed the way it is, I would probably have to answer, no, at least not in a God as commonly understood in our Western hemisphere. As one of the consequences of my NDE, I have doubts about and objections to the Judeo-Christian anthropomorphic God of judgment. During my experience, I only found total non-judgmental acceptance and love—none of the fire and brimstone of the Old Testament. On the other hand, do I deny the existence of God? No, of course not, how could I? I simply don't know."

"So, what power or being was responsible for your near-death experience?"

"I'm not sure, it seemed to be a natural part of the life-and-death process. I call *Universe* what I think other people call God. To me the term 'Universe' is more comprehensive, there's less historical, theological, and philosophical strife associated with it, I think. The 'Universe' gave me life, and I respect and nurture it."

"So you are not a religious person."

"I consider myself a very spiritual person, however I am not associated with any denominational creed. My spirituality did not unfold overnight after my NDE, but it developed—slowly but surely—and is still expanding today."

"Are there any messages you would like others to have based on your experience?"

"I came back feeling that I had to learn, that I had to absorb like a sponge as much as I could. It was as though I was charged with a duty to learn."

"What do you mean, charged?"

"When I was floating through the tunnel, I understood that it was important and dutiful that I learn all that I could. I no longer could afford to be a superficial teenager. As a matter of fact, before my NDE, I was not all that excited about school. Within a few years of my NDE, I became, and remained, a 4.0 student. From that point on, I have been thirsty to read and learn about a variety of subjects."

Analysis of the Three Experiences

As will be evident from further discussion concerning patterns in NDEs, all three of those interviewed followed in the footsteps of many we have interviewed in using certain words and actions. The words were: light, love, peace, no pain. Both Sylvia and George also spoke of the remarkable colors which they saw, again, a common element in many NDEs.

Perhaps not as common, but a transforming event for those who do experience it, was the music which Sylvia heard. It was interesting that both Sylvia and another lady that Carol and I interviewed spent considerable effort trying to find a duplicate of the music they heard upon returning. Both found a piece which approached, but didn't quite reach, the level of ecstatic sound they had experienced.

One of the more common elements in near-death experiences, and one which I will discuss in more detail later, is the light. All three of our candidates spoke of the marvelous and remarkable light.

Only Sylvia went through a tunnel. This, too, fits a pattern. In my previous work only 22 percent of those I interviewed had the tunnel experience, usually those whose NDE was fairly extensive.

Both Sylvia and Dan were given a choice of staying or returning. And immediately upon making that choice they found themselves, either back in their body as with Dan, or rapidly on the way to their body as in the case of Sylvia. This, too, is a common pattern.

As with essentially all pleasant near-death experiences—as contrasted with unpleasant ones—each of our candidates felt of the enormous peace and acceptance that accompanies such experiences. This aspect of the experience was so profound that it was indelibly imbedded in their memories as a real event—as real as anything they have experienced in life on earth.

Dan's sense of mission, and yet inability to know exactly what that mission was, is also customary in NDEs. Many of those having undergone an NDE are extremely frustrated over the fact that they know they are supposed to accomplish something with their remaining life, but they cannot remember what it is. A few remember that they were told they would forget exact knowledge of their mission. In a sense, Sylvia's feeling that her mission was to learn is somewhat atypical.

Two aspects of Dan's experience deserve special attention. The first has to do with his vivid memory of the event after these many years and from such a youthful age. In his own words he remembers it as, "probably one of the most deeply entrenched experiences and mental images that I've ever had in the fifty years I've lived." Numerous other people I have interviewed who had their NDEs at a very young age have reported their experience in a similar manner. It is almost as if the reality of the event has been burned into their memory.

The second item that is especially noteworthy has to do with the profound commentary that came from Dan when I questioned him about life and death. Dan's formal education was limited, yet he enunciated these thoughts instantly and with complete assurance. I later asked him where the ideas originated; had he read some sophisticated philosophic treatise, or had his previous religious training contributed to what he told me? He assured me that he had not read any philosophic books, and the thoughts had not originated from his religious background. He said, "I don't know where they came from—they are just inside of me."

Dan's explanation for his inner thoughts are almost the exact words that Theresa—whose story is told in later chapters in this book—expressed when I queried her concerning her understanding of opposition, such as pain, fear and grief. Her reflections on opposition are given in Chapter 7. She, too, had limited formal education, yet her ideas were philosophic and erudite in the extreme. My observation at the time was that it was as if she had been pre-programmed to respond to certain questions in this manner. The same was true of Dan.

George was the only one of the three NDE candidates to see other people during his experience. From his description they were in human form and dressed in long flowing robes. They traveled by "gliding," and they were elevated from the floor. This is how such spiritual beings are usually depicted by those having NDEs. From my own research, 55 percent of those having NDEs see other spirit beings in human form, 40 percent know the individuals that they see, and 28 percent recognize them as deceased relatives.

Sylvia was the only one of our candidates to have a life's review— although a diminished one as such reviews often occur—and she was astonished that it could happen in what seemed her entire life in real-NDE- time, even though it must have been only a second or so between bounces. This, too, is not unusual in NDEs. Most participants feel that time during their NDE is vastly different from time in our earthly existence. One man whom I interviewed had a life's review while his car was traveling through the air after a crash. An unusual facet of Sylvia's life review was its complete self-centered nature. In the overwhelming majority of life reviews the person having the review feels empathy for, and even the pain of, other persons when their repeat life again interacts with those other persons.

Also in Sylvia's case, a very unique element in her NDE was her observation that immediately after entering the tunnel she was in the form of a "Medusa" type character with flowing appendices instead of arms and legs. She also said that she could see out the top of her head, and she assumed, therefore, that she had eyes there. Several people speak of being able to see from all parts of their bodies during their experience. Some describe their vision as being through a 360 degree range.

As for Sylvia's medusa-type body, that particular description is unusual, but the idea that spirit beings can appear in a number of forms is not. Howard Storm, who had an extensive NDE, saw many other spirit individuals as sparkling radiant formless shapes who asked him if they needed to appear in human form. He assured them that their glory was so beautiful that they need not change.[2] I shall comment further on this aspect of Sylvia's NDE in Chapter Three.

Both Dan and Sylvia understood, from their NDEs, the importance of learning. Dan saw this life as a preparatory school for the next stage in his development, and Sylvia felt that she had been charged to learn all she could during mortality. She also had a recollection of great knowledge pouring into her during her NDE; knowledge, which at the time, made the universe and her place in it seem obvious. Dan and Sylvia both also understood how precious each moment of life was.

An amusing part of our interview with Sylvia was when she became aware, because of a question I asked her, that her body—which was being sucked backwards through the tunnel—was not the same body as her earthly one. The certainty that they were different bodies became apparent when she realized that the earthly body was still on the sidewalk while the one in the tunnel, although it had all of the normal features of head, hair, arms and legs, was a separate entity at that point. It was only after they merged when they became an obvious single entity. I shall explore this element of the dualism of living beings in the next chapter.

Several people whom Carol and I interviewed have identified their return to their earthly bodies as a sucking or vacuum experience. One lady I quizzed about whether or not she made the choice to return answered: "Well if I did, I was sucked back kicking and screaming against my will." Sylvia's sucking event fit the vacuum pattern perfectly.

Sylvia's bias against a male voice speaking to her was humorous. In this instance her previous cultural background made an obvious intrusion into her experience.

As you can see from these three experiences, the individuals came from very different cultural, religious and educational backgrounds, yet each of them felt of the inexpressible peace and joy associated with their experiences. None of them will ever be able to forget what was, to them, the most wondrous experience of their lives. Both Dan and Sylvia had impressions of great knowledge becoming instantly available.

As observed in the amusing question and answer period with Sylvia, strange electrical effects are not uncommon after an NDE. DeAnne

Shelley, whose experience is described later in this chapter, felt powerful electricity flowing through her during a remarkable healing event.

An astonishing element, to me as a researcher, has been the recognition that knowledge given to these choice individuals has nothing to do with the educational background of the individual. Some of the most profound thoughts have come from people with limited formal education, as with Dan, and later to be discussed, Theresa. But now let us turn to the question of how "real" the experiences are and what reality means.

Do the Stories Represent Reality?

To the people having these experiences, they certainly represent reality. As one lady put it, "This is the dream world, the other one is the real world." Repeatedly, near the end of each interview, I asked the individuals if their experience could have been caused by a dream or an hallucination, or did it seem real? The response was always vehemently the same. To give you a feel for how these individuals reacted to their experience and to that question let me recreate much of what Stephanie LaRue told Carol and me of her NDE. Stephanie's NDE followed her operation for a hysterectomy when she began to hemorrhage. Her husband was holding her in his arms in the hospital bed shortly after he called for emergency medical assistance. Our interview follows:[3]

"All of a sudden, within the blink of an eye, I left my body. It was so fast and so natural. I wasn't afraid—of course I didn't know that this was death."

"How did you know that you had left your body?" I asked.

"I turned around and saw myself in the bed."

"What did you look like?"

"I remember saying: 'That's not the real me,' and I pointed at the hospital bed. 'This is the real me; that's only a shell,' and I pointed back, again, at the hospital bed."

"Could you see your husband?"

"I could see my husband, and I could see myself. . . .

"About this time I had an experience that I'll never forget. It was an experience of complete tranquility, peacefulness, wholeness—whatever the word wholeness means; like mind, body, and soul. Also a feeling of total, total knowledge without asking.

"It's like you and me sitting here, now, and wondering how far the universe expands, or . . . just questions we have on earth about the geography of the earth, craters, or anything. This feeling I had of total knowledge was just that, I knew everything without asking. It was an incredible feeling.

"I turned around and looked at my body again, and I knew why I was there; I didn't have to ask. The only way I can relate to it is to observe that I was more alive in that realm than I am talking to you, here, now. Another way to relate to it is . . . like you and I are more awake now than when we are asleep at night. That's how much more aware I was in the other realm."

". . .When I left my body I was encompassed with a higher power. It felt like complete wholeness, tranquility, peacefulness, . . ."

"Love?"

"Oh definitely love, definitely. It . . . there are no words in the English language to describe it. It's more than love; the word love is just the tip of the iceberg, so to speak."

"When you had that feeling, did you have any understanding about where the feeling was coming from, or what was driving it?"

"It was everything. It was an accumulation of everything that ever lived—like the trees, the flowers, every human being, animals, anything that lives or breathes, a blade of grass. It was a totality of everything. Also, when I came back into my body I knew that everything had its place, its purpose, and there was a reason for everything. Even poor children that die of cancer at a young age, somebody's life that is taken; everything has a reason. But you don't know that until you are on the other side."

. . . "Do you feel that the experience was truly out-of-body, and that it was a real experience and not a dream or an hallucination?"

"I'd bet my life on it."

Some Corroborative NDEs

As will be discussed in the next chapter, corroborative experiences are especially useful in demonstrating the reality of NDEs because there seems to be no other way to explain them except as an out-of-body occurrence in some other dimension or spiritual reality. The cases which I shall detail below are ones that my wife and I are personally familiar with. We have checked on the details described. In most instances we have become close friends with the individuals involved.

DeAnne Anderson Shelley—A Remarkable Healing[4]

In 1961 DeAnne contracted bulbar polio which she ultimately recovered from. Then, in 1964, after moving to Vacaville, California, she became ill again. Thinking it was a recurrence of polio, she was put in a hospital; there they diagnosed her illness as acute multiple sclerosis. The disease attacked her muscles and central nervous system, and she quickly deteriorated. She became largely paralyzed, she could only breathe with the aid of a tracheotomy, and within a short period she lost her sight.

Her doctor, John E. Parkinson, used the best medical techniques available but she continued to decline. After about five months of crisis, on one particularly critical night, Doctor Parkinson informed her husband that DeAnne couldn't last through the night.

After giving DeAnne's husband, Fred, the distressing news, the Doctor, who was an active member of The Church of Jesus Christ of Latter-day Saints, left for home. He later told Fred and DeAnne that, as he was preparing for bed, he had a strong feeling he should return and give DeAnne a blessing even though Fred and DeAnne were not members of his church.

The Doctor called the local Stake President of the LDS Church and the two of them returned to the hospital. When asked if he would allow them to give DeAnne a blessing Fred readily agreed. In the blessing DeAnne was promised that she would live and that the medicines would be effective. She was also told that she had more purpose in life that was yet to be fulfilled.

When Doctor Parkinson returned the next morning Fred was present. DeAnne awoke, and although unable to see, she began crying. When asked why she was crying DeAnne explained that she had just had a gorgeous experience and she didn't want it to quit.

She told the doctor and Fred that she had been in this beautiful place, with brightness all around, where she could see again, and where there was no anguish or pain. She met her father there, who had previously died, and he looked wonderful. He was wearing a long white robe and he was not as wrinkled as she remembered him in life. He told her that he was thrilled she didn't have to suffer so much anymore.

After seeing her father she became aware that she had to return. She awoke to find that she was back in the hospital, blind again, and in terrible pain. That was why she was crying.

In a short period she recovered her sight and over the next several months, with the aid of extensive physical therapy, reached the point where she could ride in a wheelchair. She could also walk, with some difficulty, with the aid of braces and crutches. Her limbs were atrophied from the effects of the disease, which was still with her, and from lack of use.

As a result of discussions with the doctor and others, and following much study and prayer, Fred and DeAnne joined The Church of Jesus Christ of Latter-day Saints. A few months after joining the church DeAnne asked for and received a special blessing from Patriarch John L. Murdock in Napa, California. In the blessing she was promised that one day she would lay her crutches and braces aside and would be made whole.

In February, 1965, DeAnne and Fred traveled to Oakland to go through the Mormon Temple there. She used the wheelchair in going through the temple.

The next portion of DeAnne's experience is reproduced exactly as DeAnne related it to me.

"Were you excited [to go to the temple]?"

"I'll say I was. They put me in the wheelchair so that I could move around in the temple. Everything went well until after they had started the endowment session, then I became ill."

"What do you mean you became ill?"

"There was this vibration in my body. It was as if electricity was going through it."

"Did you feel sick?"

"Yes, I felt as though I couldn't catch my breath, and that I might faint. The electricity was so strong."

"Did anyone else notice?"

"Maxine felt the vibration, and she noticed that something was wrong with me. She raised her hand and they stopped the session. One of the matrons wheeled me out and Doctor Parky followed me."

"So you went out into the hall?"

"Yes, and Doctor Parky helped me to lie down on a bench. He took my pulse and said that I seemed to be excited. He told me to remain still for a period and I'd probably be all right."

"Did you tell him how you felt?"

"I tried to but I'm not sure he understood at first. As I lay there my arms and legs began to feel . . . they felt light. They always felt so heavy after I got MS. Even to move my ankle was a big deal. If I wanted to move my legs I had to pick them up with my hands, they wouldn't move by themselves. Now, all of a sudden . . . it must have been over in five minutes. I felt like I could use my legs. My neck and back felt better too."

"Did you tell your doctor that you could move your legs?"

"Yes, and I showed him that I could lift my left leg. Maybe he understood then that I'd been healed, I'm not sure. In any event he put me in the wheelchair, and we went back in to the session."

"How long were you in the hall?"

"It couldn't have been more than ten or fifteen minutes."

"They started the session up then?"

"Yes, and they came to the part where they invite some couples to come up front. I stood and walked up, Fred saw me, and he came up."

"What was his reaction?"

"He stood with me and tears were streaming down his face. I was just happy—happy—happy!"

DeAnne never used crutches again. In subsequent years her children grew up, and married. Fred was killed in an airplane accident and DeAnne married another wonderful man, Melvin Shelley. They are living today in Arizona.

In addition to hearing DeAnne tell her story, we heard from Fred what he had witnessed. We also heard Dr. Parkinson give a detailed description of the medical crises and events over the many months of her disease. Just prior to the healing experience, medical technicians, as a regular part of following DeAnne's progress had measured her muscular deterioration. Measurements taken after the cure showed restoration of the muscles to normalcy.

Although DeAnne's story is not in the category of a corroborative out-of-body episode where the individual saw things which were later

verified, her NDE and the entire healing situation—with the Doctor verifying the different events leading up to the healing—were corroborative. DeAnne, herself, and all those associated with her whom Carol and
I met were convinced of the reality of the incidents involved.

Bill English—A Courageous Man

The president of our local IANDS chapter is Bill English. Prior to
his NDE Bill was not a religious individual and he did not belong to any
organized group. He still does not affiliate with any particular religion,
but unlike his previous orientation, Bill is now a very spiritual individual. He is an example to all who know him.

In July 1991 Bill and his brother, Bob, were riding their ATVs (All
Terrain Vehicles) in the sand dunes near Saint Anthony, Idaho. Bill's
machine threw him and he landed on his head, breaking his back at
about the nipple level. After removal by helicopter to a local hospital,
and later being transported to the University of Utah Medical Center in
Salt Lake City, Bill's medical emergency deepened. His brother was
told that Bill probably would not live, and if he did live he would be paralyzed and need help for the rest of his life. Bill was comatose for over
four weeks. During that time he had two out-of-body experiences. The
first one occurred on the afternoon of the day following the accident.
Bill was able to determine the specific time because of the nature of his
NDE.

Following is our interview from this point in his experience:[5]

At the University Medical Center they did a number of other tests.
By that time I had gotten Adult Respiratory Distress Syndrome
(ARDS), which is usually fatal, and my heart was erratic. They put an
external pacemaker on me to keep my heart beating regularly as well
as other equipment to keep me alive. Then I developed pneumonia, and
I got a staph infection in the blood. I was on a ventilator and I had tubes
attached to various parts of my body; by this time I was comatose and
the medical prediction was that I would not live.

Bob called a couple of my relatives who were LDS and asked if
they would come and give me a blessing. My cousin, and Bob's brother-in-law, who were both active in the Church, came to the University
hospital and gave me a blessing. Medically, when they gave me the
blessing, I was in a coma and could not hear what they were saying.
The fact is, however, I could almost repeat verbatim what they said. I

have, since, lost some memory of their words, but at the time I was totally aware of what they were saying.

I still remember them laying their hands on my forehead and asking that I be given peace to accept whatever was the Lord's will. There was no specific request that I be allowed to live or that I be healed; rather it was that I would be granted peace and acceptance.

As the blessing proceeded I felt hands on me—hands from those giving the blessing, but also other hands as well. The peculiar thing was that it was almost multi-dimensional—I could feel their hands, and I was looking at the scene as if from the perspective of a balcony. And . . . and there was this tremendous feeling of peace and well being that came into my body.

From this elevated position I first saw my cousin and Bob's brother-in-law with their hands on my head. Then, as I looked at the scene, I saw other less distinguishable people around me; and I had the feeling that their hands on me were healing hands.

Next, it was as if I shifted perspective from a balcony position to a position directly above my body. Looking down, I saw me, my body, with the people around it. Being somewhat quizzical, and trying to figure out what was happening, I looked, and . . . and I found that they were praying over me. It still wasn't clear why they were doing this, but I was filled with an awesome peace and calmness.

It was strange, I could feel this warm peace in my body, yet I was looking at myself from above. The most fascinating aspect of the scene was that physically I only saw two people in the room besides me—my cousin and Bob's brother-in-law, who were giving the blessing. Surrounding the bed, though, were all these other people with their hands on me; I could feel their hands on me. I couldn't distinguish them clearly, but I felt . . . I had a sense that they were relatives that had gone before me.

I can't tell you if my other experience was chronologically next, or how close it was to the experience with the blessing. I can pin the time down for the experience with the blessing because my cousin told me of the time—it was the afternoon of the day following the accident—but I can't do that with the next experience. All I know was that it was sometime during the four-and-one-half week period that I was comatose.

The experience began when I found myself in a beautiful meadow; it was . . . I can't describe it. The meadow was incredibly beautiful, and

I was walking along a path. The colors were vivid, and there was every color imaginable. It was just . . . I've tried to describe it to other people, and I couldn't—its beauty was beyond description.

As I walked along the path in the meadow I came to a stone archway. It seemed almost as if I were called, or drawn, to the archway. I walked through it and entered a courtyard where I saw my father. He was dressed all in white, and he was bathed in sort of an iridescent white light.

We approached each other, and I remember telling him that I was feeling lost and confused. I realized at that point that I was either in the process of dying, or I had already died. My confusion centered on my earthly life. I was feeling a great loss because of my children, and I was sharing that feeling with my father. Additionally, I wasn't sure that I wanted to live in the paralyzed state that the doctors said I would live in.

My father said to me: "You aren't going to be lost or confused any longer. Everything will be fine. It's not time for you to be here, now, but when it is I will be here." Then he embraced me—there was an enormous outpouring of peace—and he took me back to the archway. As I entered the archway, I had the feeling that everything would be okay. That's the last thing I remember until I came out of the coma.

When I came out of the coma, my youngest brother, Tom, was there, and my mother. They asked me if I knew where I was and what had happened. I remember telling them that I had been with Dad, in response to which they looked at me strangely.

During Bill's first NDE his cousin, Tom Christenson, wrote a detailed description of what he witnessed during that period when he was giving Bill the blessing. Many of those details coincided with what Bill described when he later was well enough to tell what had happened to him. Tom has outlined these details for our local IANDS group. What Tom did not see during the blessing were the other spiritual individuals—deceased relatives—which Bill was able to observe from above his body.

Today, although Bill is paralyzed from the chest down, he is athletically involved. He regularly rides and races in a three-wheeled hand-driven tricycle. He is a marvelous man who gives help to many people.

Susan—An NDE From Multiple Perspectives[6]

Susan's NDE was described at a local meeting of IANDS of Utah in August 1994. This was a unique meeting with numerous people explaining what happened during the NDE from their different perspectives. The participants were: Susan, who had the NDE; Cory, her husband; Dianne, her sister; Doctor Rick, the anesthesiologist who was present during the NDE; and Betty, one of the nurses present during the NDE.

Susan told us that as a child her parents divorced, and she retained anger for her father for many years—because she felt abandoned by him. She still felt anger as an adult.

In May 1992 she had a caesarean section in order to deliver twins, a boy and a girl. She and her husband, Cory, already had four children, so this made six.

After the delivery of the children, Susan suddenly felt that she could not breathe—she had a heart attack. Then, she was relieved of pain and found herself watching the doctors and nurses work on her.

Feelings of great peace enveloped her, and she noticed that her body was no longer pregnant. She felt embraced by a loving warmth, and then she saw her deceased aunt. There was a marvelous reunion, and her aunt acted as her guide during her NDE. A second lady of light appeared and said: "Consider well the choice you make."

As she studied the room she was in, she saw the health workers giving her CPR and frantically trying to resuscitate her. She also saw other spirit helpers working to assist the professional medical staff. Her aunt said: "They [the spirit helpers] are there to help facilitate your return—should you choose to return."

At first Susan didn't know that she was dead. When she realized that she was dead, Susan told her aunt that she needed a blessing. The aunt said: "That is being taken care of." Looking at her body, Susan saw three spirit men about to give her a blessing. Her father was not one of the men and Susan felt anger that he was not there. Her aunt told her, "He can't be here right now, Susy, but don't worry, he's okay" (he had committed suicide when Susan was fifteen).

Susan said that she carried all of her earthly emotions with her during her NDE, as when she was angry with her father for not being present. On each occasion, her aunt told her to "search her heart," and reject negative feelings. She was told: "Fear and doubt will hold you back. In order to progress you must conquer them." At first, she rejected the advice, and she could feel all knowledge being withdrawn, as if she were in a lead box that blocked all knowledge. Then, as her aunt continued to help her, and she felt of the love, she was able to eliminate the anger and fear, and the knowledge she obtained returned in a rush.

At one point in her NDE, Susan asked why she was born where she was—where her father could hurt her when he left her at age six by divorcing her mother. A loving voice said that such choices were made in her premortal life.

Finally, she had to choose whether or not to go back. By then she had decided she didn't want to return to the pain and problems of earth. She was told that if she didn't go back it would hurt both the health professionals who were laboring to bring her back, and her children. Not returning would also hurt her extended family. She returned to great pain.

Cory, Susan's husband explained how radically different Susan was upon return. He said that her personality and life values had been radically rerouted. He explained it as an overwhelming change that the parties had to struggle through. He said that he was suddenly faced with six children, two of whom were twin babies, and a wife that was "off in *La-La Land*." He observed that the adjustment has not been easy for either of them.

Dianne, Susan's sister, described the new Susan as her enlightened sister who had to be dragged kicking and screaming to her blessings. She said, as a result of the new Susan, the family is much closer than it was before.

Dr. Rick, the anesthesiologist, explained that everything went normally until after the cesarean delivery when suddenly Susan remarked that she couldn't breathe—she became unresponsive. Within 5 to 10 seconds there was no pulse and no blood pressure reading. Dr. Rick asked the surgeon to begin CPR, and the nurse pressed the code button.

It took 10 to 15 minutes to reestablish a blood pressure reading. Since the brain function is damaged after 3 or 4 minutes without a heartbeat, the doctors expected severe brain damage. They were astonished, later, when Susan began to recover.

After her experience, Susan described to Dr. Rick what she saw in the operating room. He said that her eyes had been taped shut during the emergency, and there was no way that she could have witnessed what she saw unless she was out of her body.

Later, in a visit to his home, Susan examined a photo album of ancestors and various deceased relatives of Dr. Rick. To both his and her surprise, she identified one of his ancestors as one of the "helpers" in the room during the emergency.

Betty, the nurse, confirmed that she was unable to feel a pulse. She pushed the code button and helped in the team response when the medical personnel with the emergency cart arrived. She was very emotionally affected during the event because she, too, was pregnant. She was surprised and delighted at Susan's near-complete recovery.

Maria—The Shoe on the Ledge[7]

This is probably the most famous story of a corroborative type of NDE. It is extremely difficult to explain in any other way than as a spiritual out-of-body event. Kimberly Clark Sharp expounded on the details of the story in one of our IANDS of Utah meetings. She has also written about Maria's experience in her book *After the Light*.

Maria was a middle-aged Hispanic migrant worker who was admitted to the Coronary Care Unit of Harborview Hospital in Seattle where Kimberly was employed as a clinical social worker. Maria had suffered a massive heart attack and was hooked to cardiac monitors when Kimberly first met her in 1977. Maria began to improve physically, and although she could only speak Spanish and a weak version of English, she and Kimberly became friends over the three days of her recovery. Then, on the fourth day, as Kimberly was having coffee and completing paper work, Maria's monitors alarmed and she "flatlined" with cardiac arrest.

An emergency resuscitation succeeded, but as Kimberly was getting ready to leave the hospital she got a request to come immediately to Maria's station. Maria seemed agitated and the nurses felt that Kimberly could calm her.

When Kimberly reached her Maria was in an extreme state of agitation. Her arms were flailing and she was speaking rapid Spanish trying to communicate something. In time she calmed enough to point to the ceiling and let Kimberly know that she had been up there. With difficulty, but gradually, she was able to communicate how she had seen the medical personnel working on her, including details of what they did—and what Kimberly had also seen the resuscitation team do.

Maria then described how she had left the hospital and been in an elevated position beside an outside wall. There was a ledge running around the wall three stories above the ground. On the ledge, and invisible from below, was a man's dark blue tennis shoe, scuffed on the left side and with the shoelace caught under the heel. Maria was upset because she wanted someone to get the shoe in order to prove that her experience had been real.

Kimberly went from room to room of the hospital, pressing against windows and looking for the shoe. Finally, on the west side of the hospital she found the shoe on the ledge, with the shoelace tucked under the heel just as Maria had described it. Kimberly opened the window and extracted the shoe. Kimberly later expressed in her book Maria's reaction to the shoe when it was brought to her:

"Oh, my God! Dios mío! Maria cried, beside herself with bilingual joy. "The shoe! Lo encontraste! You found it! El Zapato! Gracias, gracias! Oh thank you!"

Maria was catapulted to instant hospital fame as her story spread from nurse's station to nurse's station. Doctors, nurses and orderlies came to pay homage to the humble Hispanic woman who had seen a shoe on a ledge.

Some Summary Thoughts About NDEs

These were people—experiencers and in one case a researcher—whom Carol and I interviewed and knew personally. We knew them to be honest, intelligent and responsible persons. They each had a profound spiritual experience which changed them forever. Each of them shifted their priorities toward what, to them, were more purposeful pursuits.

From these experiences we get a glimpse of a reality that surpasses what we normally designate as real. For those who traveled to that realm the events they went through were more vivid and increased their

awareness of their being, and their position in the universe, significantly compared with anything they had known in earth life. If reality is
measured by the acuteness of our senses, and by our knowledge and
understanding of why we exist, how we fit in the universe, and how we
should interact with others, then that ethereal reality exceeds our present
version of reality.

We could expand these examples almost indefinitely with equally
interesting, and in many cases, enthralling tales of travel to a distant
world. It is a world of infinite variety, and apparently a world of opportunities for infinite growth in an unlimited future. A world governed by
love, truth, mercy, justice and light, and a world of unsurpassed beauty.
Impressions of that world awakens in our soul hidden memories of a
former home and a glory that we long to revisit.

William Wordsworth wrote:[8]

> Our birth is but a sleep and a forgetting:
> The soul that rises with us, our life's star,
> Hath had elsewhere its setting,
> And cometh from afar:
> Not in entire forgetfulness,
> And not in utter nakedness,
> But trailing clouds of glory do we come
> From God, who is our home . . . .

2
Near-Death Experiences—
Research

Why a Chapter on NDE Research?

You have just read the stories of people who attempted to explain the ineffable joy they had when they were exposed to eternity. These stories may have challenged some of your cherished beliefs concerning whether or not there is a life after this life and what that life consists of. These, and other equally inspiring experiences, certainly challenged some of mine. An almost inevitable question concerning the experiences, then, is: What is the status of near-death research and is it in accord with modern science? An equally interesting question is: What impact is this work having on various branches of science—and on the religious community? Finally, the most important question of all: If the stories really do represent reality, what are the implications?

History and Early Work

In the Introduction I described how I got started in NDE research and I listed some of the pioneers in the field. Although it was Raymond Moody's work described in his book *Life After Life* which sparked modern-day interest, Moody himself got interested because of what he heard as an undergraduate philosophy student from one of his professors—a clinical professor of psychiatry in the University of Virginia school of medicine. The professor, George Ritchie, described an amazing experience of how he "died" from a severe case of pneumonia while on an Army base in World War II. Ritchie's story so impressed Moody that he continued with his studies, got his Ph.D. in philosophy and later entered medicine and became a psychiatrist, at least in part to perform studies of individuals who had undergone what he later came to call near-death experiences (NDEs).[1]

Although Moody, Ritchie and Kenneth Ring were probably the most important individuals behind modern-day interest in NDEs, they were by no means the first. Doctor Elisabeth Kübler-Ross worked with dying patients for decades and has studied hundreds of cases of people all over the world who had been declared clinically dead and who later returned to life.[2]

Probably the first researcher to perform a serious study on NDEs recorded in the early and recent history of The Church of Jesus Christ of Latter-day Saints was Duane Crowther. In his book, *Life Everlasting*—first published in 1967 and still in print—Crowther was able to document dozens of such experiences happening to early Mormons and to correlate many of the experiences with LDS teachings.[3]

Going further back in time, Carol Zaleski, in her book *Otherworld Journeys—Accounts of Near-Death Experience in Medieval and Modern Times*, was able to describe experiences recorded by ancient writers from Plato to Pope Gregory the Great (in the sixth Century).[4] Ian Wilson, in his book *The After Death Experience—The Physics of the Non-Physical*, also traced NDEs into ancient times citing such examples as the Tibetan's Book of the Dead, the *Bardo Thodol*.[5]

One of the more interesting descriptions of a historic account of an extensive epiphany was provided by Emanuel Swedenborg who lived from 1688 to 1772. Swedenborg was an Enlightenment thinker of penetrating intellect, and he spent his first fifty-five years as a scholar, scientist, inventor and statesman. He was an active member of the Swedish House of Nobles. In 1744 he had an extensive vision of life after death in which he described an encounter with Christ.[6] His experience was not an NDE as such, but rather was a spiritual journey in which he was taken through the process of death by angelic guides. Over the next several years he had numerous visions and spiritual experiences of which he wrote expansively. His most prestigious work was probably the book *Heaven and Hell* which is often quoted by NDE researchers and authors. In *Heaven and Hell* he explained in detail what his visions showed him about heaven and hell.[7]

One can also find accounts in the scriptures of events which parallel many of the descriptions of NDEs. Paul's encounter with the Light in which he saw Christ—described in Acts—has similarities to NDE type events.[8] In the Book of Mormon there is an analogous experience to that of Paul by Alma as he set about to persecute the Saints of God. He, too, was overcome after he was accosted by an Angel, and he completely changed his life thereafter.[9] Although the descriptions in Acts and Alma do not include most of the elements listed by Kenneth Ring in his definition of what constitutes an NDE, they do include a primary event in which the individual had a dramatic vision or experience with some ethereal being, was reminded of past sins (a life review), and came back with a completely changed perspective about how to live.

So, NDE accounts are not new in the literature. What is new is the attention being given to the phenomena by many modern scientists—and by the resultant thrust of their research on the subject. A glance at the bibliography of this book illustrates this extensive and thorough world-wide interest.

Some Initial Researchers

In the Introduction I described how Kenneth Ring sought out and interviewed near-death candidates. That early work, and the founding of the International Association for Near-Death Studies in 1980, precipitated a great deal of follow-on work by others. Initially the work was produced by medical professionals, psychologists and sociologists—and by people who had undergone an NDE (and sometimes by a combination of both).

In addition to the physicians George Ritchie and Raymond Moody, two other physicians who collected information on their patients and those of other physicians were Maurice Rawlings and Michael Sabom. In 1979 the Bantam Edition of Rawlings' book *Beyond Death's Door* was published. Rawlings was a cardiologist, and he documented NDEs which illustrated both happy or euphoric experiences and frightening experiences. His book had chapters devoted to the subjects Ascending to "*Heaven*," and *Descending to "Hell."* Rawlings is a Protestant Christian, and he attempted to show correlations between Biblical scriptures and the NDEs which he had documented. His book was one of the first to provide considerable detail on frightening experiences.[10]

In 1982, Michael Sabom, also a cardiologist, detailed the results of his findings on 116 cases, mostly his own patients, who had NDEs.

Sabom's work was especially useful since he took the trouble to document out-of-body (OBE) experiences where corroboration could be obtained. In particular, he sought to obtain data from medical professionals and other witnesses who could corroborate what the NDE claimants said they saw while they were out of their body. During periods, for example, of a medical emergency the patients' eyes are often taped shut to protect them. Where the patients were able to see the medical professionals performing specific tasks on their bodies, these actions by the medical people were later verified by Sabom.[11]

In 1990, Melvin Morse, a pediatrician, in collaboration with Perry, published his book on children's NDEs in the book *Closer to the Light.* This book was unique in that it reproduced the innocent and often matter- of-fact comments by children as they described how they went to heaven and saw Jesus.[12]

In 1988 Phyllis Atwater's book *Coming Back To Life—The After-Effects of the Near-Death Experience* was published. In the book Atwater detailed how, during a hemorrhaging miscarriage in 1977, she had an extensive NDE—actually three separate NDEs—which profoundly affected the rest of her life.[13] As a result she set out to do research on the lasting effects of NDEs. She has written several books and articles on the subject and has frequently been a speaker at IANDS conferences

Dr. Cherie Sutherland was a Sociologist at the University of New South Wales in Australia. In 1971, while giving birth to a son she had an NDE and, as with many such experiences, she was given a choice to stay or return to life. She chose to return to life for the sake of her two children and for her own sake. Since that experience she began a long and extensive effort to research numerous NDEs in Australia and elsewhere. She, too, has documented frightening NDEs. Two of her best known books are *Reborn in the Light*[14] and *Within the Light.*[15]

Kimberly Clark Sharp is a clinical social worker and the founder of the local Seattle group of IANDS, one of the first and largest of the local groups in the United States. In 1970 she collapsed outside an office in Shawnee Mission, Kansas, and she had an NDE where she was encompassed by the Light. This set her on a course of finding out what such experiences were all about. She has illustrated some of the most splendid NDE cases in the literature. She wrote the book *After the Light—*

What I Discovered on the Other Side of Life That Can Change Your World.[16]

The Nature of Early Research

By its very nature, early research consisted primarily of the gathering of anecdotal stories. This led to both one of its weaknesses and one of its strengths. The weakness came about because researchers could not fix the parameters of data that they gathered with such techniques as double-blind studies and sophisticated pre-test statistical gathering methods. The strength of the anecdotal method resulted from the publishing of vast numbers of experiences with the details recorded of each event. In social science this type of early study is called an "Exploratory Study." Researchers later, therefore, studied the recorded anecdotes and performed more sophisticated work, such as searching for patterns of repeatability.

Much criticism has arisen from this method of gathering anecdotal evidence, and some of it may be justified. Kenneth Ring, for example, attempted to change research methods somewhat by introducing more statistical gathering techniques (as in Heading Toward Omega), and in his more recent work with blind people who have had NDEs he deliberately sought corroborative data of the sort gathered by Sabom.[17]

Some of the criticism appears misplaced, however, and reveals something of the philosophy of the criticizer. If, for a moment, it is assumed that near-death experiences are in fact spiritual events—as most of those having an NDE claim—then anecdotal evidence makes perfect sense. Presuming that, just possibly, there is a creative higher power aware of and involved in the affairs of men, isn't it the epitome of arrogance to assume that such a higher power would craft NDEs for the convenience of researchers—instead of for the benefit of the person undergoing the NDE?

Another criticism of early NDE research was the lack of peer review. A rebuttal to this criticism might be that in those early days there were no peers—at least in the sense that there was no large group of professionals who were familiar with the NDE phenomenon. In recent years the IANDS organization, and in particular Professor Bruce Greyson at the University of Virginia, have attempted to correct this particular weakness. Greyson is the editor of the quarterly publication

Journal of Near-Death Studies which publishes technical articles dealing with all aspects of the near-death experience. Each article is subjected to extensive review before it is accepted for publication.

Another effort to improve on the quality of near-death research has been the attempt to determine patterns from an accumulation of events described by those having had NDEs. Phyllis Atwater, for example, has done a broad study of the aftereffects of NDEs on the lives of those who lived through them.[18] The Sociologists Craig Lundahl and Harold Widdison did an extensive categorization of events into various subjects known to be a part of many NDEs. Their book, *The Eternal Journey*, lists such categories as: *Pre-Earth Life and Its Purposes, Earth Life and Its Purposes, The Death Transition, Death: Crossing into the World of Light, The Nature of the Spirit Body, The City of Light*, and *The Realm of Bewildered Spirits*. They catalogued numerous events from NDEs which shed light on these various subjects.[19] Widdison is a professor of medical sociology at Northern Arizona University, and Lundahl is chairman emeritus of the department of Social Sciences and professor emeritus of sociology and business administrations at Western New Mexico University.

A fascinating study was done by Evelyn Elsaesser Valarino, the head of the law library at the University of Geneva in Switzerland. In a five year effort she studied NDE accounts so as to become relatively expert in the subject. Then she interviewed eminent personnel in diverse scientific and religious disciplines to obtain their perspectives on the NDE phenomenon. Those that she interviewed included: Kenneth Ring, the pioneer NDE researcher, Michel Lefeuvre, a professor of philosophy, Louis-Marie Vincent, a biology professor, Régis Dutheil, a professor of theoretical physics, Paul Chauchard, a neurophysiologist, and Lord Bishop Jean Vernette, advisor to the Vatican.[20]

In terms of recent work, Kenneth Ring's book, *Lessons from the Light—What We Can Learn from the Near-Death Experience* illuminates his decades of research in the field. Ian Wilson, who wrote the masterful book *The After Death Experience*, said of Ring's recent book: "A thoroughly gripping read, this is unquestionably the most important book on the subject since Moody's *Life after Life*."[21]

LDS authors, in addition to Duane Crowther, who have attempted to provide insight into possible correlation of NDEs with LDS teachings and scriptures include Brent and Wendy Top,[22] Craig Lundahl and Harold Widdison,[23] and me. Several other LDS authors have written about aspects of the NDE without attempting to correlate with LDS teachings or philosophy.

From this brief tabulation of research effort concerning NDEs it is apparent that since its modern inception in the early- to mid-1970s there has been an explosion of interest in the subject. Although initial research effort was crude, it has been improving in technique and sophistication since that time. And, a spiritual dimension has been added to the research effort as recognition has been gained that the very nature of the NDE may be due more to a spiritual than a physical phenomenon.

Attempts to Explain the NDE by Current Science

In 1998 Craig Lundahl and I submitted the paper "Near-Death Studies and Modern Physics" for publication in the *Journal of Near-Death Studies*. In the paper Lundahl performed a comprehensive review of the many attempts to explain what was happening in an NDE. Much of what was reported in that paper is repeated in Appendix A.

To an increasing extent recent NDE literature has described cases where the most likely explanation is that the human personality exists as both a physical body and a spiritual (or other-worldly) body. In many of these cases the out-of-body nature of the experience is demonstrated where the individual saw things which could not have been seen from the physical body—either because of position or because of the physical state of the body—and the things which the individual claimed to have seen are later verified by the individual or others. As noted previously, both Sabom and Ring identified such accounts which Lundahl and I chose to call *Corroborative NDEs*.

To this point Corroborative NDEs have not received much attention from the scientific community. As their cumulative evidence becomes more obvious they will undoubtedly receive increased research effort from various groups.

Today, the NDE still lacks a technical explanation acceptable to the scientific community at large despite the fact that considerable data has been accumulated on the phenomenon for almost a quarter of a century. Physicians, psychiatrists and others continue to generate what they hope will be a model or explanation of the NDE that will stand up to scientific scrutiny, so far unsuccessfully. An interesting case in point was exhibited in the Fall, 1997 *Journal of Near-Death Studies.* The entire edition was devoted to an article by Karl L. R. Jansen and to the responses by other medical practitioners and researchers to his article. The title of his article was *The Ketamine Model of the Near-Death Experience: A Central Role for the N-Methyl-D-Aspartate Receptor.*[24] In his article and in his follow-up response[25] to the commentaries of others, Jansen argued that his Ketamine theory might explain NDEs and eliminate the need to ascribe NDEs to some spiritual out-of-body event. Most of his respondents were favorably impressed with Jansen's work. Then, just before publication of the *Journal,* Jansen forwarded a post-script which was added as the last note in the publication. A portion of his postscript is as follows:

> I am no longer as opposed to spiritual explanation of near-death phenomena as my article and this response to the commentaries on it would appear to suggest. . . .
>
> My forthcoming book Ketamine will consider mystical issues from quite a different perspective, and will give a much stronger voice to those who see drugs as just another door to a space, and not as actual-ly producing that space. After 12 years of studying ketamine, I now believe that there most definitely is a soul that is independent of expe-rience. It exists when we begin, and may persist when we end. Keta-mine is a door to a place we cannot normally get to; it is definitely not evidence that such a place does not exist.

The principal problem with the majority of scientific explanations of the NDE in the past has been their attempt to use a material cause to describe what may, in fact, be a spiritual phenomenon. This has caused "hard science" investigators to rely on techniques that work fairly well in describing our physical universe, but seem unable to adequately explain what may be a different kind of world or universe.

Another NDE Explanation—The Unbound Spirit

Melvin Morse in a letter to *Vital Signs* (a publication of IANDS) commented that "near-death experiences are clearly localized to an under-used area in our brain in the right temporal lobe." In the same arti-cle he wrote, "We do not want to wait until we die to understand that there is a loving God who we have the ability to communicate with."[26]

This is similar to the observations of Karl Jansen, discussed above, where he noted that the natural drug ketamine may play a role in providing a "door to a place we cannot normally get to," but that there is a soul which survives death and is independent of the ketamine door.

These commentaries would suggest that there is both a physical and a spiritual component to the near-death experience. The physical component may be a triggering mechanism which can stimulate some part of the brain and induce a separate spiritual component to become activated as an independent entity. In such an event, it should be possible to bring on near-death type symptoms without the individual actually being clinically close to death. Instead of physical trauma common in most NDEs, the triggering event might be emotional trauma, Yoga fasting and meditation, extreme fear, prayer, or some other analogous mechanism. After this triggering event it should be possible for the spiritual component to separate from the physical body and make out-of-body observations which can later be verified as in corroborative NDEs.

A model of this type would be consistent with my own research findings. Although not in the majority, there were numerous individuals that my wife and I interviewed where there was no threat of death, yet a fairly comprehensive NDE type of experience occurred.

Julie was one of those we interviewed. As a teen-age child she was awakened and found herself standing in a brilliant light in the kitchen. Standing in the light were two individuals, one of them being her cousin who had been fighting in the jungles of Vietnam. He informed her that he had "come home." When the vision ended, Julie told her mother. Two weeks later the military identified the body of her cousin, Alan, who had been killed at roughly the same time that Julie saw him.[27]

Dee was in a bad marriage which completely traumatized much of her life. She had two separate experiences where she left her body during periods when her emotions became overwhelming. One of the experiences was a pleasant one where she traveled to a distant city and saw a girl friend with a new-born baby—the girl friend did not see Dee. Dee was able, later, to verify much of what she saw during her spiritual journey. The second event was a terrifying one where she was chased by evil spirits who seemed intent on destroying her.[28]

Joy lost her husband, her brother and her father within a two-year period. She eventually remarried, but recurring periods of grief became a consuming part of her life. One afternoon as she lay on a couch, resting, she left her body and went to some other spiritual dimension where she met with her deceased husband, brother and father. She had a joyous reunion and was able to return to life refreshed and capable of functioning normally.[29]

Vern Swanson was an Assistant Professor of Art History at Auburn University in Alabama when his wife and baby son were killed in a tragic automobile accident. Although Vern was ultimately able to emotionally cope with his wife's death he could not accept that of his son. He suffered extensive and almost continuous bouts of melancholy. One night after retiring he found himself instantly out of bed in the presence of his wife who was bathed in light. She was holding their son and she insistently demanded that Vern acknowledge the death of their son. After this experience Vern became his normally joyful self.[30]

During World War II Doris joined the Navy. She became disenchanted and decided to try and get out. In order to force the Navy to release her she went on an extensive fast. On the eleventh day of her fast, as she was walking toward her barracks, she suddenly found herself floating above her body which continued walking. She was astonished and debated how to get back in her body, which continued on its way as though nothing were wrong. She said of this surprising incident, "I wanted out of the Navy, not out of my body." Suddenly she found herself back in her body and the incident was over.[31]

Each of these events, except for Julie's, seem to have been triggered by some type of emotional or physical distress. Julie's was more in the nature of an urgent message delivered from another world to inform and calm close relatives of a recently deceased individual. All of the incidents resulted in an out-of-body experience. None of them were triggered by impending death.

Considerably more research needs to be done to verify this type of model. Nevertheless, from the above data and from Morse's and Jansen's observations, it seems reasonable to postulate a model where both physical and spiritual causative factors are involved in NDE types of experiences. The physical mechanism could be some kind of process, perhaps chemical in origin, which activates a part of the brain with an unusual stimulus. The brain, in turn, stimulates a spiritual entity, which is normally tightly bound to the physical body, to loosen its tight binds.

In many instances the binding of the spirit entity to the physical body may completely break. Upon termination of the NDE or analogous type of experience, the spiritual entity resumes its place and tight binding with the physical body—and life as we know it continues.

This kind of model would eliminate many of the current arguments by researchers that the NDE is *either* a physiological or a spiritual event. In fact, it appears to be *both*. For purposes of continued dialogue with other researchers I shall call this the *Unbound Spirit* model.

In a sense, this model is similar to that proposed by J. Kenneth Arnette in two articles which appeared in the "Journal of Near-Death Studies." Arnette called his model *The Theory of Essence*.[32] Arnette's model establishes a duality of the human being with a physical body which expires at death and an "essence" that survives. The essence includes the ego or consciousness of the individual and after death it separates from the body and exists in a real, though different dimension. Arnette also suggests, as I do in the Unbound Spirit model, that the "essence must have some aspect that we would call physical in order for essence/body interaction to occur; the body must possess something essential as well. Essence and body are extremely different, and in this sense the term dualism is appropriate. But the two must in some way speak a common language in order to communicate."

What Impact is Near-Death Research Having?

In the general public the impact is enormous, largely driven by the mass media. From Oprah Winfrey to the internet it is difficult to miss the continued and often sensational references to individuals who have returned from death. Consequently there is a general awareness now, which was not evident in my youth, of the NDE phenomenon.

In some portions of the scientific community the impact has been large. Those scientific disciplines associated with physiology, psychology, sociology, and psychiatry, in particular, have had to address the subject because of the increasing evidence of certain peculiar NDE events. The now recognized widespread nature of the phenomenon demands a serious and sophisticated response by scientists working in these areas.

In the so-called "hard sciences" such as physics, mathematics, cosmology, astronomy, chemistry, geophysics and geology, until very recently, there has been little impact. The reasons are complex and are as discussed in Appendix A. As near-death research material has invaded the scientific literature, however, there has been an awakening by the hard sciences to the existence of a body of evidence which cannot readily be discarded.

The fact that physicists and others in related fields are having increasing difficulty explaining certain events in the macro- and micro-universe, such as its anthropic nature and "quantum weirdness," has had a humbling effect on many such scientists (discussed in later chapters). Their own dilemmas have forced some of them to reach for answers in hitherto forbidden areas—even in the previously scorned regions where psychologists, physicians and sociologists fearlessly tread.

It is in the religious community, though, where the NDE is having a large and peculiarly troublesome impact. As Kenneth Ring points out in the Foreword to this book, many religions are now attempting to "hitch a ride on the NDE wagon and take over its reins." This has not always been so. In the early days of near-death research many of those now seeking admission to the NDE club were adamant in their condemnation of it. Why this sudden change of heart?

The changed attitude in the religious community has much to do with the same reasons that the scientists are having to reconsider their positions concerning NDEs. Those involved in the research—and especially those who have had near-death experiences—have communicated a powerful enough message that it cannot be silenced. Whereas previously individuals who had such experiences rarely spoke of them, either due to religious inhibitions or because the scientific community so universally ridiculed them, that is no longer the case.

Many religions are now having to deal with members who claim to have had near-death and similar spiritual experiences. It is no longer as easy for the hierarchies to authoritatively dismiss such claims. So, in defense of their theological positions, they have attempted to match their claims with what researchers have found in the NDE field.

This is not an altogether unhealthy trend. It is only when religious apologetics become so enthusiastic that they distort or change the near-death research data in order to force-fit it into their particular theological framework that it becomes injurious to the cause of truth.

Kenneth Ring also points out in the Foreword that there is much in the near-death experience that has a natural home in the traditions, beliefs and scriptures of the great religions of the world. Among other things, therefore, this book is a plea for greater collegiality between the different religions. It is in my view perfectly acceptable, even healthy, for competing religious beliefs to be compared with the research findings from the near-death field—so long as those comparisons are made with a reasonable measure of objectivity.

As you, the reader, are by now aware I believe that my own Mormon religion measures well against NDE research. But, as you read the juxtapositions which I make of the religious doctrine and the historical record of the early LDS Church against the near-death discoveries, you be the judge.

What are the Implications of Near-Death Research Findings?

In the course of my work in the near-death field I have come in contact with many of the early researchers listed in this chapter. *All* of those that I have become acquainted with agree that God is the author of much of what we find in the course of our research. Indeed, some researchers discover that they are in the same category as Kenneth Ring where he "found that the atheism of my younger years was insupportable and, mirabile dictu, I no longer had any doubt about God's existence and in fact came to believe that God was intimately involved in the orchestration of NDEs."

The implications of this trend by a scientifically educated and professionally skeptical audience are vast. For it is just such a group that has the power to influence and persuade a vast audience from other scientific disciplines and from the general audience. Later chapters will therefore illustrate—as my own intellectual and spiritual journey confirmed—that science and religion are really not antagonists. Rather they are partners in an eternal search for truth, and they can join hands in proclaiming that God's fingerprints are found everywhere we look.

Final Thoughts on Near-Death Research

In the process of my own research work I have interviewed two small children who went through remarkable near-death experiences. They told their stories in such innocent matter-of-fact ways that it was a delight just to sit and be taught by them. There was no denying the reality of their experiences, as for example when Rocky visited Jesus and Jesus gave him an apple.[33]

Perhaps no one has done as much research on the near-death experiences of children as has Melvin Morse. Let me end this chapter by describing an event where one of the children he had interviewed asked about the reality of the experience. The child's name was Chris.

> Suddenly Chris stopped.
>
> "I have to ask you a question," he said with the sophistication of someone ten years older. "How do I know that what happened was real? How do I know that I really went up to heaven? How do I know that I wasn't just making it all up?"
>
> I had focused on that very question myself for ten years. From the day that I heard my first near-death experience and a little girl patted me on the hand and confidently told me, "You'll see, Dr. Morse, heaven is fun," I have sought to answer the very question that Chris was asking me.
>
> I looked around the living room as everyone waited patiently for my response. Even with the years of research I have done on this topic, this is a difficult question for me to answer. I cleared my throat and smiled nervously at Chris.
>
> "Chris, what happened to you is as real as it gets." [34]

3
Questions About NDEs

Commonly Asked Questions

Since getting involved in NDE research I have been asked many questions dealing with the reality of NDEs. Some of the most common questions are the following:

> But Arvin, how do you know they were telling you the truth? Maybe they thought it was a real experience, but couldn't it have been some type of dream or hallucination? Couldn't their experience have been from the effects of the medication they were taking? Why in the world would anyone tell you a story like that—what was their motivation? Did you offer to pay them money for their stories? Do you really believe all of these stories? Aren't there a lot of nuts who call you with screwy stories—how do you separate them from the authentic experiences? Why do some people have near-death out-of-body experiences, and others with equally serious injuries or illnesses, do not? Why do individuals have such varied experiences—doesn't that prove that they are just figments of the mind? How do you explain some of the bizarre things that occur in some NDEs? Do you think that these experiences prove that there is a life after death? Could reincarnation explain some of the experiences? Are all the experiences pleasant? There doesn't seem to be much repentance and judgment associated with NDEs—isn't that at odds with the scriptures? Are angels a part of the NDE, and if so, what do they do? What about those who claim to have seen Jesus or God, doesn't that show that they were confused?

Interestingly, these kinds of questions are most often asked by people who have not taken the trouble to read much, if anything, on the subject of near-death experiences. Those who have read extensively on the subject are equally curious, but their questions are centered more on what our research findings show. It is clear from these, and other questions, that the subject has created substantial interest with the public.

In Appendix A I shall examine numerous attempts to explain the NDE as solely a psychological or physiological event. Similarly concerning the question which keeps appearing concerning reincarnation, that subject is considered in Appendix A. Other questions, however, deserve an answer and will be treated here.

Do Those Who Have an NDE Always Tell the Truth?

Of course not. Untruths are uttered for a number of reasons. Quite a few interpreted the fact that they lived before this life—which they discovered during their NDE—as evidence for reincarnation. In this instance their factual untruth was not the result of a deliberate lie.

A few individuals who have had an NDE allow themselves to be exploited by sensationalizing TV commentators and talk-show hosts. Publishers also take advantage of these individuals. In the process, the individuals occasionally expand on what they saw and heard during the experience. Sometimes they confuse their earthly beliefs with what they saw and heard. An unfortunate few use their temporary fame as an ego building exercise.

Outright fabrications of NDEs are fortunately, rare, but they do occur. Kenneth Ring investigated a published account of a blind woman who had an NDE. It turned out that the entire account was false.[1] In addition, there is one high-profile case of an individual who claimed to have had an NDE that is suspect.

What is the Motivation for Telling About an NDE?

People responded to our advertisements and came to see us for several reasons, but none of the reasons had anything to do with money. Of the hundred or so people we interviewed, only three or four asked if there were a fee involved. When I explained to those few that such a fee would make the story itself suspect, they understood and dropped the subject.

The reasons that most people came were: to talk to someone who was sympathetic to what they had to say; to find out about others who had had similar experiences; and to help others by sharing what the respondent knew about death. Many of them, after the interview was completed, questioned Carol and me for an hour or more about others we had interviewed. They were thrilled that we accepted their stories for what they were—a profound spiritual experience—and they were extremely curious about others. Equally important to those we interviewed was the possibility of having their stories published in a manner that would help others. In many instances they felt an obligation to bear witness to what they had seen and heard.

Which People Have NDEs?

There is no definitive answer to this question, but there have been studies that examine which people, and what percentage of the population, are more likely to have NDEs.

Kenneth Ring summarized the pertinent research with these words:

> Taking into account all the relevant research so far published then, and allowing for the possibility that Gallup's own figure may reflect a minimum value for the population, I would propose that somewhere between 25 and 35 percent of those who come close to death would report NDEs.[2]

In summarizing the research about whether one group of people is more likely to have an NDE than another, at least in Western societies, Dr. Ring said the following:

> Demographic characteristics such as age, sex, race, social class, educational level, occupation, and the like seem to have no particular relationship to NDE incidence. . . . I found no relationship for such demographic variables as social class, race, marital status, or religious affiliation.
>
> . . . There is, in fact, no difference in either the type or incidence of NDEs as a function of one's religious orientation—or lack of it. To be sure, an agnostic or an atheist might—and actually appear to—have a more difficult time coming to terms with the experience and may be less likely to interpret it in conventional terms than a believer, but the form and content of the NDE will not be distinctive.[3]

Why Such Varied Experiences?

Many who have had NDEs give detailed descriptions of a remarkable and colorful world on the other side. Their descriptions—unfortunately from the point of the researcher—are not consistent. Some speak of marble and gold buildings and streets; a city of light. One English

lady told of her mother's wonderful house in the spirit world with nas-
turtiums around it. The building was a prefab building of the type used
to shelter people in England during WWII.

Some individuals tell of an incredible being of light and love who
spoke with them. Many are certain that the being was Jesus Christ. Others, usually from non-Christian beliefs, describe the being as the Great
Spirit, or as in the case of one atheist that I interviewed, "an image made
of light particles in human form."

Why these differences? No one knows. Some speculate, however.
My own speculation, and that of Howard Storm[4] and Kenneth Ring[5] is
that the Lord provides us with a glimpse of the spirit world which is
suited to our needs. The Lord knows us better than we know ourselves,
and if in his wisdom he decides that we should see a deceased grand-
parent as a young and vibrant individual, that is what we see.

What About the Bizarre Happenings in Some NDEs?

People occasionally express disbelief about certain elements in
some NDEs which, to them, seem bizarre. I have been asked, for example, about a giant double-cone-shaped object in the sky which Forrest
Hansen saw during his NDE when he found himself in space. He understood this double-coned shape to represent the spectrum of possibilities
in the past, present and future for the universe. Despite my misgivings
about this aspect of his experience I included it in its entirety in the book
Glimpses of Eternity.[6] Then later I read Phyllis Atwater's account of a
similar event in her NDE[7] with almost identical meaning to that
assigned by Forrest. When I called Forrest and explained what I had
read in Phyllis's book he was interested, and he had never heard of Phyllis or her book.

Many people wonder at what appears to be evil spirits which occur
in some NDEs. George Ritchie, in his extensive NDE, described many
beings confined to a state that can only be described as hell.[8] And
Howard Storm described bizarre beings who attacked him during his
NDE.[9] Howard's account was very similar to that of one described by
Dee whom Carol and I interviewed in 1991. Portions of her experience
are described in the next section.

I mentioned in the preceding section that people have NDEs which
seem deliberately tailored to their particular needs. This is especially

true concerning how they see themselves and other persons whom they
encounter during the NDE. Most frequently they see themselves or others in a human form, but not always. Moreover, even in the human form
these appearances vary. Some see relatives, for example, in a younger
or older age than when they knew them on earth. For deceased grandparents and other relatives they usually appear in a younger form than
when they were known by the person during mortality. The opposite is
true of little children.

Similarly, when individuals see themselves, they are usually at the
prime of their life in the NDE even though they may be extremely disabled in their physical state. During my interview with DeLynn he told
me how he deliberately felt of his face and body to be assured that it was
complete and without the physical blemishes that plagued his cystic-
fibrosis-ridden physical body. He found that he could feel his face and
other features, and for the first time in his life he could breathe with no
difficulty. His arms and legs and other portions of his body had substance to them, and they looked normal except that there was a glow to
them. He was dressed in a white jump-suit type of garment.[10]

It is interesting when individuals see themselves or others in something other than a human form during the NDE. As I observed in Chapter One, Howard Storm saw beings who appeared as radiant sparkling
formless shapes. When I interviewed Forrest Hansen about his NDE he
said this: "It was just me. Now this was a . . . I wasn't aware of any body
whatsoever. It was strictly a mental experience."[11]

Phyllis Atwater saw herself and others in much the same way that
Howard Storm saw spiritual beings. She said: "For the first time I
looked upon myself to see what possible form or shape I might have,
and to my surprise and joy I had no shape or form at all. I was naught
but a sparkle of pure consciousness, the tiniest, most minuscule spark of
light imaginable. And that is all I was. . . . Everywhere around me were
sparkles like myself, billions and trillions of them, winking and blink-
ing like on/off lights, pulsating from some unknown source."[12]

When Sylvia (Chapter 1) described the body she initially found herself in as a Medusa-type body, with flowing appendices, it did not surprise me. Later in her experience she was, again, in human form—so
much so that she thought it must have been her physical body. Although
her Medusa-type experience was unusual, even for NDEs, I have

learned from my research to expect the unexpected and not to prematurely discount it.

Another aspect of Sylvia's experience which seemed unique when she first described it to Carol and me was the beautiful translucent yellow and purple bubbles which she saw in the tunnel. She had no idea what the bubbles were, nor did I. Then I remembered something I had read from Phyllis Atwater's experience and I decided to check her book again. In one of Phyllis's NDEs she found herself free of her body and wondering what happens next. This is her account of that portion of her experience:

> . . . What happens now? Where is anybody? Am I supposed to do something or say something? Hey, anybody, somebody, what comes next? Where do I go? What do I do? Hello? Hello?
>
> As my thought produced questions, blobs began to form around me. Blobs again, only this time they were more like shimmering pastel bubbles, fully pliable, transparent, and translucent. This time they were pretty and I liked them. I finally recognized the blobs to be my thoughts jelled into substance but devoid of specific direction, size or shape.[13]

The remarkable congruence between what Sylvia saw with her beautiful bubbles and Phyllis's experience is typical of NDE research. Had I not recorded that portion of Sylvia's encounter with the bubbles, or had I not remembered something similar in Phyllis's story, it could have been dismissed as just another bizarre element of the NDE scene. What may seem bizarre at one time, or to some individuals, becomes a reasonable occurrence as more information is gathered. That is the nature of research.

Are All NDEs Pleasant?

By no means. Most NDEs reported in the literature are positive in nature. Individuals who have had them report feelings of peace, bliss, joy, love and euphoria. Many are reluctant to return to this life because of the wonderful feelings they had in the other world.

That is not universally true, however. Increasingly, researchers are reporting different types of frightening, or hell-like experiences.[14, 15] My own research divulged a number of unpleasant experiences. A portion of Dee's experience is detailed below. Another disagreeable NDE is given in a later chapter.

To the individuals going through unpleasant NDEs the events in them are just as real—although terrifying—as are those who have pleasant NDEs. In Dee's case she was shaking as she relived the horror of her experience while Carol and I watched in empathetic fascination.

The next thing I knew was . . . there was something behind me, and I was afraid. I felt this awful presence—and I knew that it was after me. I looked back and I saw that my string, which I was hooked to, was getting tight. I was afraid, and I was thinking: *What is this thing behind me?* I started to circle, because I knew I had to get back to the house.

The thing was coming after me fast, and I had the feeling it could kill me. I was moving through the tops of the trees, and I was thinking that I couldn't break my string, and I had to get back quick.

This . . . this thing, this awful, this terrifying thing—I could feel it on me. It was pushing me away from the house, and I could see the string getting tighter. I was sure I was going to die. I was frantic for Sara, frantic over the idea that if I died she would be stuck with my husband. I felt I had to get back, but the thing kept trying to push me away from the house.

Every time I would circle and try to get back to the house the thing would come up behind and push me. I knew I was going to die. I could feel the tug at my string. I was being chased by something that was the personification of evil. And it wanted me. It wanted to destroy me. I was terrified and I was crying, and I remember thinking: Oh God, help me, help me God. I got all my strength to go as fast as I could—I could actually feel this thing on the back of my neck.[16]

Proof of Life After Death?

Most near-death researchers argue that the NDE does not prove the existence of life-after-death. I agree with that position—particularly since my religion teaches me that the Plan of Salvation (discussed in *Chapter 7*) provided that perfect knowledge would be removed from us during our mortal probation. In order for us to have freedom of choice it was necessary that our memory of a previous life and our knowledge of a future life be incomplete. Complete proof would tend to invalidate the Plan of Salvation. Concerning proof by science, the tools are simply inadequate to provide such proof.

Despite the inability through scientific methods to *prove* the existence of a life after this life, the NDE does offer substantial evidence that there *could* be something beyond this life. The evidence comes in several forms. One of the most fascinating forms of evidence is that provided by the witnesses themselves. Most of those who have had an NDE, when they tell of their experience (especially if they have not told it frequently before), are extremely moved by the experience. There is an awe about them that is obvious to anyone observing them. In many instances they tend to relive the experience, their emotions overcome them, and they are unable to continue with their discussion for a time. This is true whether or not the experience was frightening or uplifting, whether or not they are male or female, and independent of their cultural and educational background. The only exceptions that Carol and I observed seemed to be small children. They simply told their experiences in a matter of fact manner, as if to say: *Of course I saw Jesus—doesn't everybody?*

Another form of evidence involves patterns of behavior by those being interviewed. Although the stories, by their very nature, are anecdotal and therefore not subject to the rigor of repeatability that characterizes most scientific research, there are certain aspects that are repeatable. Certain words, for example, were used by the respondents we interviewed repeatedly, almost as if the people were programmed to use them. Words such as *peace, warmth, love,* and *light* were used with such frequency—and with a scriptural context or meaning—that they clearly represented a significantly high pattern of usage.

A subtle form of evidence derives from the method I used to create the final written version of the experiences. After each experience was taped and transcribed into a computerized printed version, I forwarded that version to the respondents for their corrections. Invariably, they would return the copy with what to me were trivial corrections that had nothing to do with the substance of their stories. Yet, the respondents were adamant that the changes needed to be made in order for the stories to be correct. Typical of these changes was one by a lady who said: "When I told you the story, I got the order of two events wrong. That wasn't the way it was. The first thing that happened was . . ." These kinds of small corrections, and the insistence of the respondents that I make the changes, gave further evidence that they, at least, had a sense of the reality and order of the events.

What About Repentance and Judgment?

Repentance and judgment will be treated in considerable detail in Chapter 7. For the moment, though, it is useful to review a particular event that frequently occurs in extensive NDEs. That event is the life review.

There are numerous types of life reviews, and not all of them are pleasant. In general they occur in the presence of other spiritual and loving beings who help the individual understand and get through the emotions of reliving portions of his or her life. Usually, as the life review unfolds, the person sees, hears and feels each of life's twists and turns exactly as they occurred—except that this time they often also feel the emotions, good or bad, that they afflicted on those interacting with them in life.

Although the spiritual being or beings witnessing the life review with the person undergoing it show mostly love toward the individual, there is a form of judgment. The person having the NDE understands with great clarity where they exceeded or fell short of how they could have behaved. They are also aware of the pleasure or disappointment felt by their loving spiritual witnesses, and they have an intense desire to please those witnesses. It becomes an enormously effective teaching tool—witnessed by the changes in life goals and purposes by those returning from an NDE with a life review. In effect, the individuals passing through this form of ethereal schooling become their own judge.

John Stirling is an intelligent, sensitive man and those characteristics became evident during our interview in 1991. His NDE and life review display the basic goodness of the man. For a good portion of the interview John was in tears as he struggled to explain what had happened to him. His recovery from his physical injuries after the accident was remarkably swift. John was not surprised since he understood in his NDE that he would heal.

In September 1978 John's wife left him and took his son. It devastated him, and he did not feel that life was worth living. He got together with a friend and they took a motorcycle ride on John's Yamaha 650 up Emigration Canyon just east of Salt Lake City, Utah. He and his friend were traveling very fast when they hit a bump. John's story, as he told it to me follows:[17]

The bump bounced the motorcycle off the road and into the gravel. It was about eleven-thirty at night, and as I fought for control in the dark I considered heading the motorcycle up the mountain instead of staying in the gravel. I opted to do that, to go up the mountain, so that gravity would slow us down.

We headed up the mountain a short distance, then I saw that the mountain had been discontinued where road work had been performed. I yelled at my friend, that he had to get off. We were still going fast—about fifty-five, and he wouldn't get off. I leaned back and knocked him off.

I then hit the rock, where it had been blown away, and I thought to myself: *Well this is it.* The right side of my body crashed into the rock where it had been, kind of, curved. The bike rolled over on top of me and stuck the rear view mirror on the top of my head—I didn't have a helmet on. Then the bike continued to tumble and ended up about two-hundred-and-fifty feet away.

I remember the crash and the bike tumbling, then I remember laying there, for just a split second, and thinking: Well this is it, I'm leaving. I turned around and looked, and I saw a body that seemed familiar. It looked like me, but I had no emotional involvement with the body laying there.

I then felt great relief and joy—that I was leaving, and that I didn't have to endure, any more, the pain of the divorce, or the pain of missing my child. So I immediately, without any further thinking about it, took off. Because it was what I had been wishing would happen.

I could feel an ability in my spirit body to move at great speed, and I wanted to get where I was going as quickly as possible. I was going to a place that I knew. It was the place that I had come from. I wanted to get there as quickly as possible.

I started traveling fairly slowly, in real time, when I first started. Then, as I got farther away from earth I traveled much faster. The stars started to look like the stars in "Star Wars," with a long trail, because of my speed.

A voice came to me, as I was traveling at that high rate of speed, and . . . and I was so peaceful and comfortable. All the emotional pain that

I had been feeling was gone. I looked at my hand, and I saw the shape of a hand, but . . . but it had an aura around it. It wasn't the same hand as an earthly hand. There was an energy field that defined it.

And the voice . . . the voice asked me if I was done. And I knew the voice and it was . . . John had difficulty continuing as he wiped away the tears. It was a comfortable voice—a voice full of love.

I said: "Yes, I'm done. I don't want to go back there. I don't ever want to go back there." The voice asked me a second time: "Are you done?" And I said: "Yes, I'm done. I don't want to go back." The voice asked me a third time if I was done, and again I said that I was.

Then the voice said: "Well, let's look at your life." And I saw . . . I saw my life flashed before my eyes. Everything from when I was a child up to the present time. And every emotion that I had during my life, when I saw the scene, I felt the same emotion. I could feel the reasons that I did things as I saw the scenes unfold.

I felt very comfortable with my life as I looked at it. It was all in color and three dimensional, and it flashed in a circle as if it were a deck of cards. I felt very comfortable that I would not have to come back to earth.

The review continued until it came to the previous Friday, when I had had my son over, on Friday night. And it . . . the review traveled all the way up to that time.

The scene, you can call it a card that came up for me to see, or, the vision that came to my view, it . . . my eyes locked onto that night. And the life review stopped. When that Friday scene first flashed up it looked as if it was going to go by, but when my eyes locked on it, then I knew I had to come back.

So I . . . I said yes I would come back. Because I knew I had to raise my son as best I could. There was no further contact with the voice after I said I would return. I came back to my body so much faster than when I left. It was almost instantaneous. I can remember reversing in space and then waking up in my body.

The first thought that came to me when I was back in my body was that I had to find Richard, my friend who was on the motorcycle with me. So I stood up and started screaming for him. He answered and came down. When he saw me his face showed fear. I asked him to show me where he was hurt. He had scraped his elbow and his shin a little bit.

I told him I would go get some help from one of the houses in the canyon. He told me to stay put and he would go get the help. I told him that he should stay, since he was hurt, and I raised my hand to brush away what I thought was sweat from my eyes. I saw that the sweat was actually blood—then I looked closer at my arm. My hand was at a right angle to it.

At that point I told him: "Well, okay, I guess I'm hurt worse than you. You go get some help." As he left, and I waited, I looked a little closer at myself. I saw that both of my feet were folded underneath at the ankles—I was walking on my ankles. I didn't feel any pain at all. I had the same peace with me, that everything would be okay, as I'd had when I first left my body.

As I mentioned, John recovered unusually fast from his serious injuries, and the peace stayed with him. Today he is actively involved in living a full life—with a close relationship to his son—and he retains an essence of spirituality that is obvious to those who know him.

Are Angels a Part of the NDE?

Without debating what constitutes an angel, what their duties are, how they are selected, or how many can stand on the point of a pin, there were numerous occasions where Carol and I interviewed individuals who claimed to have been helped by angels. One of the more striking cases was that of Ann whom we interviewed in 1991.[18]

Ann had two NDEs, one when she was a child of four years as a result of leukemia, and the other as a young woman of twenty-eight as a result of spinal meningitis.

I shall reproduce our conversation concerning the first NDE. Ann had been returned home from the hospital so that she could die at home with her parents. This NDE is of interest since, although Ann was an adult when she told Carol and me of her NDE, the experience occurred when she was a child and it reflects a child's perspective. Again, Ann was extremely moved as she shared her story with us. On several occasions she could not continue.

"I was tired, listless, and generally sad of heart. My parents loved and cared for me, but I couldn't seem to communicate to them how badly I felt on this particular occasion. My father was having severe back problems and this may have accounted for their seeming indifference.

"Anyway, on this one night my mother put me to bed and tucked me in. She was worried about my Dad and didn't seem to notice that I had a hard time climbing into bed. I felt so tired that . . . that I simply wanted to get to sleep. I lay there for a moment waiting to go to sleep when I noticed a light coming into the room. It was a beautiful golden-white light which seemed to appear in the wall to the left of my bed."

"Did you notice anything besides the light?"

"Not at first. And I wasn't afraid, just curious about the light. It was about three feet up from the floor and mid-length of the bed, which was located near the wall. As the ball of light grew the pain and feeling of illness suddenly left me. I had no idea what was happening, but I felt at peace."

"I sat up and watched the light grow. It grew rapidly in both size and brightness. In fact the light got so bright that it seemed to me that the whole world was lit by it. I could see someone inside the light. There was this beautiful woman, and she was part of the light; in fact she glowed."

"Did the light hurt your eyes?"

"No, even though it was bright by mortal standards."

"Tell me more about the lady in the light."

"Her body was lit from inside in a way . . . it's very hard to explain what she looked like. It seemed as if she were a pure crystal filled with light. Even her robe glowed with light as if by itself. The robe was white, long-sleeved, and full length. She had a golden belt around her waist and her feet were bare. Not that she needed anything on her feet since she stood a couple of feet off the floor."

"Were you frightened by her?"

"No, just the opposite. I had never seen such kindness and gentle love on anyone's face such as I saw in this person. She called me by name and held out her hand to me. She told me to come with her—her voice was soft and gentle but . . . but it was more in my mind. Communication was easier than when you verbalize thoughts. At the time I thought of it as 'mind talk.'

"I asked her who she was and she explained that she was my guardian and had been sent to take me to a place where I could rest in peace. The love emanating from her washed over me so that I didn't hesitate to put my hand in hers.

"As soon as I was standing beside her we moved through a short darkness to a beautiful, even brighter, light. And then I saw . . . there was this astonishingly beautiful world before me. It was like nothing else I have since seen on earth. Somehow I knew, inside of me, that the earth had been left behind. I had no idea where I was, and I didn't care. I felt a deep, profound peace . . . no, it was more than that. It was a world of peace and love.

"The new world looked sort of like the world I had left behind, but it was also very different. Everything glowed from the inside with its own light. The colors were beyond anything on earth—they were more vibrant, brilliant, and intense. And there were colors I had never seen before—don't ask me what they were. There were shrubs, trees and flowers, some of which I had seen on earth, like evergreens, and others which I hadn't seen before, and I haven't seen since. They were beautiful, beautiful.

"I asked my guardian why she took me to this place. She said that I needed the rest because life had become too hard for me to live.

"There was also grass all around, and a little hill with sand at the base in a sort of play area where several other children were playing. My guardian took me to the area and left without my knowing it. I immediately joined the children in play. There were toys in the sand and we built castles and roads and played with the toys. I was totally immersed in this new world of love, peace and play."

"Did you stay with the children very long?"

"It seemed long in one sense; in another, it seemed timeless. I felt thoroughly refreshed, enlivened and spiritually rejuvenated. I was filled with a zest for life. It is impossible to explain what it felt like to be lighter than air, with no pain, and totally at peace with everyone and everything around. I simply accepted my existence in the new world and lived.

"When my guardian returned I thought we were going to another part of this fascinating and wonderful world. Calling to me, she gently took me by the hand and said that I had to leave. When we started back the way we came I realized that we were returning to the earth, and

I asked her why I had to go back. She told me it was time to return, and it would be easier for me to live on the earth now.

"We came back through the darkness, as before, with the surrounding light making a sort of tunnel through it. The peace followed me and I was content. We emerged back in my bedroom. My guardian smiled at me, and suddenly I was back in bed without the slightest idea of how I got there."

"Could you still see your guardian?"

"Yes, but the light was diminishing. I waved at her, and she smiled and waved back. Then the light sort of gathered around her and she was gone. I went into a peaceful sleep content in the knowledge that someone loved and watched over me."

"Did you tell your parents?"

"Not until years later when I told my mother. I didn't think they would believe me. The next time they took me to the hospital for a checkup my blood tests showed that I was normal."

"So you must have been healed during or after your experience?"

"I think it was during the experience."

"During your experience did you feel like you had a body like the one on this earth?"

"No, it was lighter."

"But you had arms and legs?"

"Sure, I could touch the other children, and I could feel and smell. I played in the sand and made sand castles with my hands. As we were playing, sometimes I would walk, and other times, when we went as a group, we just floated."

"It's amazing that you remember all those details after so many years."

"It's because it was so real. I still remember it as one of the more realistic events in my life. I was able to do things that I never did in any dream. It was real."

What About Encounters with Deity?

This is a particularly interesting question because of the religious implications. There are many accounts in the NDE literature of individuals who saw or talked with Jesus Christ, and a few who were in the presence of God the Father. Several that Carol and I interviewed had such encounters. My own father was in the presence of Christ.

Many of those of a Fundamental Christian persuasion have problems with the concept of people being in the presence of or viewing deity. They often take their position based upon scriptures such as that from Exodus, "No one may see me and live."[19] Other scriptures which appear to contradict that statement are usually not quoted. The Bible also says, for example, "And the Lord spake unto Moses face to face, as a man speaketh to a friend. . . .,"[20] or from Deuteronomy 5:4: "The Lord talked with you face to face in the mount out of the midst of the fire."

Mormons *must* acknowledge that man can see God and live, otherwise they cannot explain the Joseph Smith story—as will be described in detail in Chapter 6. There are several LDS scriptures on this point, including from the Doctrine and Covenants which says: "For no man has seen God at any time in the flesh, except quickened by the Spirit of God."[21]

With regard to that scriptural quotation from the Doctrine and Covenants, it is interesting to compare it with an account taken from an interview with a blind lady who had an NDE in which she expressed the limitless joy she felt when she saw and was embraced by Jesus. She was not LDS and had no knowledge of the above scripture. The following portion of her interview was taken from Kenneth Ring's book, *Mindsight.*

> Interviewer: Was there a brightness associated with Jesus?
> Vicki: Much more than anybody there. He was the brightest of anybody there at all.
> Interviewer: Was it a hard brightness to look at? Was it unpleasant?
> Vicki: No. It wasn't unpleasant, but it was incredibly beautiful and warm. It was very intense. I know I couldn't have stood it if I were myself ordinarily, but because I knew I was not myself ordinarily, I knew I could stand it.[22]

Without commenting further on the religious implications of deity being viewed by those having NDEs, let me merely reproduce some representative cases. In each of the experiences described below, when the interviewees came to the point where they told of their encounter with Deity, they were overwhelmed by their emotions. They had a difficult time continuing with their story. The awesome reality of what they had witnessed was all too evident in their every demeanor.

Elizabeth Marie[23]

Elizabeth was a lovely young lady who I interviewed in1993 in the home of her mother. A portion of the interview follows:

"Describe the light in the room."

"It was light like in the tunnel. It was bright, but not nearly as bright as the light that came after He called my name."

"Where did the bright light come from?"

"It was high up and distant when I first saw it. The room boundaries seemed to disappear."

"What did the light look like?"

"When it got close to me, it was brighter than the sun. The sun is yellow, but the light was white. Yet I could look at it with my eyes."

"What happened to the light?"

"It came down and stood a few inches in front of me. It was a man."

"There was a man in the light, then?"

"I didn't see a man, but I knew He was there."

"Who was He?"

"It was Jesus."

"How did you know it was Jesus?"

"I just did." Elizabeth paused for a period to control her emotions. She continued: "I don't have words for it, but I knew it was He."

"You felt Him embrace you?"

"Yes. He put His arms around me and hugged me, just as my father would. The feelings I had at that point were extremely intense. My children and my parents, for example, I love with all my heart. Yet in this life I couldn't produce a small portion of what I felt in His presence. The love was a mutual feeling between us, and it went through my whole body."

Mike[24]

Mike was a thirty-one year old man when I interviewed him in his home in 1993. He had his NDE as a nine year old child when he fell off a cliff. A portion of our interview follows:

"Coming out of nowhere, while I was puzzling the whole situation, a giant cone of light appeared. It was off in the distance, and I started going toward it. . . .

"Something in the light seemed more important to me than anything else. . . . I was drawn to it.

"When I reached the edge of the light, I could see the shape of a human in it. A man in the light reached out his hand, and I reached to touch him. Upon touching him, I knew immediately who He was. The confusion that I had felt, and every fear, left me.

"This wonderful Being called me by a name, not my earthly name, but some other name. I knew He was addressing me, but it was not a name that I had been called while on earth. I have since forgotten it."

"The cone of light that you saw, can you describe it more fully?"

"That's the thing . . . it wasn't there, and then it was. It was sort of in the middle of my vision. Above the cone it was black, and below the cone it was black. It just appeared and I felt drawn to it."

"Can you describe the figure that was in the light?"

"The figure was a man; he was in a white robe, he was transparent, and he was very bright. Instantly, upon His touching my hand, I knew it was the Lord. I was filled with peace, I felt calm, and there was an assurance that the peace would stay with me. There was an overpowering love coming from Him to me—I could feel it. The warmth I felt . . . . There is no experience in life that can duplicate what I experienced there in His presence."

"How did you know it was the Lord?"

"There were the love and the comfort that He gave. He was radiantly beautiful, dressed in a white robe, and He had long brown hair. His dress and appearance were that of the Lord, and . . . and He showed me the nail prints in his hands."

"Where were the nail prints?"

"They were on his wrists."

"Was there anything else about the Lord that was unusual?"

"There was the music, and there were angels. When I was in His presence, I heard this wonderful music. It was beautiful."

"Describe it."

"I can't."

"What kind of music do you listen to here?"

"Country-western."

"Was it like country-western?"

"No. There were a multitude singing something like hymns, or humming. The sound was unbelievable . . . it is hard to explain."

"What do you mean, a multitude?"

"There were angels, thousands of angels, dressed in white robes and singing. They were kneeling down with their arms outstretched, and they were singing."

Theresa

After the birth of her child, Theresa developed blood clots which ultimately led to a heart attack. In her subsequent extensive experience Theresa was brought into the presence of deity where she saw and felt the love of God. Other portions of her experience will appear in later chapters. She said of this portion of her experience:

> My excitement and joy were intense, but amidst these feelings was also the recognition that everything around me had a peaceful silence about it—and there was a feeling of radiant energy in the atmosphere. A person then stepped into view whom I recognized as Jesus Christ.
>
> . . . He was a magnificent being who was like the perfect combination of a person—He was beautiful. His hair was golden-brown, and there was a white glow to Him. His magnificent blue eyes seemed to have the ability to peer into my soul. He was clean-shaven. The white glow that came from Him radiated a considerable distance beyond His body.
>
> [I just knew it was him.] The recognition came from my heart. I never asked Him who He was. I didn't need to.
>
> He drew me to Him, and . . . [Theresa couldn't continue for a while, and she apologized for her tears.] He put his hands to me, and there was a peaceful smile on His face. Bringing me closer to Him, the love I felt was unbelievable. Looking into His face, I was so grateful to be there—because I was home.
>
> I was home . . . I felt as though I had returned home—and I had missed Him. I missed Him, you know. I . . . I loved Him so much.
>
> Drawing me close to Him, everything got very quiet, and He asked me to look at my life. In an instant, everyone, all the people in that room—no, it wasn't a room—everyone in that space saw and felt and truly experienced my whole life. Just like I did. . . .

Other Questions About NDEs

Appendix A addresses other questions often asked about NDEs. In particular, researchers have spent decades attempting to explain the NDE as something other than a spiritual event reflecting a duality of life. Those attempts and their lack of success are described there. Also, the reasons for the continued interest in reincarnation amongst researchers and NDE participants is explored.

Numerous other questions could be investigated, and some are in the following chapters, but these should be sufficient for the moment. Let me end this chapter by describing an interesting episode that occurred in one of our local IANDS meeting in 1994. In that meeting Janet, an emergency response nurse who attended patients at crash sites and on return trips on the helicopter, brought one of her patients with her.

Janet and the helicopter crew had been called to respond to a head-on crash with a car and another car pulling a horse-trailer. The accident occurred on the road to Bear Lake at the border of Idaho and Utah.

After picking up Kyle, a teen-ager and the most seriously injured individual, Janet battled to keep him alive. He kept slipping away and Janet repeatedly shouted at him, "Don't you leave me."

When Janet finished telling our group what medical procedures she followed to keep Kyle alive, she asked him to tell us what he remembered of the incident.

Kyle then described how he left his body and traveled with the helicopter, all the time watching his body and Janet as she shouted at him. He had a peaceful feeling, with no pain, and he felt the presence of some spiritual being with him. He said that he could see the trees below him, and everything seemed to have its own light.

Both Janet and Kyle shared in the joy of the moment as they celebrated, with us, Kyle's healthy return to life.

4
The Creation

To My Readers

At this point in my story the message is arranged for two different types of readers. This chapter and the next one presents in concise form the primary evidence for a God-centered universe. It is the major evidence which influenced me in my own intellectual and spiritual journey. You, as a reader, may therefore follow this condensed version of the path that I took and determine if it is a persuasive path.

The science of the creation is not a simple story, however. By necessity the evidence gathered by physicists, cosmologists, biologists and others working to understand how and why life came to be follows a twisted path. During the years that I worked in the development of nuclear energy I came to appreciate and to love the challenge of the twists and turns involved in the evolving scientific story. For those readers who wish a more complete understanding of what science has to say, further elaboration of the story is provided in the Appendices to this book. The rest of you may find that you are content with the detail which follows.

The Bible and Other LDS Scriptures

In the beginning God created the heaven and the earth. And the earth was without form, and void; and darkness was upon the face of the deep. And the Spirit of God moved upon the face of the waters.

And God said, Let there be light: and there was light. And God saw the light, that it was good: and God divided the light from the darkness. And God called the light Day, and the darkness he called Night. And the evening and the morning were the first day.[1]

My faith teaches me that Moses was the author of Genesis—after having had a vision of the entire act of creation by God. And Moses' account of the creation was inspired by God. How then, if I accept current scientific findings regarding the creation of the universe do I reconcile certain apparent contradictions? Moses, for example, records that God completed his work of creation in six days, and he rested on the seventh. Yet, current science places the time required for creation of the universe at 15 billion years.

Shortly I shall present a fictional version of how a modern Moses might speak of the creation. For the moment, though, let us suspend judgment concerning the truth or falsehood of either account. Let us first consider Moses' situation as described in *The Pearl of Great Price*.[2]

> The words of God, which he spake unto Moses at a time when Moses was caught up into an exceedingly high mountain, And he saw God face to face, and he talked with him, and the glory of God was upon Moses; therefore Moses could endure his presence. And God spake unto Moses, saying: Behold, I am the Lord God Almighty, and Endless is my name; for I am without beginning of days or end of years; and is not this endless? And, behold, thou art my son; wherefore look, and I will show thee the workmanship of mine hands; but not all, for my works are without end, and also my words, for they never cease.
>
> And it came to pass that Moses looked, and beheld the world upon which he was created; and Moses beheld the world and the ends thereof, and all the children of men which are, and which were created; of the same he greatly marveled and wondered. . . .
>
> And it came to pass, as the voice was still speaking, Moses cast his eyes and beheld the earth, yea, even all of it; and there was not a particle of it which he did not behold, discerning it by the spirit of God.
>
> And he beheld also the inhabitants thereof, and there was not a soul which he beheld not; and he discerned them by the Spirit of God; and their numbers were great, even numberless as the sand upon the sea shore.

We see from this account that Moses had this remarkable vision in which he spoke with God and beheld God's handiworks from the beginning to the end of time. According to the account Moses was overwhelmed by what he saw.

Moses was not an ignorant peasant. His preparation for his monumental task began in his youth. Raised in Pharaoh's court, Moses "was learned in all the wisdom of the Egyptians" and he became "mighty in words and in deeds."[3] In addition, of course, he was taught by the greatest of all teachers, God. Nevertheless, he lived at a time when science as we know it had not yet been invented. Archaeologists place Solomon's temple, for example, in the tenth century b.c.e.[4] It was a time of crude technology and extensive use of slave labor.

In this environment Moses set about to record what he had seen in a document that would be intelligible for his time as well as for future generations. In addition to telling the story of the mighty creative epochs of God, it must, above all testify to the greatness and glory of God which Moses had seen and felt.

To illustrate the problem that Moses faced, let us try an experiment. Instead of Moses writing Genesis let us assume that a modern scientist was given that assignment by God. Under those circumstances Genesis might begin something like this:

> In the beginning there was a singularity. And God saw the singularity, and it was not good. So God spoke and created the universe as a single point smaller than a mustard seed. At Planck time of 10^{-43} seconds, time had started and the temperature was 10^{32} degrees Kelvin. And God saw that the universe was stuck at an awkward place since it was not expanding properly, so God created inflation to speed up the expansion.
>
> And the universe was mostly photons and neutrinos, and it was very hot. So God speeded the expansion and it began to cool. And the time was 10^{-32} seconds, and God slowed the inflation.
>
> And it was 10^{-6} seconds and God created quarks and antiquarks so that protons and neutrons could form. It began to get cooler.
>
> And it was one minute since God had first spoken and nuclear reactions began to occur. So God spoke and the neutrons and protons obeyed and interacted. And the universe became 75 percent hydrogen and 25 percent helium.
>
> At 300,000 years the temperature dropped to 3,000 degrees Kelvin and the earth was without form and void and darkness was everywhere. And God said: "Let there be light," and free electrons disappeared, and matter and radiation separated, and there was light.

This alternative beginning for a modern-day Genesis, although necessarily very abbreviated, is more technically correct according to contemporary science than is the Moses version. Which version, however, would better stand the test of time throughout the many generations since Moses?

At least one reputable scientist has made a detailed comparison of the events as recorded in Genesis and those accepted in the scientific community. Gerald L. Schroeder did undergraduate and graduate work in physics at the Massachusetts Institute of Technology. He obtained his Ph.D. in physics and then did biblical research under Rabbi Herman Pollack in Israel, where Dr Schroeder and his wife now live.

In the two books: *Genesis and the Big Bang—The Discovery of Harmony Between Modern Science and the Bible*, and *The Science of God—The Convergence of Scientific and Biblical Wisdom*, Dr. Schroeder explores apparent conflicts between science and the Bible and concludes that there really are no contradictions when one considers the dilation of time as expressed in Einstein's general and special theories of relativity. His conclusion is that the events of the billions of years that cosmologists say followed the big bang and those of the first six days described in Genesis are, in fact, one and the same—identical realities described in vastly different terms.[5]

Before we leave this discussion of the creation as recorded in Genesis, let us consider a most interesting example of obedient universe behavior. It has to do with night and day.

In 1823 Heinrich Olbers, a German astronomer, posed what came to be known as Olbers's paradox.[6] If the sky is filled with essentially an infinity of stars stretching uniformly in all directions, shouldn't the light from these stars radiate into our space so that there is no darkness at night? It turns out that the age of our universe (about 15 billion years) coupled with its rapid expansion is just right so that light from distant galaxies has not reached us yet. Thus our dark night sky. If the universe were very much younger, then the dust from the big bang would still be gathering and no life would be possible. If the universe were much older, or the rate of expansion slower, or the density of stars greater, then their radiation would have reached us, the night would be bright, and no life would be possible because of excessive radiation. Genesis has this to say about night and day.

> And God said, Let there be lights in the firmament of the heaven to
> divide the day from the night; . . . And God made two great lights; the
> greater light to rule the day, and the lesser light to rule the night . . . .[7]

Serendipity?

Before proceeding with a description of the expansion and creation
of the universe, it is useful to consider the fortuitous circumstances
which result from certain fundamental forces having the exact values
that they do (see Appendix B for a more detailed description of the four
fundamental forces which govern our universe). Why these particular
forces exist and why they have the exact values that they do is a mystery.

As a start, the big bang had to proceed very rapidly when atoms
were first formed—described as the inflationary period—and a weak
nuclear force, which governs the fusion of protons, had to be weak
enough so that atomic fusion would not be too rapid. Were this not so,
essentially all of the matter in the universe would have been burned to
helium before the first galaxies started to condense and long-lived stable stars with heavy elements would not be possible. Hydrogen, water
and life would not exist.

On the other hand, if the weak nuclear force had been slightly
stronger, then there would also have been little if any hydrogen so
essential to life. At the early moments in the big bang expansion it was
extremely hot and neutrons and protons were about equally common—
at such high temperatures the higher mass of neutrons was not conse-
quential in their abundance compared with protons. The weak force can
make neutrons decay into protons, and this force was just sufficiently
strong to assure an excess of protons—leading to about 70 percent
hydrogen in the early universe. Without this proton excess there would
have been helium only, and life would not be possible.[8] So, as with
other forces in nature which we shall consider, the weak nuclear force
seems precisely tuned so that our universe would start as an abundant
hydrogen containing universe—one that could have water and support
life. Was it just a happy accident that there is a weak nuclear force and
that it is tuned just right for hydrogen and helium to exist in the proper
ratios?

The strong nuclear force, which binds neutrons and protons to their atomic nuclei, also must be neither too strong nor too weak in order for our universe to have life. If the strong force were increased by, say, two percent, then the formation of protons from quarks would be blocked, and the existence of hydrogen and other atoms could not occur.[9] Life would not be possible.

Slight decreases in the strong nuclear force would be equally catastrophic. The deuteron, a combination of a neutron and a proton, is essential for certain nuclear reactions in stars. This neutron-proton combination is weakly bound. Dropping the strong force by about five percent would unbind it leading to a universe of hydrogen only.[10] There would be no oxygen or other heavy elements and no life would be possible.

The electromagnetic force holds electrons in discreet atomic orbits. Chemistry would not be possible without this force. Moreover, most stars fall in a narrow range between blue giants and red dwarfs. If the electromagnetic force were only slightly stronger, all stars would be red and too cold for life to begin. If the force of electromagnetism were slightly weaker, all stars would be hot blue giants which would burn out before life could emerge.[11]

The strength of gravity played an enormous role in how our universe expanded. During the early moments of the big bang the universe struggled with the competing effects of the expansion and the tug of gravity. Had the vigor of the big bang been slightly less, then gravity would have predominated and matter would have collapsed on itself before stars and galaxies could have formed. If gravity had been stronger, than a similar result would have occurred.

If gravity had been weaker, or the explosion vigor greater, then matter and energy would have been dispersed so rapidly that galaxies could not have formed. Paul Davies has computed that at Planck time of 10^{-43} seconds—the earliest moment when space and time has meaning—the matching of gravity against the explosive vigor "was accurate to a staggering one part in 10^{60}."[12]

Another example of fine tuning involves matter and anti-matter. Anti-matter is the mirror image of matter and they are close relatives. All the particles of regular matter—quarks, neutrons, protons, and others—exist as anti-matter except with opposite charge from matter. They exist in theorist's equations and in collider experiments, but rarely in nature. When matter and anti-matter interact they destroy each other. Current theory holds that early in the big bang matter and anti-matter existed in about equal quantities. Exactly why matter survived and anti-matter did not—or why they both did not destroy each other and the early universe—is a puzzle.[13]

These examples of the fine tuning of nature's constants so that everything seems pointed to the goal of human life could be expanded almost indefinitely. Other examples will be considered in future chapters. This kind of serendipity led one physicist, Fred Hoyle, studying the subject to state: "The universe is a put-up job."[14] To say that it is a put-up job is an understatement. Who or what was it that established these forces in just the right way so that there would be an Anthropic Universe with life?

Science's View of the Creation of the Universe

Singularity and Planck Time

A singularity is physics-speak for "I don't know." It is intended to describe a time just before the beginning of the big bang when the universe was compressed into an infinitely high density and an infinitely small space. It is a point where all the laws of physics fail and we cannot describe just what is there.

The first instant of time after the big bang starts when we can commence to describe what is happening is known as Planck time. From time zero to Planck time is known as the Planck epoch.

The Planck time is derived from the Planck constant and is a brief period from time zero to 10^{-43} seconds when spacetime foam would have played a dominant role in all events. During the Planck epoch every particle was so energetic that the warping of spacetime around each particle was powerful enough to influence particle interactions as profoundly as did the normally much stronger electromagnetic and nuclear forces.[15]

Early Expansion

Why the universe began its expansion no one knows. Immediately following Planck time the universe was the size of a speck of dust and the temperature was 10^{32} degrees Kelvin. By comparison the center of the sun is about 15 million (15×10^6) degrees Kelvin; the surface of the sun is only 5,800 (5.8×10^3) degrees Kelvin.[16]

In these very early times, and at these enormous temperatures and pressures, matter did not exist as we know it. Even the tiny particles known as quarks could not exist. There was colossally high energy and little else.

For some reason from within the core of this fiery furnace a repulsive force was generated which caused an accelerated expansion to occur. This accelerated expansion was faster than the speed of light (one of the very few events where the speed of light can be exceeded) and in microseconds it flung energy and mass into its own space-time bubble. The period of rapid expansion was called inflation. During the inflationary epoch the universe expanded by a factor of 10^{50} until inflation ended at 10^{-33} seconds and the universe—which was then about 10 centimeters in diameter—began to cool from the rapid expansion.[17]

During this rapid expansion phase, when the temperature dropped to about 10^{27} degrees Kelvin—and in the presence of the Higgs field—certain symmetries of nature were broken with resultant enormous particle production.[18]

At 10^{-12} seconds the temperature of the universe fell to 10^{15} degrees Kelvin and the weak and electromagnetic forces separated. At between 10^{-6} seconds and 10^{-4} seconds quarks and antiquarks stopped destroying each other and protons and neutrons were formed.[19]

During the first seconds of the universe the temperature was still several billion degrees Kelvin—too high for nuclei to stick together. In effect there was a high temperature stew of neutrinos, protons, neutrons and electrons, and this stew was dominated by radiation.

After about a minute nuclear reactions began to occur so that neutrons and protons could make heavy hydrogen or deuterium, which in turn could capture a proton to form helium. At this time the universe consisted of about 25 percent helium and 75 percent hydrogen. The temperature of the universe was still too high for free electrons to interact with the nuclei of atoms.[20] Opaque radiation dominated the infant universe.

From Years to Billions of Years

At 10,000 years the temperature had fallen sufficiently so that matter rather than energy dominated the universe—in that photon radiation was losing energy from expansion (wave lengths were increasing) and the mass density of particles exceeded the mass density of photons. By the time 300,000 years had expired the temperature had fallen to 3,000 degrees Kelvin, matter and radiation decoupled and the formation of stable atoms began. Thermal equilibrium of matter and radiation had ceased, and the resulting decoupling left the residue of the background radiation for scientists to find some fifteen billion years later in the COBE satellite. The universe became transparent for the first time since its formation.[21]

After about one million years, all of the protons and electrons had combined into hydrogen atoms, and photons were able to travel freely. The universe emerged from its dense fog, and as the scriptures say, "there was light."[22]

Gravity dominated and caused local condensations of gas to clump together. These clumps gradually accumulated into larger rotating gases which over millions of years formed galaxies. Gravity caused the accumulating matter to be compressed locally and the temperature in these compressed regions of hydrogen and helium gas began to rise. At about one billion years some of these compressed regions reached stellar fusion temperatures, and the first stars appeared.

At around 7.5 billion years our sun was formed from the Milky Way Galaxy and our solar system began to be formed.[23] At about 10.5 billion years the formation of our earth reached a point where the earth's crust cooled, and at somewhere around 11.7 billion years after the big bang the first life appeared on earth in the form of single-celled organisms.[24] At 14.4 billion years multi-cellular creatures appeared,[25] and at 15 billion years a scientist marveled at the stars in the heavens and developed a theory on how it all began. The heavens at which the scientist was gazing extended for at least 15 billion light-years—or about 88×10^{20} miles.

Energy, Work and Power from Different Perspectives

What is at Issue?

You have just read a brief description of the creation as understood by science. Once the big bang got started everything that happened was governed by Einstein's famous equation of the equivalence of mass and energy and by the fundamental forces which seem to have been specifically selected for our benefit.

But, again, who or what arranged this mighty cauldron and triggered the release of such prodigious amounts of energy? Engineers and scientists define energy as the ability to do work. Work, in turn, is defined as force times distance, and power is the time-rate of doing work—that is, how fast is the work being done?

It is clear that the during the big bang work was being done mighty fast. Enormous forces flung matter and energy great distances quickly—faster than the speed of light. Unbelievable power was somehow unleashed in a very precise way.

In the Appendices I describe various theories which science has advanced in an attempt to explain how this might have happened without the handiwork of God. For the moment, though, let us revisit some of our friends who have had near-death experiences and see if they have anything to tell us about energy and power.

Godly Power?

One of the most fascinating interviews I had with people who had undergone an NDE was with Berta and her son Rocky. When he was four years old Rocky fell from a window on the second floor of his house to the concrete below. His head hit the concrete and he underwent severe skull and brain damage.

During his recovery, which lasted months, he had to learn to walk, control his arms and legs and to talk again. As he gradually began to speak he informed his mother that he had been to heaven with Jesus. Then, to his parents' supreme astonishment, he began to quote scriptures from the Bible. Berta assured me that although she had taught the children some of the Bible stories and read short sections from the Bible they had never been exposed to serious Bible study. Their church attendance was sporadic.

It was usually when Rocky was frustrated with his ability to explain what he had seen on the other side that he resorted to quotations from the scriptures. One such example was when he attempted to help his mother understand what he knew to be true about God's power. He said that Jesus and Heavenly Father had power. Berta told me that she kept looking through the Bible until she found Mark 12:24 where it says: "And Jesus answering them said unto them, Do ye not therefore err, because ye know not the scriptures, neither the power of God?" Rocky agreed that this was what he meant.

One of the most ubiquitous comments by those having NDEs is the awesome power of the Light. In a following chapter I shall delineate an LDS scriptural basis for attributing the Light, as seen and felt by these choice individuals, to the power of God. Light, in terms that scientists would agree to, is a form of energy—electromagnetic energy. As such it has the capacity to do work and to generate power.

In Chapter 1 John Sterling's near-death experience is described. During his experience John looked at his hand. He described what he saw in this manner: "It wasn't the same hand as an earthly hand. There was an energy field that defined it." Also in Chapter 1 portions of Theresa's story is told. At one point in our interview Theresa explained how it felt to be in the presence of deity: "The energy and the light were so bright that it . . . it was hard to make out pertinent features or color. He was just brilliant. He was more . . . He was beautiful beyond description." While she tried to put into words the transcendent nature of her experience Theresa was racked with sobs. She relived portions of the wondrous majesty and power which she had been privileged to witness—if but for a moment of eternity—and it was overpowering even in retrospect.

Godly Power Made Manifest

Carol and I met Jake when he came to our home in 1996 to be interviewed by Sandra Cherry, a near-death researcher doing work for her Master's thesis. Jake had previously called me from Colorado after having read one of my books. On that occasion he explained, over the telephone, what led to his NDE. His experience was sufficiently interesting that our local chapter of IANDS invited Jake to tell his story at one of our meetings.

Jake was a large man, several inches taller than my six-feet-two inches. He had an athletic build and moved with the easy grace of some-one at home with his own frame. He spoke with a quiet humility not uncommon in large men. His appearance and demeanor were not sur-prising, though, since he had already told me of his occupation. He was a member of an elite fire-fighting group called "Hotshot;" a crew whose job it was to be dropped into particularly troublesome forest fires and bring them under control.

During a wilderness fire in 1989 a helicopter dropped Jake, as crew boss, and two 20 person Hotshot crews onto a fire at the top of a steep mountain. The fire was burning below the crews in thick Ponderosa Pine and Oak brush. The wind was blowing the fire downhill away from the crews. The decision was made to try and construct a fire line down-hill towards the existing fire with one crew, and have the second crew follow, starting a back-fire into the main blaze.

Creating a fire line involved clearing a path six feet wide down to mineral soil by using power saws and other hand tools. The second 20 person crew—whose job it was to initiate the back fire—started light-ing any unburned fuel in front of the newly constructed fire line. The fire they were lighting was supposed to burn ahead of them with the wind down the slope toward the primary blaze thus stopping the main fire from advancing any further.

The slope of the hill the men and women were working on was about 40 degrees. They worked their way down the steep slope, when, part way down, to their horror, the wind changed to an upward direc-tion. The trees in front of the men and women traveling down the hill erupted into flames with explosive force.

Jake explained how fire-fighters have a fire-resistant pack that is car-ried on their web gear. The pack includes an aluminum foil-type mate-rial which they can throw over themselves as they crouch to the ground in an emergency. These foils are only effective if the people can deploy the shelters after properly preparing the ground by reaching mineral soil with no residual flammable organic materials. The problem in this case was that the enormous winds caused by the inferno erupting all around them and the immediacy of the crisis made the shelters useless.

The panic stricken crews started to try and go back up the trench-trail they had built. Trees exploded and fire engulfed the immediate area, and oxygen feeding the conflagration was sucked from near the ground where the people struggled to breathe. One by one the men and women fell to the earth suffocating from lack of oxygen. They were reduced to crawling on their hands and knees while they attempted to get back up the hill to a safer area.

Suddenly Jake had the thought: *This is it. I am going to die.* And with that thought in mind he found himself looking down on his body which was lying in a trench. The noise, heat and confusion from the inferno surrounding them was gone and Jake felt completely at peace. As he looked around Jake saw other fire-fighters standing above their bodies in the air. One of Jake's crew members had a defective foot which he had been born with. As he came out of his body Jake looked at him and said: "Look, Jose, your foot is straight."

A bright light then appeared. Jake described the bright light in this manner: "The light—the fantastic light. It was brighter than the brightest light I had ever seen on earth. It was brighter than the sun shining on a field of snow. Yet I could look at it and it didn't hurt my eyes."

Standing in the light was Jake's deceased great-grandfather. His great-grandfather acted as Jake's guide throughout his NDE. Jake met with others of his ancestors and had an extensive experience. Only the portions pertinent to this discussion are repeated here.

His great-grandfather ultimately communicated by mind thought to Jake that it was Jake's choice whether or not he should return to earth. Not wanting to come back from the beautiful and peaceful place that he was in, Jake argued with his great-grandfather. Explaining that it would be devastating to return to a horribly burned body, Jake pled with his great-grandfather to remain. Jake said that all of this communication was by questions he would think of and have instantly answered in his mind.

Jake was informed that neither he, nor any of his crew who chose to return, would suffer ill effects from the fire. This would be done so that "God's power over the elements would be made manifest."

Returning to his body was one of the more painful events of his life. When I asked Jake why it was painful he said: "When I was there, everything was so perfect, and my spirit body, it . . . it was so free. It felt like everything was limitless. When I came back, well you know, there's always something plaguing you, like arthritis, or sore muscles, or . . . but not there. Getting back into my physical body felt cramped—held back. For example, when I used to play football for a few days after a game or hard practice I was always sore. The same thing was true after coming back into my physical body. I hurt and felt constrained, and it was hard to get used to for some time."

Finding himself, again, in his body Jake looked around and noticed that some of the metal tools they had used to fight the fire had melted. Despite this intense heat, and the fire still raging around him, he was able to walk up the hill in some sort of protected bubble. He did not hear nor feel the turbulence around him. Upon reaching the relative safety of the hilltop the noise of the fire was again evident, and he saw other members of the crew also gathering there.

The entire happening was so profound that upon escaping from what they had supposed would be sure death the group of saved people knelt in prayer to thank the Lord for their deliverance. All of the crew escaped and the only visual evidence on them of what they had been through was a few singed hairs.

Jake said that in comparing accounts of their different episodes the men and women were astonished that they had each undergone some type of near-death experience. And this happened to a diverse ethnic and religious group of Hispanics, Caucasians and American Indians. Throughout the summer as the crew worked together they continued to discuss the miraculous adventure which they had lived through. Others of the crew confirmed, for example, that they also felt the ill effects of returning to their physical bodies. They, too, had met with other members of their deceased families and were given the choice of remaining where they were or of returning to earth.

Ultimate Cause and Effect

I began this chapter with a few references to scriptural accounts of the creation. In those references the great prophet Moses revealed a portion of the stupendous vision he had when he was granted the privilege of seeing the creation from beginning to end. At the end of this vision he wrote:

> And God saw every thing that he had made, and, behold, it was very good. And the evening and the morning were the sixth day.
>
> Thus the heavens and the earth were finished, and all the host of them. And on the seventh day God ended his work which he had made; and he rested on the seventh day from all his work which he had made.
>
> And God blessed the seventh day, and sanctified it: because that in it he had rested from all his work which God created and made.[26]

In addition to the biblical account I presented a different vision of the creation. It was a vision expressed in the language of the scientist, and it is a vision of the architecture of the universe which is no less majestic than that of Moses. The scientist, too, was aware of and used the tools of his calculus to describe the almost indescribable work, energy and power that birthed the universe. And, like Moses, the scientist gazed at the heavens and marveled at what he saw, and he knew that it was very good.

Near the end of the chapter I presented still another vision of existence—and by implication, creation—which now and then escapes from a hidden realm in a brief blaze of power and glory. This collective vision by hosts of those who have glimpsed eternity is expressed in the language of the spirit, a language from the heart to the heart. It is a language even more beautiful than that of the scientist and it, too, staggers under the burden of attempting to describe the indescribable. Yet, occasionally, there is a burst of light where the marvels of the work, power, energy and glory of the creation are plainly exhibited. Then the transformed individual also knows that this creation is very good.

As you read further in this book you will see more of these three visions. As stated before, my own journey illuminated each of these visions as I gradually came to understand that they were the same vision—they merged into one. Perhaps you also, as you travel with me, will see the merging of these paths or visions into one path. Let me end this chapter by quoting from a Psalm of David:

O LORD our Lord, how excellent is thy name in all the earth! who hast set thy glory above the heavens. . . .

When I consider thy heavens, the work of thy fingers, the moon and the stars, which thou hast ordained; What is man, that thou art mindful of him? and the son of man, that thou visitest him?

For thou hast made him a little lower than the angels, and hast crowned him with glory and honour.[27]

5
The Probability of Life

Why Probability is Important

In the Introduction I mentioned how probabilistic analysis is used to determine the behavior of massive numbers of atoms in a nuclear system. Although it is impossible to predict the action of any individual atom, taken collectively and analyzed by probabilistic mathematics, the average behavior of the massive group of atoms being studied can quite effectively be determined.

The same is true of many other systems in which large numbers of events are involved. Thus insurance companies can do statistical analysis on large numbers of people and determine average lifetimes of different groups. Then, using probabilistic techniques, they can determine with a high degree of assurance whether or not they will have to pay a life policy on an individual based upon his or her age and other factors important to the probabilities involved.

As the previous chapter demonstrated, much is known about the various factors important to the creation of our universe—such as how much hydrogen is needed for stars to form. Similarly, as will be discussed in this chapter, much is known about the factors important in the formation of life—such as the need for abundant carbon. The problem is that very little is known about the precise cause of many events, such as why the abundant hydrogen was formed just as it did, or what causes various amino acids to arrange themselves so that proteins—and life—can exist. Taken collectively, however, and subjected to probabilistic analysis, much can be learned about whether or not life could have developed under particular circumstances.

How Probability Works

Any high school boy, when asked to choose heads or tails of a coin toss, knows that he has a one out of two or 50% chance of being a winner. Most folks also understand that if a single die, with six numbers on its six faces, is tossed, there is a 1/6 or 16.67 percent chance of hitting any particular number. Others understand that if the single die is tossed twice, the probability of coming up with the same number two times in a row is 1/6 x 1/6 = 1/36, or one chance in 36 tries—which is equal to .02777 or 2.77 percent of the time.

It is seen from the above that simple probabilities are multiplicative.

This has important implications concerning the rapid decline of hoped for success as multiple events are considered. For example, the probability of the single die being tossed and coming up with the same number six times in a row is 1/6 x 1/6 x 1/6 x 1/6 x 1/6 x 1/6 = 1/46,656 or one chance in 46,656 tries. This corresponds to .0000214 = 2.14 x 10^{-5}, or a probability of 2.14 x 10^{-5}.

Time also plays an important part in probabilities. Let us assume that you wish to come up with a number on the single die six times in a row, but you have a limited time to do it because your wife is waiting in the hotel room to go out to dinner. You promised her that you would pick her up in two hours, and you need to win your bet in order to pay for the hotel room and the dinner. It takes you 7 seconds to throw and retrieve the die each time you toss it. But you have to toss it 46,656 times to have just one chance of winning. The total time required for that one chance is 7 x 46,656 = 326,592 seconds, or 90.72 hours.

The hotel clerk relayed a message. Your wife said that she had gone home to her mother. Of course, probabilities are not assurances, and you might have hit the six rolls on the first try—which would have been so unlikely that you most probably would have fallen over with a heart attack.

Probabilities can rapidly get more complicated as multiple events are considered, and as conditional events are included. Conditional events are those events which can occur, but only if some other event has occurred first. Further more complex situations and sample calculations are given in Appendix C. In addition the Appendix will include some of the arguments that scientists use to establish that life *could* have developed by chance.

A Warning to my Readers

This chapter will have more numbers and more scientific terminology in it than any other chapter in the book. The language of science is often the language of mathematics, chemistry, biology, geology and physics. While I will not display the detailed arithmetic or equations used to obtain the final values reached, by necessity I will show the answers in the numerical format and in the language of the scientist.

This may seem like dull reading for some, but the presentation in this manner is important in order to answer questions about the complexity of the processes and the magnitude of different probabilities. In other words, how likely is it that life could have been started accidentally by a lightning bolt striking a mud-puddle several billion years ago? And even if the lightning bolt did, by some means, cause amino acids to be created and join themselves so as to form, say, a lovely green slime, how likely is it that your Uncle Willie could have evolved from that slime? Or, as some scientists have suggested, how likely is it that life may have started in space and been transplanted to earth, or perhaps started in the oceans where early volcanoes spewed their chemical stews into the deep?

So, dear reader, please be patient and follow me on another journey in the search for truth. As we travel on this path I will pause at various places to emphasize where we are and what it means. And at the end of the chapter I will summarize the importance of what we found. For those interested in a more detailed—and a more complex path—I refer them to the Appendices.

Argument Against a Happenstance Universe

In the last chapter I showed some of the unique natural laws and constants which seem precisely selected from the beginning of the big bang so as to make possible life on the earth. In Appendix D I give information on how black holes are formed. Paul Davies considered the early formation of the universe and made the following observation:

> . . . Given a random distribution of (gravitating) matter, it is overwhelmingly more probable that it will form a black hole than a star or a cloud of dispersed gas. These considerations give a new slant, therefore, to the question of whether the universe was created in an ordered or disordered state. If the initial state were chosen at random, it seems

exceedingly probable that the big bang would have coughed out black holes rather than dispersed gases. The present arrangement of matter and energy, with matter spread thinly at relatively low density, in the form of stars and gas clouds would, apparently, only result from a very special choice of initial conditions.[1]

Roger Penrose calculated the odds against the observed universe appearing in its present form rather than as a cosmos filled with black holes and little if any stars and galaxies. He estimated a figure of 10 raised to the 10^{30} power as the probability against our universe appearing as it is instead of multiple black holes.[2] Understanding that impossibility is usually accepted as the odds of 10^{50} to one against an event, the number of 10 raised to 10^{30} power certainly falls into the category of impossible.

The Probability of the Spontaneous Creation of Life

The Miracle of Life

The miracle of life itself still needs explaining. Given that we have a universe which is conducive to life, we are still left with the question of how did life begin? And that question is independent of the question of how the universe came to be. Regardless of whether the universe was created by God or by chance, life itself needs explaining.

In terms of probabilities, we can assess the probability of life developing spontaneously—and we then have a conditional probability. That is, life being generated spontaneously is conditional upon a universe properly tuned for life. The compound nature of these probabilities, depending upon their outcomes, can assist us in evaluating the overall probability of an accidental universe coupled with the spontaneous eruption of life.

Carbon

Before life could even be hoped for on earth, the primary elements and molecules for its existence must be present. The fundamental building block of all life is carbon. Our bodies are mostly carbon and water. The problem for physicists is how did the carbon get here. As noted previously, early stars and matter in the universe were mostly hydrogen and helium. In a "fortunately-unfortunately" story the magic circumstances required so that our earth got abundant carbon happened in the following manner.

Fortunately, under certain circumstances three helium nuclei can fuse to form carbon. Unfortunately, the simultaneous reaction of three helium atoms is extremely unlikely. Fortunately, it turns out that there is a resonant (tuned) energy at which they will react to form carbon. Unfortunately, it is a rather narrow energy band. Fortunately, this resonant energy is precisely tuned to the thermal energy (temperature) at which many large stars burn. Unfortunately, the carbon would be expected to be converted by collision with another helium nucleus to form oxygen, thus eating up all the carbon. Fortunately, there is another resonance, which again is precisely tuned to the thermal energy of many large stars, that prevents carbon from turning into oxygen. Unfortunately, the carbon is trapped in distant stars. How does it get to our earth and other planets? Fortunately, as stars burn up their fuel, many of them explode and scatter their dust throughout the universe. Unfortunately, this dust is randomly distributed. How does it get to our earth in sufficient quantities? Fortunately, our solar system was properly arranged to accumulate by gravity this dust into planets, one of which was our earth with abundant carbon, oxygen and other heavy elements.

In terms of probabilities, the likelihood of all of these events occurring in just this manner by chance is vanishingly small. It should be recognized, of course, that I have been illustrating carbon based life. That is the only form of life we have experience with on planet earth. Some scientists, such as Carl Sagan,[3] have theorized the existence of a different type of life on some other distant planet—a life based on, say, silicon, magnesium, or some other element. Since we have no evidence of such life forms, that postulate must remain as pure speculation.

DNA Magic

When considering the spontaneous development of life it is important to understand the complexity of the living cell and how it replicates itself. A detailed description of the miraculous chemistry of life regeneration is beyond the scope of this book, but a rudimentary description follows.

It is clear that all matter is made up of atoms. Atoms, bonded together, form molecules, as for example two atoms of hydrogen and one atom of oxygen bonded together form a water molecule. Almost all biological molecules are made of the atoms of just six elements: carbon, oxygen, nitrogen, hydrogen, phosphorus and sulfur.[4] DNA works its magic to assemble these various molecules in life replicating cells.

In 1962 Maurice Wilkins, James Watson and Francis Crick shared the Nobel Prize for describing the structure and chemical composition of deoxyribose nucleic acid (DNA).[5] All living forms contain DNA. Your DNA is unique to you and precisely determines the color of your eyes, your disposition towards hay fever and whether or not you will have a tendency to be overweight. It also ties you to your parents, grandparents, great-grandparents and distant ancestors. Only identical twins have the same DNAs.

The DNA structure has been observed in modern microscopes in which it appears as a long wormlike structure. A DNA molecule consists of a twisted double string of linked amino acid molecules in different specific combinations which determine the genetic makeup of a living cell. The double-helix shape of a DNA molecule with interconnecting links resembles a ladder with rungs attached to double corkscrew rails. The building blocks of the DNA molecule are the amino acid chains which make up the genes, which in-turn are linked to form the complete DNA.

In the human body there are trillions of cells but they are separated into only about 200 different types.[6] The living cell builds most of the molecules that it contains, and it does this by means of the master controller, the DNA, acting through the genes which are a part of it. Essentially every cell has a nucleus which contains the same DNA as every other cell. Human DNA contains about 100,000 genes. The genes, and all other proteins, including the enzymes which act as catalysts to accelerate the chemical reactions in the cell, are synthesized by the DNA. Each gene is responsible for assembling a different protein. It does this by providing the coded information necessary for combining the appropriate combination of amino acids present in the cell.[7]

The DNA manufactures proteins in its cell factory by means of a helper. The helper is ribonucleic acid, or RNA. This is a whole class of molecules whose structure is determined by the gene that is being copied.

The RNA helps the DNA by copying a particular gene and then escaping the nucleus where the DNA is housed in a membrane. The RNA is small enough to escape through the membrane whereas the DNA is not. After escape, and by using the enzymes, the RNA accumulates amino acids on its surface and links them together in just the right combinations to replicate the desired protein from the original DNA.[8]

Cells can divide and duplicate themselves. In this process the DNA is replicated by being split into its two component strands. Each of the separated strands acts as a template for the assembly of a complementary strand. By this method each molecule of DNA generates two exact copies of itself. Thus, through billions of such duplications, the original DNA of our mother's fertilized egg is passed on to all of the cells in our body which have a nucleus.[9]

Mutations can also occur in cells. Typically these mutations happen when some of the gene portions of the DNA are damaged. If the damage is not too severe the DNA can duplicate itself in its changed form. By far the largest cause of change in the DNA, however, results from the mixing of genes during the sexual reproduction process. Evolution by natural selection is, in fact, evolution of the DNA.[10]

From this necessarily abbreviated picture of the chemistry of life we can see how, once began, life can continue through replication of itself. The basic problem is how did it get started? Brian Silver in his book *The Ascent of Science* said:

> This brings us up against a fundamental problem. We have seen that DNA is responsible for the replication of the cell. *If a primitive cell contained only proteins, it would have no future.* Proteins cannot replicate themselves. Such a cell would eventually age and die without progeny.
>
> On the other hand, imagine a primitive cell with only nucleotides [DNA]. We know that DNA can direct duplication of the cell, initially by duplicating itself. *But that duplication needs certain enzymes,* and in a cell with no proteins, DNA could not duplicate—remember all enzymes are proteins. Neither could such a cell direct the synthesis of proteins—a process that itself requires enzymes.[11]

So we are left with a quandary. Scientists can explain in great detail the mechanics and chemistry of life propagation but not how it came to be. Material which follows and in Appendix C will consider various theories about the beginning of life. As you read that material, and particularly as the probabilities of the chance development of life are considered, please bear in mind the immensely complicated chemistry of biological systems. And continue to ask yourself the question, could the incredible complexity of the human body with its multitudinous specialized functions have come into being completely by chance or is it another fingerprint of God?

Evolution and Some Problems

In Appendix C there is an explanation of the Darwinian theory of evolution. In my view, the problem with evolution by natural selection is not that it doesn't answer certain questions in a scientific way—it does. The problem is that in a desperate attempt to avoid attributing any functions concerned with the creation and development of life to God, more is claimed by some of the supporters of natural selection than it can logically respond to.

One of the problems, as discussed in Appendix C, has to do with how to explain the explosion of life as demonstrated by the fossils found in the Burgess shales of Canada. More confirming evidence of this Cambrian time period explosion was later found in fossils from Sirius Passet, Greenland and from Yunnan, China. The explosion occurred over about a 10 million year period, far shorter than the hundreds of million—or even billions—of years previously believed to be necessary for natural selection to do its work. It is possible, of course, that earlier life forms simply were not fossilized for some reason, but the mounting evidence of this rapid appearance of many life forms does pose serious questions. In 1993, after working with a team of researchers studying the time line of these Cambrian fossils, Samuel Bowering of the Massachusetts Institute of Technology said this: "We now know how fast fast is, and what I like to ask my biologist friends is, How fast can evolution get before they start feeling uncomfortable?"[12]

In his book *Darwin's Black Box—The Biochemical Challenge to Evolution*, Michael Behe, Associate Professor of Biochemistry at Lehigh University, pointed out many of the problems associated with evolution as it is accepted by most biologists. In particular he argued that the chemistry in many complex living organisms cannot have evolved over time. The detailed chemistry of the eye and of blood clotting in the body, for example, requires complex systems which, if any part failed, the entire system would fail. These complex systems seem to have arrived fully functional—there appears to be no way that portions of the systems could have evolved with a gradual improvement of functionality. He describes such complex systems in this manner:

> What type of biological system could not be formed by "numerous, successive, slight modifications?"
>
> Well for starters, a system that is irreducibly complex. By *irreducibly complex* I mean a single system composed of several well-matched, interacting parts that contribute to the basic function, wherein the removal of any one of the parts causes the system to effectively cease functioning.
>
> . . . Since natural selection can only choose systems that are already working, then if a biological system cannot be produced gradually it would have to arise as an integrated unit, in one fell swoop, for natural selection to have anything to act on.[13]

If Behe is right, then it becomes increasingly difficult to argue that all of life's functions can be explained by natural selection processes. This brings us again to the possibility of some type of a master designer—God?

Conditions Necessary for Life to Begin

I have already presented the arguments for an anthropic universe and for a planet with abundant carbon. In addition, after initial formation of the earth about 4.6 billion years ago, for an initial period the earth was too hot and too many meteorites were bombarding it for the emergence of life. So the earth had to cool and the crust solidify before life could begin. Liquid water appeared between 3.4 and 3.8 billion years ago.[14, 15]

Next, the chemistry had to be just right. In those early stages there was no oxygen (or only traces of it) in the atmosphere of the young earth. Initially oxygen appeared in the oceans as tectonic forces unleashed huge earthquakes and volcanoes thereby releasing the previously rock-bound element.[16] Atmospheric oxygen had to await later photosynthesis from algae and other plant life to create the abundance that we know today.

In 1953 Stanley Miller, a graduate student at the University of Chicago, performed experiments in which he directed electrical discharges, simulating lightning, through a gaseous mixture of methane, ammonium, hydrogen, and water vapor in a flask. The early planet could have expected these gases to be available in the atmosphere. The result of Miller's experiment was the production of amino acids, urea, and other organic molecules.[17]

Since amino acids are the building blocks of proteins, it seemed that he might have found the secret to how life began. Newspapers hailed the event as the key to explaining the beginning of life. Other scientists quickly rushed to exploit this phenomenal find with research of their own.

In 1954, the biochemist and Nobel laureate George Wald reviewed the present state of biochemical science and wrote the following in an article in *Scientific American:*

> Time is in fact the hero of the plot [in the generation of the first form of life]. . . . What we regard as impossible on the basis of human experience is meaningless here. Given so much time, the "impossible" becomes possible, the possible probable, and the probable virtually certain. One has only to wait: time itself performs the miracles."[18]

In other words, if we had the right "chemical soup," and if we waited long enough, then the laws of probability would work in our favor and we would have spontaneous generation of life. Evolution could then take over to create the multitude of life forms that we see around us. Or, at least, that is what Wald thought. Let us now consider some of these issues.

Fossil Evidence of Early Life

Mayr described the evidence for early life in this manner:

> From the origin of life (about 3.8 billion years ago) until about 1.8 billion years ago, only prokaryotes existed [forms of bacteria]. . . . Around 1.8 billion years ago the first one-cellular eukaryotes originated . . . . The first fossil records of multicellular organisms appeared as recently as about 670 million years ago.[19]

As noted previously, atmospheric oxygen in concentrations suitable for multicellular life did not exist shortly after the earth cooled. It was rich in carbon dioxide from volcanic eruptions, however, and early plant life, such as algae, gradually produced oxygen in the primordial oceans through the process of photosynthesis. Concentrations in the atmosphere reached values similar to what we have today about 100 million years before the Cambrian era—between 650 and 700 million years ago—thus making multicellular life possible.[20] These high oxygen burning creatures could use food energy much more efficiently than the single-celled anaerobes of the previous era.

Referring back, now, to Wald's comment that "time is the hero," the fossil record shows that from the time when the earth's crust was solid and meteorite activity was subdued until the first rudimentary bacteria appeared was about 1.2 billion years.[20] This was between 3.4 and 3.8 billion years ago.

For from 1.3 to 2 billion years nucleus-free bacteria (blue-green algae) were the only representatives of life on the earth, that is between 25 and 43 percent of the present age of the earth. Eukaryotes—one celled life forms with a nucleus—appeared between 1.8 and 2.2 billion years ago and persisted as a major life form for from 200 to 300 million years. Then somewhere between 1.7 and 2.0 billion years ago the first multicelled algae appeared. Single and multi-celled algae were the primary life forms for about 1.5 billion years when the first multicelled animals exploded into dominance in about a 10 or 20 million year period. This was at the beginning of the Cambrian period 543 million years ago.[21, 22] There was a brief period of 20 or 30 million years just before the Cambrian period, called the Vendian period, when strange fond-shaped organisms existed and then disappeared. Not much is known of them.[22]

From this fossil record, the most time that we have available for rudimentary life to develop is 1 to 3 billion years, and for muticellular animals we have a few tens of millions of years. This narrow window of time for life to have developed gives substantial difficulties for scientists who search desperately for some method—other than a Godly one—for life to have come into being. A 1999 article in *Scientific American* put it this way: "In other words, only 100 million years or so after the earliest possible point when Earth could have safely supported life, organisms were already well enough established that evidence of them remains today. This narrow window of time for life to have emerged implies that the process might have required help from space molecules."[23] The possibility of life originating in space molecules, as suggested in the article, is discussed in *Appendix C.*

Remembering, now, that when George Wald made his comment in 1954 that time was the "hero of the plot," he was assuming that there were many billions of years for the self-induced beginning of life. What are the probabilities that life could have been spontaneously generated in the much shorter time periods currently known to have been available?

The Probabilities of Different Life Forms Developing

In 1968, Professor Harold Morowitz, a physicist at Yale University, published the book *Energy Flow in Biology.* In the book he presented calculations of the time required for random chemical reactions to form a simple bacterium. He based his calculations on optimistically rapid rates of reactions. He determined that the calculated time for the bacterium to form by random processes exceeded the 15-billion year age of the universe, never mind the 1.2 to 2 billion years that the fossil record shows for bacteria to appear.[24]

The astronomer Sir Fred Hoyle, who helped develop one of the cosmological models to explain the universe, and an atheist, together with his colleague, Chandra Wickramasinghe, calculated the probability of one simple enzyme forming by chance. The enzyme was much simpler than even a bacterium. The two scientists determined that there was only one chance in 10^{20} of this simple enzyme appearing. Then, since they recognized that to form a single bacterium like E. coli would require 2,000 enzymes, each performing particular tasks, they needed to compute the compound probability of a single bacterium forming. The odds against the formation of a single bacterium were determined to be $(10^{20})^{2000}$ to one, or $10^{40,000}$ to one. Remembering that impossibility is defined as 10^{50} to one (100,000, 000,000,000,000,000,000,000,000,000,000,000,000,000,000,000 to 1), it is seen that the calculated value most assuredly represents an impossible situation. Wickramasinghe later made the following analogy concerning their calculations: "The chances that life just occurred are about as unlikely as a typhoon blowing through a junk yard and constructing a Boeing 747."[25]

In 1992, Herbert Yockey, an information theorist and biologist from Cambridge University, published the book *Information Theory and Molecular Biology*. In the book he provided the calculations for a fairly sophisticated chemical process for the beginning of life. He noted, for example, that because all amino acids are not equally probable, a correct calculation cannot simply multiply the number of functionally equal amino acids at each site to arrive at the number of sequences (as Hoyle and Wickramasinghe did). Yockey chose iso-l-cytochrome c as a model protein with known functionally equivalent amino acids, and he proceeded to calculate the generation of one single molecule of that specific protein. The probability was calculated to be 2×10^{-44}, and he observed that the actual probability would be much worse due to the many non-proteinous amino acids in the prebiotic soup. In commenting on his calculation he wrote:

> Let us remind ourselves that we have calculated the probability of the generation of only a single molecule of iso-1-cytochrome c. Of course, very many copies of each molecule must be generated to form the protobiont. . . . And so we see that even if we believe that the "building blocks" are available, they do not spontaneously make proteins, at least not by chance. . . . The extremely small probabilities calculated are not discouraging to true believers . . . or to people who live in a universe of infinite extension that has no beginning or end in time. In such a universe all things not *streng verboten* will happen. In fact we live in a small, young universe generated by an enormous hydrogen bomb explosion some time between 10×10^9 and 20×10^9 years ago. A practical person must conclude that life didn't happen by chance.[26]

In 1994 Walter L. Bradley and Charles B. Thaxton wrote an article for the book *The Creation Hypothesis* in which they also calculated the probability of the random formation of 100 amino acids into a protein. Their calculations showed a probability of 10^{-191}.

Bradley and Thaxton stated their agreement with Yockey's conclusions. They further concluded that if all the carbon on the earth were available as amino acids and chemically reacted at the greatest possible rate of 10^{12} reactions per second for one billion years, the chance formation of one functional protein would be the mathematically impossible value of only 10^{-65} [27]

For those readers interested in seeing how a simplified probability calculation may be carried out concerning the chance creation of life, a representative analysis is given in Appendix C.

The Lightning Bolt and Uncle Willie

So where does this leave us? Could a chance lightning bolt into a mud-puddle have created the slime from which Uncle Willie evolved some four billion years later? Or perhaps, as discussed in Appendix C, Uncle Willie's ancestors could have been spawned in some ancient volcanic undersea eruption. I think not. The evidence against such events are irresistible. Moreover, the probabilities against many of the complex life functions evolving by natural selection are equally formidable in my view. To quote Michael Behe as he summarized the results of his studies on the chemistry of life.

> The result of these cumulative efforts to investigate the cell—to investigate life at the molecular level—is a loud, clear piercing cry of *"design!"* The result is so unambiguous and so significant that it must be ranked as one of the greatest achievements in the history of science. ... The observation of the intelligent design of life is as momentous as the observation that the earth goes around the sun or that disease is caused by bacteria or that radiation is emitted in quanta.[28]

Still Other Perspectives

We have now traveled the probabilistic path on our scientific journey. That path has illumined another view of the truth. It is a view that repeatedly speaks of the creation—a creation of the universe, a creation of our earth and a creation of all living things thereon.

May we once more turn to our friends who have visited other spheres and see what we can learn from them about life and the creation? Perhaps they have a more ethereal understanding of how things work.

Kenneth Ring interviewed Beverly Brodsky, an atheistic Jewish lady who, as a result of a motorcycle accident, had an extensive NDE. The experience forever changed her life and her perspective about life. In one part of her experience she said:

Now I was treated to an extraordinary voyage through the universe. Instantly we traveled to the center of stars being born, supernovas exploding, and many other glorious celestial events for which I have no name. The impression I have now of this trip is that it felt like the universe is all one grand object woven from the same fabric. Space and time are illusions that hold us to our plane; out there all is present simultaneously. I was a passenger on a Divine spaceship in which the creator showed me the fullness and beauty of all of his Creation.[29]

Jenette is another NDE participant that Carol and I interviewed at her home in 1992. During a trip to a hospital in 1988 for a physical problem the doctors told Jenette that she needed a heart operation. A portion of our interview follows:

Which hospital was this?

Holy Cross in Salt Lake. . . . My Doctors decided I needed a mitral valve replacement and a double bypass. The mitral valve had gone sour, because as an infant I had had scarlet fever.

The original surgery was scheduled for early in the morning of February 28, 1988. And I wasn't fearful at all. After the surgery I went into Intensive Care where they determined that bleeding was occurring. They rushed me back into surgery to find the source of the bleeding. That was at five P.M. on the same day.

This was bleeding in the heart?

Yes—it turned out my heart was misshapen and in the wrong place. Instead of a normal heart's shape, my heart looks like a mushroom. So the bleeder was on the back side of the mushroom instead of where they expected to find it. There was a vein towards my back rib leading to the valve and that's where the bleeding was coming from.

The original team of surgeons tried to correct the problem on the second, afternoon surgery. They thought they had it corrected and put me back in Intensive Care. Eight to ten hours later I was still hemorrhaging. So for the third time in twenty-two hours I went back into surgery, this time with a new team of surgeons. And this time they found the problem, but it was during this third surgery that I had my experience.

I was on the operating table and I could see the doctor's faces, and I could hear a few words of what they were saying. I could see inside myself where the problem was. I tried to tell them, "Look under that lip edge." Of course, being anesthetized I couldn't tell them anything, but mentally I was trying to tell them, "That's where the bleeder is, that's where the bleeding is coming from."

Could you see them as this was going on?

I could see them—it's like I came out of my body and was two feet above them. And I could see what they were doing, and I could see the heart, and I could . . . I just knew where the bleeder was before I even rose up from my body. It just came to my mind . . . I just knew where it was.

I wanted to explain where the bleeder was, but I couldn't, and in my anxiety to express it I came out of my body. I tried to communicate to the doctors, but I couldn't communicate, and I could see what they were doing. There were three surgeons and four nurses all working together.

I finally decided that there was no use, the doctors weren't hearing me. And I kind of floated up to the top of the room. Like I was looking down from a distance, and still more distance, at them.[30]

These two experiences give us a dual view of the creation—both that of the universe and that of life itself. Similar to the view of the scientists wrestling with the probabilities of a tuned universe and of spontaneous life forms it is a view marked with wonder. Wonder of the marvelous circumstances in which we reside and live. It leads us to ask, are these probabilities and NDE interpretations of reality in conflict with each other or are they simply illustrations of the different fingerprints of God?

6
Mormonism—The History

Why a History?

Mormonism is inextricably connected to its history. Joseph Smith, Jr., the first prophet, claimed to have seen God, Christ and angels in a series of spiritual events or visions which mirrored those of ancient Biblical prophets. These claims were so extraordinary that any consideration of Mormonism *must* address them. Either what Joseph Smith claimed did happen as he described it, or it did not and he and most of his early followers were frauds. There is no middle ground for Mormonism.

Obviously, a complete and detailed history of The Church of Jesus Christ of Latter-day Saints is beyond the scope of this book. Abbreviated, but important events in the history of the Church will be delineated. These abbreviated portions will place emphasis on some of the more dramatic visions recorded in early Church history.

There is another reason that I include these portions of the history. One cannot read LDS Church history without seeing parallels between what is recorded there and what in recent years has been recorded in accounts of near-death experiences. The parallels and the frequency of their occurrence are so obvious that comparisons become inevitable. Moreover, these parallels are not restricted to early Mormon Church leaders. Such experiences were and are ubiquitous among the members. A more detailed account of these historic LDS epiphanies is given in Duane Crowther's book, *Life Everlasting*.[1]

The fact that those early Mormon visions and experiences occurred starting in the early 1800s makes for some interesting comparisons. I have already described how NDEs can be traced back to medieval or even Biblical times. This pattern of repeatability leads naturally to the question, could most or many of these experiences be authentic, or are they largely fraudulent—or is there some other explanation? The readers can form their own conclusions from some of the evidence presented in this book.

The First Vision

Joseph Smith, Jr., the Mormon Prophet, was born on December 23, 1805 in Sharon, Vermont. The family moved to New York in 1816 where they farmed a one hundred acre unimproved plot of land two miles south of Palmyra. Young Joseph's education was limited; school was held in his home, except for periods in Vermont where he attended "common schools," and where he learned to read, write and cipher. In his home schooling Joseph was largely taught from the Bible by his mother.[2] From his early youth Joseph and his brothers, Alvin and Hyrum, labored diligently to help the family and to obtain money by hiring themselves out.

Bible reading and family prayers were a daily practice in the Smith home, and Joseph was aware of basic Christian beliefs. He was confused, however by the numerous religious sects which contended for members in the area. He had his initial vision when he was fourteen years of age. His account of what happened follows:[3]

> While I was laboring under the extreme difficulties caused by the contests of these parties of religionists, I was one day reading the Epistle of James, first chapter and fifth verse, which reads: If any of you lack wisdom, let him ask of God, that giveth to all men liberally, and upbraideth not; and it shall be given him. Never did any passage of scripture come with more power to the heart of man than this did at this time to mine. It seemed to enter with great force into every feeling of my heart. I reflected on it again and again, knowing that if any person needed wisdom from God, I did; for how to act I did not know, and unless I could get more wisdom than I then had, I would never know; for the teachers of religion of the different sects understood the same passages of scripture so differently as to destroy all confidence in settling the question by an appeal to the Bible.
>
> At length I came to the conclusion that I must either remain in darkness and confusion, or else I must do as James directs, that is, ask of God. I at length came to the determination to "ask of God," concluding that if he gave wisdom to them that lacked wisdom, and would give lib-

erally, and not upbraid, I might venture. So, in accordance with this, my determination to ask of God, I retired to the woods to make the attempt. It was on the morning of a beautiful, clear day, early in the spring of eighteen hundred and twenty. It was the first time in my life that I had made such an attempt, for amidst all my anxieties I had never as yet made the attempt to pray vocally.

After I had retired to the place where I had previously designed to go, having looked around me, and finding myself alone, I kneeled down and began to offer up the desires of my heart to God. I had scarcely done so, when immediately I was seized upon by some power which entirely overcame me, and had such an astonishing influence over me as to bind my tongue so that I could not speak. Thick darkness gathered around me, and it seemed to me for a time as if I were doomed to sudden destruction. But, exerting all my powers to call upon God to deliver me out of the power of this enemy which had seized upon me, and at the very moment when I was ready to sink into despair and abandon myself to destruction—not to an imaginary ruin, but to the power of some actual being from the unseen world, who had such marvelous power as I had never before felt in any being—just at this moment of great alarm, I saw a pillar of light exactly over my head, above the brightness of the sun, which descended gradually until it fell upon me.

It no sooner appeared than I found myself delivered from the enemy which held me bound. When the light rested upon me I saw two Personages, whose brightness and glory defy all description, standing above me in the air. One of them spake unto me, calling me by name and said, pointing to the other—This is My Beloved Son. Hear Him!

My object in going to inquire of the Lord was to know which of all the sects was right, that I might know which to join. No sooner, therefore, did I get possession of myself, so as to be able to speak, than I asked the Personages who stood above me in the light, which of all the sects was right (for at this time it had never entered into my heart that all were wrong)—and which I should join. I was answered that I must join none of them, for they were all wrong; and the Personage who addressed me said that all their creeds were an abomination in his sight; that those professors were all corrupt; that: "they draw near to me with their lips, but their hearts are far from me, they teach for doctrines the commandments of men, having a form of godliness, but they deny the power thereof." He again forbade me to join with any of them; and many other things did he say unto me, which I cannot write at this time.

When I came to myself again, I found myself lying on my back, looking up into heaven. When the light had departed, I had no strength; but soon recovering in some degree, I went home.

The Angel Moroni

Joseph told his parents and his siblings of his vision and they believed him. He also told others, including Christian Ministers, for which he was soundly derided. However, on the evening of September 21, 1823, Joseph retired to his bed "in quite a serious and contemplative state of mind."[4] His account of what happened next follows:[5]

> . . . After I had retired to my bed for the night, I betook myself to prayer and supplication to Almighty God for forgiveness of all my sins and follies, and also for a manifestation to me, that I might know of my state and standing before him; for I had full confidence in obtaining a divine manifestation, as I previously had one.
>
> While I was thus in the act of calling upon God, I discovered a light appearing in my room, which continued to increase until the room was lighter than at noonday, when immediately a personage appeared at my bedside, standing in the air, for his feet did not touch the floor. He had on a loose robe of most exquisite whiteness. It was a whiteness beyond anything earthly I had ever seen; nor do I believe that any earthly thing could be made to appear so exceedingly white and brilliant. His hands were naked, and his arms also, a little above the wrist; so, also, were his feet naked, as were his legs, a little above the ankles. His head and neck were also bare. I could discover that he had no other clothing on but this robe, as it was open, so that I could see into his bosom.
>
> Not only was his robe exceedingly white, but his whole person was glorious beyond description, and his countenance truly like lightning. The room was exceedingly light, but not so very bright as immediately around his person. When I first looked upon him, I was afraid; but the fear soon left me.
>
> He called me by name, and said unto me that he was a messenger sent from the presence of God to me, and that his name was Moroni; that God had a work for me to do; and that my name should be had for good and evil among all nations, kindreds, and tongues, or that it should be both good and evil spoken of among all people. He said there was a book deposited, written upon gold plates, giving an account of the former inhabitants of this continent, and the source from whence they

sprang. He also said that the fulness of the everlasting Gospel was contained in it, as delivered by the Savior to the ancient inhabitants. . . .

The angel gave further instructions to Joseph Smith, and he quoted
extensively from Malachi, Isaiah, Acts, Joel and other scriptures from
the Bible. Then as the instructions from Moroni seemed about to cease,
Joseph Smith recorded this:[6]

> After this communication, I saw the light in the room begin to gath-
> er immediately around the person of him who had been speaking to me,
> and it continued to do so until the room was again left dark, except just
> around him; when, instantly I saw, as it were, a conduit open right up
> into heaven, and he ascended till he entirely disappeared, and the room
> was left as it had been before this heavenly light had made its appear-
> ance.
>
> I lay musing on the singularity of the scene, and marveling greatly
> at what had been told to me by this extraordinary messenger; when, in
> the midst of my meditation, I suddenly discovered that my room was
> again beginning to get lighted, and in an instant, as it were, the same
> heavenly messenger was again by my bedside. He commenced, and
> again related the very same things which he had done at his first visit,
> without the least variation. . . .

Moroni repeated this same message a total of three times. As part of
these messages Joseph was told that at the proper time he would be
given the golden plates and, through the power of the Lord, would be
able to translate the ancient writings contained on them. After these vis-
its to Joseph by Moroni, which took most of the night, daylight broke
and Joseph went to the field to harvest the grain as usual. His father
observed that Joseph was not able to vigorously work as he normally
did, and thinking him ill, told him to go home. Joseph left and in
attempting to climb a fence collapsed. Immediately he heard a voice
speaking his name. Looking up he saw Moroni who repeated the same
message from the previous evening, and he told Joseph to tell his father
what had transpired.[7]

The Gold Plates

In his vision Joseph had seen where the golden plates were buried in
a hill four miles south of Palmyra. Joseph went to the spot of the vision
and was able to find the plates and other materials. He attempted to

remove them but was unable to do so as he was commanded by Moroni, who again appeared, to leave them until he was given permission to remove them. He was told to visit the hill each year, on September 22nd, to be instructed further.[8]

Joseph did as he was instructed for four years, and on September 22, 1827, accompanied by his wife Emma, Joseph was given the plates by the Angel Moroni. He was cautioned that he would be responsible for the record, and should the record be lost through his neglect God would cut him off. In addition to the plates Joseph was given a Urim and Thummim, which was an ancient translating device, and which would later aid him in the translation. He took the plates home and hid them.[9]

Martin Harris, a friend of the Smith family and a well-to-do farmer, was told by the Smiths prior to receipt of the plates that they would be given to Joseph. Word apparently leaked to the surrounding neighborhood and soon the Smiths were besieged with people trying to find and steal the plates. In order to protect them, as Moroni had instructed, Joseph and Emma left New York in great secrecy for Harmony, Pennsylvania where they would stay at the home of Emma's parents, the Hales. They arrived in December, 1827.[10]

Joseph wrote this description of the plates:

> These records were engraven on plates which had the appearance of gold, each plate was six inches wide and eight inches long, and not quite so thick as common tin. They were . . . bound together in a volume as the leaves of a book, with three rings running through the whole. The volume was something near six inches in thickness, a part of which was sealed. The characters of the unsealed part were small, and beautifully engraved. The whole book exhibited many marks of antiquity in its construction, and much skill in the art of engraving.[11]

Translation of The Book of Mormon

Joseph and Emma moved into a small house on property owned by Emma's brother, and Joseph began translation of the plates. In April, 1828, Martin Harris became Joseph's scribe. By June they had translated 116 pages of manuscript on large foolscap paper. Due to the loss of these pages through Martin's carelessness Joseph lost the power of translation for a period. It was restored in September, 1828, but Joseph was instructed to cease translating for a time. In April, 1829, Oliver

Cowdery, a school teacher who had heard of the metal plates and Joseph's findings, and had some spiritual experiences related to those findings, joined Joseph as his new scribe. Work proceeded rapidly on the translation until May, 1829, when threats of violence caused Joseph, Emma and Oliver to move to the home of their friends, Peter and David Whitmer, who lived in Fayette, New York. The translation was completed there by June, 1829.[12] The total elapsed time for the translation was about ninety days.

As to the method of translation, Joseph said that he translated the plates "by the Gift and Power of God." A number of witnesses have described how the process worked. A summary of the process is as follows: Joseph Smith viewed the interpreters (either the Urim and Thummim or a seer stone) and dictated for long periods of time without reference to any books, papers, manuscripts, or even the plates themselves. Joseph also spelled out unfamiliar Book of Mormon names. After each dictated sequence, the scribe read back to Joseph what was written so that Joseph could check the correctness of the manuscript. Joseph started each dictation session without prompting from the scribe about where the previous session had ended and without notes.[13]

Throughout the translation of the Book of Mormon the plates stayed with Joseph Smith except for a brief period when Moroni retrieved them, then later returned them to Joseph. Upon completion of the translation Moroni reclaimed the plates from Joseph.

The Witnesses

During the translation of the Book of Mormon, Joseph and Oliver Cowdery discovered that some of the text spoke of witnesses who would "bear record of same." Ultimately eleven witnesses would be chosen, eight who would view and handle the plates, and three who would have the greater privilege of an angelic visitation. The three chosen witnesses were Martin Harris, Oliver Cowdery and David Whitmer. The eight witnesses were Christian, Jacob, Peter, and John Whitmer, Hiram Page, Joseph Smith, Sr., and Joseph's brothers, Hyrum and Samuel Smith.

In June of 1829, as the translation was almost complete, Joseph took Martin, Oliver and David into the woods where they prayed to have a vision. Notwithstanding their prayer, nothing happened, and Martin asked to be excused so that he could pray separately. He was excused and Oliver, David and Joseph resumed praying. Joseph described what happened next in this manner:[14]

> ... When presently we beheld a light above us in the air, of exceeding brightness; and behold, an angel stood before us. In his hands he held the plates which we had been praying for these to have a view of. He turned over the leaves one by one, so that we could see them, and discern the engravings thereon distinctly. He then addressed himself to David Whitmer, and said, "David, blessed is the Lord, and he that keeps His commandments;" when immediately afterwards, we heard a voice from out of the bright light above us, saying, "These plates have been revealed by the power of God, and they have been translated by the power of God. The translation of them which you have seen is correct, and I command you to bear record of what you now see and hear."

After this experience, David and Oliver left and Joseph went in search of Martin. He found him praying a short distance away. They joined in prayer and Martin and Joseph then had a similar experience.

A few days after these experiences the Whitmers and Hiram Page visited the Smiths in Manchester. The Prophet invited them, his father and brothers into the woods where Joseph took the plates from a cloth container and laid them before the eight men. They saw and handled the plates. There was no vision or voice that spoke to them—just the plates.[15]

All of the eleven witnesses signed statements bearing witness to what they had seen and heard. The statements appear at the beginning of each Book of Mormon. Later in their lives some of the witnesses left the Church for various reasons, but they never denied their testimonies.[16]

Organization of
The Church of Jesus Christ of Latter-day Saints

While translating the Book of Mormon Joseph and Oliver discovered that baptism for the remission of sins was mentioned several times by prophets described in the text. The mode of baptism prescribed was baptism by immersion. They also determined that baptism was for those eight years of age and older—for those capable of sinning. Little children and those not capable of sinning were saved through the atonement of Jesus Christ without baptism.

As a result of these passages of scripture, on May 15, 1829 they retired to a riverbank on the edge of the Susquehanna River where they commenced to pray for enlightenment. They had scarcely commenced their prayer when a heavenly messenger descended in a cloud of glory, surrounded by light which surpassed the glitter of the May sunbeams and shed its brilliancy over the face of nature.[17]

The messenger introduced himself as John the Baptist, and said that he was acting under the direction of Peter, James and John—Christ's Apostles from the Old World—and that he was to bestow upon them the Aaronic Priesthood which held the keys of the ministering of angels, and of the gospel of repentance, and of baptism by immersion for the remission of sins.

Oliver Cowdery, the school teacher, and scribe of the Book of Mormon, was one of the more eloquent speakers and writers in the early Church. He later wrote an account of what he felt and saw during this experience. His description follows:[18]

> I shall not attempt to paint to you the feelings of this heart, or the majestic beauty and glory which surrounded us on this occasion; but you will believe me when I say, that earth, nor men, with the eloquence of time, cannot begin to clothe language in as interesting and sublime a manner as this holy personage. No; nor has this earth power to give the joy, to bestow the peace, or comprehend the wisdom which was contained in each sentence as they were delivered by the power of the Holy Spirit! Man may deceive his fellow-men, deception may follow deception, and the children of the wicked one may have power to seduce the foolish and untaught, till naught but fiction feeds the many, and the fruit of falsehood carries in its current the giddy to the grave; but one touch with the finger of his love, yes, one ray of glory from the upper world, or one word from the mouth of the Savior, from the bosom of eternity, strikes it all into insignificance, and blots it forever from the mind. The assurance that we were in the presence of an angel, the certainty that we heard the voice of Jesus, and the truth unsullied as it flowed from a pure personage, dictated by the will of God, is to me past description, and I shall ever look upon this expression of the Savior's goodness with wonder and thanksgiving while I am permitted to

tarry; and in those mansions where perfection dwells and sin never comes, I hope to adore in that day which shall never cease.

Having received the authority of baptism, and upon instructions by the angel, Joseph baptized Oliver and Oliver baptized Joseph. Immediately upon emerging from the water they experienced the glorious influence of the Holy Ghost. Later Peter, James and John appeared to Joseph and Oliver and bestowed the Melchizedek Priesthood upon them with its "keys of my kingdom, and a dispensation of the gospel for the last times; and for the fulness of times, in the which I will gather together in one all things, both which are in heaven, and which are on earth." [19]

Having the Melchizedek Priesthood with its keys of the kingdom, on April 6, 1830, in the log house of Peter Whitmer, and with about fifty persons present, the Church of Jesus Christ of Latter-day Saints was organized. It was a spiritual event for all concerned, and many people were baptized and had hands laid upon them for receipt of the Holy Ghost. Others received the Melchizedek Priesthood.[20]

A Vision of Heaven

By 1831 most of the Church was centered in Ohio where many of the new converts were located. In February, 1832, following a conference at Amherst, fifty miles west of Cleveland, Joseph returned to Hiram, Ohio, and with Sidney Rigdon as scribe, was working on the translation of the Bible. As they pondered scriptures related to "Heaven," they both had a vision in which they saw into the Lord's realm. They saw that before the creation of the earth man was in the presence of God. They also saw that through Jesus Christ—who was chosen to be the lamb slain before the foundation of the earth—man was destined, according to how he exercised his agency, to climb to exaltation. Heaven was not a single place, but had three degrees of glory reserved for individuals according to their different degrees of righteousness. From this glorious vision it was revealed that man had the potential to become as God: "Wherefore, as it is written, they are gods, even the sons of God—Wherefore, all things are theirs, whether life or death, or things present, or things to come, all are theirs and they are Christ's, and Christ is God's."[21] A basic philosophic doctrine which followed from this revelation was that all men and women are sons and daughters of God, and all are involved in an eternal adventure of creation and infinite growth—or limited growth—depending upon their choices.

The Kirtland Temple

Joseph and other leaders of the early church were very aware of the Biblical record of Solomon's Temple and of its importance in religious history. In addition, the Book of Mormon and other revelations spoke strongly of the need for baptism and for other priesthood ordinances. Therefore, despite growing opposition to their movement in Ohio and Missouri, and in response to a revelation to Joseph, they purchased property for a temple in Kirtland in June, 1833.[22] By July 1833, the Prophet and twenty-three brethren laid the foundation stone for the House of the Lord.[23] By sacrificing enormously, and notwithstanding increasingly intense persecution, the Saints completed the temple by 1836.[24]

On Sunday, April 3rd, while in the temple, a marvelous vision was revealed to Joseph Smith and Oliver Cowdery. Joseph described what happened in these terms:

> In the afternoon, I assisted the other Presidents in distributing the Lord's Supper to the Church, receiving it from the Twelve, whose privilege it was to officiate at the sacred desk this day. After having performed this service to my brethren, I retired to the pulpit, the veils being dropped, and bowed myself, with Oliver Cowdery, in solemn and silent prayer. After rising from the prayer, the following vision was opened to both of us.
>
> The veil was taken from our minds, and the eyes of our understanding were opened. We saw the Lord standing upon the breastwork of the pulpit, before us; and under his feet was a paved work of pure gold, in color like amber. His eyes were as a flame of fire; the hair of his head was white like the pure snow; his countenance shone above the brightness of the sun; and his voice was as the sound of the rushing of great waters, even the voice of Jehovah, saying: I am the first and the last; I am he who liveth, I am he who was slain; I am your advocate with the Father.
>
> Behold, your sins are forgiven you; you are clean before me; therefore, lift up your heads and rejoice. Let the hearts of your brethren rejoice, and let the hearts of all my people rejoice, who have, with their might, built this house to my name. For behold, I have accepted this

house, and my name shall be here; and I will manifest myself to my people in mercy in this house. . . .[25]

After the vision of the Savior, Moses appeared and committed to Joseph and Oliver the keys of the gathering of Israel from the four parts of the earth; Elias appeared and committed the dispensation of the gospel of Abraham, and Elijah appeared saying: "Behold, the time has fully come which was spoken of by the mouth of Malachi—testifying that he [Elijah] should be sent, before the great and dreadful day of the Lord to come—to turn the hearts of the fathers to the children, and the children to the fathers, lest the whole earth be smitten with a curse."[26]

The Martyrdom of the Prophet

As the Church grew rapidly in Ohio and also in Missouri, persecution grew commensurately. Ultimately, after a tragic massacre of many Mormons at a small settlement called Haun's Mill in Missouri,[27] and after the governor of Missouri, Lilburn Boggs, issued his infamous "Extermination Order," to drive from the state or exterminate any Mormons,[28] the Saints purchased and developed a piece of land along the Mississippi River in Illinois. They developed a thriving city there which they called Nauvoo. By July 1841 there were 1200 homes in Nauvoo with hundreds more being built.[29]

Nauvoo continued to grow and flourish for a time. It became the largest city in Illinois, but the politics changed as the Saints became more numerous. Moreover, increasing popularity of Joseph Smith as a political figure increased the hatred of his enemies in Illinois and Missouri. They promoted a campaign to poison the minds of the populace against the Mormon leader and his people. During the winter of 1843-1844, "indignation" meetings were held in Carthage, Illinois to decide what action should be taken to eliminate the Mormons.[30]

A charge was brought against Joseph Smith for inciting a riot when he, as mayor, and upon orders of the city council, authorized the city marshal to shut down an inflammatory paper, *The Expositor*. The printing press was destroyed, and the publishers of the paper fled to Carthage. There they brought the charge against him. They argued that Joseph and his brother, Hyrum, should be tried by the legal authorities in Carthage. After much legal and political maneuvering, the instigators of the charges succeeded in getting Governor Ford to intervene and insist that Joseph and Hyrum surrender to the authorities in Carthage.[31]

On June 24, 1844, Joseph and seventeen of his brethren rode for Carthage. Turning to the men around him, Joseph said,

> I am going like a lamb to the slaughter, but I am calm as a summer's morning. I have a conscience void of offense toward God and toward all men. . . . I shall die an innocent man, . . . and it shall be said of me, "He was murdered in cold blood."[32]

On June 26, 1844, Joseph and Hyrum Smith, Willard Richards and John Taylor were imprisoned in the upstairs room of the Carthage Jail. Despite assurances from the Governor that they would be protected by law enforcement officers and by the "Carthage Greys" (a pseudo military group under the control of many of those desiring to destroy the Prophet), on June 27, 1844, an armed mob attacked the jail, broke in and shot Joseph and Hyrum Smith dead and severely wounded John Taylor. Willard Richards escaped harm and managed to get John Taylor medical help.[33] John Taylor later recovered and ultimately became a president of the Church.

Aftermath

The enemies of Joseph and Hyrum thought that the death of the Prophet would destroy the Church. It did not—if anything it strengthened it. Brigham Young became the new leader. He recognized that continued antagonism would require the departure of the Saints for the West where Joseph had prophesied that they would ultimately reside. Resistance increased more rapidly than anticipated, though, and continued attacks by armed mobs forced the Saints to leave Nauvoo, at great sacrifice, in the winter of 1845-1846.

The exodus of the Saints from Nauvoo, their travel across the country by horse, ox-wagon, and handcart and their settlement of the West is one of the great stories of all time. Brigham Young has been likened to a modern Moses. That story, however, is beyond the scope of this book.

About Joseph Smith

Joseph Smith, in his $38^{1}/_{2}$ years accomplished more than most men accomplish in twice that time. He founded a new religion—or rather he helped God reestablish Christ's original religion. In that religion Joseph established, by authority of the Lord, the priesthood offices and authority that existed in Christ's pristine Church. He set into place the means to continue with that organization after his departure with follow-on "prophets, seers and revelators."

He translated an ancient record, The Book of Mormon, within a ninety day elapsed period, with no reference to other materials or sources other than those provided by the Angel Moroni. He did that with less than a fourth grade education, and he included complex materials about a complete civilization on this continent which developed from the descendants of some ancient prophets and their families who were led by the Lord from ancient Israel. The book describes Christ's visit to those peoples, and it details many other instances of the Lord's dealings with them during their periods of peace and war. It includes new information on doctrinal matters which are incomplete in the Bible. It displays evidence of being an ancient work, the technical nature of which could not have been understood by Joseph Smith when the book was written. Despite challenges by numerous scholars attempting to disprove the book or its origin, it has stood the test of time. Millions of copies have been printed in many languages and distributed throughout the world.

Joseph attracted thousands of dedicated followers, and he initiated an aggressive missionary program which survives to this day. Temples were reestablished by him as a central part of the religion—with ordinances and covenants binding man to God and God to man.

Several other documents of scripture were added to the standard works of the Church by revelation to Joseph. These included the Doctrine and Covenants and the Pearl of Great Price. The Pearl of Great Price contained additional writings of Moses and Abraham. All of these writings were to act as complements to the Bible and were additional witnesses that Jesus is the Christ.

In the area of civil and national government, Joseph planned cities, established a welfare system for the care of the needy, became mayor of the largest city in Illinois, directed the Nauvoo Legion as its commanding general, and ran for the Presidency of the United States.

During all of this time Joseph met his accusers with civility and in accordance with established laws. He defended the Constitution of the United States as an inspired document, and he met with President Van

Buren and members of the U.S. Congress in an attempt to get redress for the Saints. Van Buren's response was, "Gentlemen, your cause is just, but I can do nothing for you. . . . If I take up for you I shall lose the vote of Missouri."[34]

Quotations by Professor Bloom

Professor Harold Bloom is Sterling Professor of Humanities at Yale University, and Berg Professor of English at New York University. He has written more than twenty books. One of his recent books is *The American Religion.* Professor Bloom's religious affiliation is not given in the book, but he apparently claims to be a gnostic Jew. In this book, Professor Bloom examines the history, teachings and evolution of those religions in America that he characterizes as being uniquely American. Most of the Protestant religions are included, as are Jehovah's Witnesses, Seventh Day Adventists, and Christian Scientists. He devotes three chapters to the Mormons.

There is much that Professor Bloom gets wrong in his writings concerning the Mormons. He makes a similar mistake to evangelical Christians, for example, by contending that the Church of Jesus Christ of Latter-day Saints is not truly a Christian church.[35] His argument is that Joseph Smith is so central to the religion that he replaces Jesus Christ as the leading figure. Nothing could be further from the truth as far as Latter-day Saints are concerned. Jesus Christ is the head of the Church and, together with God the Father, Jesus is the indispensable figure of worship. Bloom also misunderstands or misinterprets the LDS position on premortal intelligences and spirits.[36] Despite these problems associated with his analysis of the LDS religion, Bloom has some interesting things to say about Joseph Smith and the future of the Church. The following quotes seem to summarize his feelings in these matters:

> Two aspects of the Saints' vision seem starkly central to me; no other American religious movement is so ambitious, and no rival even remotely approaches the spiritual audacity that drives endlessly towards accomplishing a titanic design. The Mormons fully intend to convert the nation and the world; to go from some ten million souls to six billion. This is sublimely insane, not merely because of the stunning numbers, but primarily because it means going up against such worldwide antagonists as the Roman Catholic Church and Islam, as well as

such endlessly subtle formulations as Buddhism and Hinduism. Yet the Mormons will not falter; they will take the entire twenty-first century as their span, if need be, and surely it will be.[37]

   . . . I do not qualify to pass on the rest of the Mormon creed, but I also do not find it possible to doubt that Joseph Smith was an authentic prophet. Where in all of American history can we find his match? The Prophet Joseph has proved again that economic and social forces do not determine human destiny. Religious history, like literary or any cultural history, is made by genius, by the mystery of rare human personalities. I am not persuaded by sociological and anthropological studies of Mormon history. Mormon history is Joseph Smith, and his continued effect on his Saints. In proportion to his importance and his complexity, he remains the least-studied personage, of an undiminished vitality, in our entire national saga.[38]

   . . . The God of Joseph Smith is a daring revival of the God of some of the Kabbalists and Gnostics, prophetic sages who, like Smith himself, asserted that they had returned to the true religion of Yahweh or Jehovah. If Smith was mistaken, then so were they, but I hardly know just what it could mean to say that the Kabbalists or Joseph Smith were mistaken. The God of normative Judaism and of the mainline churches, at this time, is rather more remote from the God of the earliest or Yahwist portions of the Bible than is the initially surprising God of Joseph Smith.[39]

   . . . The nation will not always be only two percent Mormon. The Saints outlive the rest of us, have more children than all but a few American groups, and convert on a grand scale, both here and abroad. I do not know what figures they project for their increase in the next generation, but my own guess is that by the year 2020 (when I will not be here), they could well form at least ten percent of our population, and probably rather more than that. Their future is immense: the Mormon people consistently are the hardest-working, most cohesive bloc in our society; only Asian-Americans rival them in zeal, ambition, and intensity. Salt Lake City may yet become the religious capital of the United States.[40]

7
Mormonism—The Doctrine

What Doctrine?

As with the previous chapter it is beyond the scope of this book to give a complete exposition of Mormon doctrine. For interested readers, that has largely been done in the four volumes of the *Encyclopedia of Mormonism*.[1] It is useful, however, to review selective doctrinal issues which seem pertinent to other material in this book. In particular, questions raised from the study of NDEs often seem to have an effective response from specific points of LDS doctrine.

Material in this chapter, therefore, will follow a format where the NDE issues will be illustrated, followed by the pertinent doctrinal point, or in some instances, the reverse of that order. The reader, thus, should be able to draw his or her own conclusions about the validity of the evidence presented.

Descriptions of the Light

Probably no part of the NDE is so universally described as is "the light."[2] Nearly every person who has undergone an extensive NDE mentions some form of bright light, and most books written about NDEs spend some time discussing it. To most of those going through an NDE the light is not an ordinary light. It has properties which produce ethereal feelings: feelings of peace, joy, and love. It is often associated with some sort of superior being, and in some cases, with a different kind of world.

Derald Evans's Description of the Light

. . . the beautiful bright-white light. It gave me a feeling like . . . almost like soft music, or something that was one-hundred percent pure. It's hard to describe in words. I had never seen nor heard anything like it before. It was not frightening, though. More softening. And it kept coming closer, getting brighter and brighter. . . . I will never forget the feeling I got from the light.

Ann's Description

I noticed a light coming into the room. It was a beautiful golden-white light which seemed to appear in the wall to the left of my bed. . . . It was about three feet up from the floor and mid-length of the bed. . . . As the ball of light grew the pain and feeling of illness suddenly left me. I had no idea what was happening, but I felt at peace.

I sat up and watched the light grow. It grew rapidly in both size and brightness. In fact the light got so bright that it seemed to me that the whole world was lit by it.

Lois Clark's Understanding of the Light

At the time that I was in the place to see the light I thought it was real. The whole thing . . . oh, there was the light, and there seemed to be soft, soft, soft, . . . you couldn't really hear it, you more felt this music. It . . . it was soft, and immaculately beautiful. There was, I guess there's no way to really describe it, there was a feeling of peace, beauty, love, and . . . it just felt like this is what I want. This is the ultimate.

Kathleen Pratt Martinez's View of the Light

The room itself was illuminated with a light that I had never seen before. It was a goldish sort of color. But it was so bright that it was—it was awe inspiring. It was like something from another world. It was soft yet it was so illuminating. I have a hard time describing it because I have never seen anything like it in this world. The closest thing I can come to it is something like a sunset—but that wasn't it either.

None of these people knew each other, nor had they communicated with each other. They were unaware of the similarity of words that they used to describe the bright light. It was fascinating to watch each of them struggle for words as they attempted to portray the light.

Scriptural References to the Light

In view of the sublime feelings associated with the light it might be expected that the scriptures have something to say about it, and they do. The light is associated with God and with Jesus Christ, as expressed in the New Testament, and as discussed in particular detail in the LDS scripture, the Doctrine and Covenants.

The First Epistle of John says of God: "This then is the message which we have heard of him, and declare unto you, that God is light, and in him is no darkness at all."[3] James says that "every good gift and every perfect gift is from above, and cometh down from the Father of lights . . . ."[4]

From John, in the New Testament, the mission of John the Baptist is described as a forerunner of Jesus Christ. In this discussion Christ is referred to as the Light.

> There was a man sent from God, whose name was John. The same came for a witness, to bear witness of the Light, that all men through him might believe. He was not that Light, but was sent to bear witness of that Light. That was the true Light, which lighteth every man that cometh into the world.[5]

Perhaps the best scriptural definition of what the light is can be found in Section 88 of the Doctrine and Covenants:[6]

> He that ascended up on high, as also he descended below all things, in that he comprehended all things, that he might be in all and through all things, the light of truth;
> Which truth shineth. This is the light of Christ. As also he is in the sun, and the light of the sun, and the power thereof by which it was made.
> As also he is in the moon, and is the light of the moon, and the power thereof by which it was made;
> As also the light of the stars, and the power thereof by which they were made;
> And the earth also, and the power thereof, even the earth upon which you stand.
> And the light which shineth, which giveth you light, is through him who enlighteneth your eyes, which is the same light that quickeneth your understandings;
> Which light proceedeth forth from the presence of God to fill the immensity of space—
> The light which is in all things, which giveth life to all things, which is the law by which all things are governed, even the power of God who

sitteth upon his throne, who is in the bosom of eternity, who is in the midst of all things.

Some researchers investigating NDEs try, in vain, to explain the light in terms of some known scientific phenomenon; or worse, as a parapsychological illusion conjured up by the person having the experience. Individuals who experience the light wonder at it and struggle to explain their feelings when exposed to it.

If the light is accepted as a spiritual phenomenon, then the scriptures cited above have special meaning. In that context the light is a characteristic of Deity. It originates with the Father and the Son. It is the power of creation, the power of life, the power of knowledge, the power of governing the earth and the stars, in short, it is the power of God.

It is not surprising that words fail individuals as they attempt to explain the light. It is more, to most of them, than just a visual phenomenon—it is a heavenly experience. It is their contact with the influence and power of God, and it is overwhelming. They never want to leave it.

The Plan of Salvation

Fundamental to The Church of Jesus Christ of Latter-day Saints is the belief that Jesus Christ and his Father developed the Plan of Salvation for all humans. In order to understand the Plan it is important to know that, in LDS doctrine, people have existed since before time was, and they will continue to exist throughout eternity. They started as individual intelligences and at some point were born as spirit children of our Father in Heaven. They continued in that form until they were born into this life, on earth, as mortal beings with both a physical body and a spirit.

Elements of the Plan

The basic elements of the Plan of Salvation, as detailed in LDS scriptures, are as follows:

1. An earth would be created upon which we could have a variety of experiences.[7] This earth would be filled with life, including humans, beginning with Adam and Eve. Adam, after being tempted by Satan, would fall from a sinless, childless, paradisiacal state in order that other humans might be born and die.[8]

2. We would take upon ourselves physical bodies by being born, and we would live a physical life on this earth. These bodies would be after the image of Jesus Christ and our Heavenly Father.[9] We would have children and be responsible for their physical and spiritual welfare.[10]

3. Memory of our previous existence would be removed from us while we were mortal and on this earth. This forgetfulness, or lack of complete knowledge of a previous life, would enhance our ability to make free choices.[11]

4. We would be allowed to choose the kind of life we lived within the constraints of physical mortality.[12] Freedom of choice would be guaranteed by providing for opposition in all things. That opposition would include suffering from illnesses, accidents and other events, some of our making and some not.[13] Our relationship with others, how we reacted to and how we treated our fellow humans would be tested.[14]

5. We would be given information about good and evil, through prophets speaking for Jesus Christ, by both the written word and by oral instruction.[15] Satan would be allowed to tempt us to do evil.[16] We would benefit by gaining knowledge while in this world.[17]

6. A Savior, Jesus Christ, would be provided who would atone for our sins, and who would make it possible for the resurrection of all individuals.[18] All would ultimately live again as resurrected beings, with their body and their spirit reunited—a gift from Jesus Christ.[19]

7. Means would be provided for saving ordinances to be performed on this earth for all persons, living or dead.[20]

8. At the end of mortal life we would die: our spirit and our body would separate, with the spirit continuing to live and the body being temporarily discarded into the tomb. The spirit would pass to another sphere, the spirit world, and would reside there until the time of the resurrection. An initial judgment would be made where spirits from righteous beings would dwell in Paradise and those from unrighteous beings would be consigned to Hell. The majority, who have never had the opportunity to learn of Christ and his atoning sacrifice, would dwell in a spirit-world area apart from both Paradise and Hell. In this separate area, those who had not been taught the gospel of Jesus Christ during earth life would be given the opportunity to hear it.[21]

9. At some future time there would be a general resurrection, and all who had lived on earth would again obtain a body which would never be lost nor destroyed.[22]

10. There would be a final judgment; and, depending upon how we lived and if we repented of our sins, we would live eternally with our Father in Heaven and his son Jesus Christ.[23] In this state we would live with our families and would have immense knowledge. We would, like our Father in Heaven, be involved in the creation of new worlds. We would experience eternal growth and happiness.[24]

11. Even those who do not live a very good life would find the new life rewarding and one which provides for growth. It would be much superior to the previous life on earth.[25]

Some NDE Correlations

In material which follows I will present certain NDEs that show evidence related to one or more of the elements of the Plan of Salvation. Only those portions of the NDE which are pertinent to the elements under discussion will be included.

Accounts of Jayne and Beverly—The Plan

In Chapter Four I noted that Carol Zaleski reported on research that she did on ancient NDEs. Actually, Zaleski, a lecturer on the study of religion at Smith College, also documented numerous NDEs of a more modern origin. One of the NDEs she recorded was from an IANDS conference where Jayne, who had an NDE during childbirth, described the following event:

It was a dynamic light, not like a spotlight. It was an incredible energy—a light you wouldn't believe. I almost floated in it. It was feeding my consciousness feelings of unconditional love, complete safety, and complete, total perfection . . . It just POWED into you. My consciousness was going out getting larger and taking in more; I expanded and more and more came in. It was such rapture, such bliss. And then, and then, a piece of knowledge came in: it was that I was immortal, indestructible. I cannot be hurt, cannot be lost. We don't have anything to worry about. And that the world is perfect; everything that happens is part of a perfect plan. I don't understand this part now, but I still know it's true. . . . Later, when I was saying the Lord's prayer, and I got to the part that says "thine is the kingdom, and the power, and the glory," I thought that nothing could describe this experience any better. It was pure power and glory.[26]

This particular experience also relates to the previous discussion of Light and what it means. More to the point of the Plan of Salvation, though, is that Jayne understood that there was a plan—a perfect plan. This portion of her experience was somewhat similar to that of Stephanie LaRue's (described in Chapter 5) where Stephanie explained her understanding of its being ". . . a totality of everything. . . . I knew that everything had its place, its purpose, and there was a reason for everything. Even poor children that die of cancer at a young age, somebody's life that is taken; everything has a reason."

A similar understanding of the purposes and perfection of a divine plan was obtained by Beverly Brodsky whose complete story is given in Kenneth Ring's book, *Lessons From the Light*. A portion of her experience follows:

I do remember this: There was a reason for *everything* that happened, no matter how awful it appeared in the physical realm. And within myself, as I was given the answer, my own awakening mind now responded in the same manner: "Of course," I would think, "I already know that. How could I ever have forgotten!" Indeed, it appears that all that happens is for a purpose, and that purpose is already known to our eternal self.[27]

Theresa's Experience—Opposition

One of the elements of the Plan was that of *opposition in all things*. Opposition was necessary so that we would truly have freedom of choice. Theresa was a young woman whom Carol and I interviewed in 1994. She was a lovely person, and she spoke in a simple and enthusiastic manner. Her vocabulary was that of a modern woman with limited formal education, and her thoughts were consistent with her background—until she began to expand on some of the things that she learned during her experience.

Theresa told us that she never completed high school, and most of her conversation reflected that kind of education. She did not claim any affiliation with organized religion, but she seemed spiritually affected.

When I asked particular questions about her experience Theresa became a different person. The manner in which she dictated the thoughts which I recorded was simply amazing, and I had to listen to the tape again to assure myself that I had heard it correctly the first time.

This process, in which the person having had an NDE speaks words or thoughts that seem to have been programmed into them I had observed before (as discussed later), but never to the extent that Theresa demonstrated it. When I asked Theresa how she did it she said she didn't know. The thoughts were simply inside her. Another person that this was true of was Dan, whose experience is recorded in Chapter 1. He was interviewed by Carol and I several years after Theresa, and again we observed thoughts emanating from him which were completely unexpected and beyond his educational abilities.

Theresa had an extensive NDE, including a life's review, due to many blood clots forming three weeks after birth of a child and a resultant heart attack. In this part of the chapter I shall only repeat that portion of her experience which relates to the subject at hand. Our interview went as follows:

"Did you see anything during your experience of a negative nature?"

"No, because there is no such thing as negative."

"What do you mean?"

"Negative is a concept that we have developed to describe things that work against our preconceived notions. Everything is both—negative and positive—and they both create energy. It works for you or it doesn't. It works for God or against Him. But they both serve a divine purpose."

"Did you see anything that worked against God."

"Yes. Even that was of a divine nature, though. It enters a person as ego—a driving force of self, to please oneself."

"How did you see that?"

"It came in the form of an angered spirit. I couldn't imagine him being so angry, but he was."

"What was happening to him, and why was he angry?"

"He was isolated within himself. The energy emanated by him created his own world, almost a separate planet. When I saw him I also heard laughter. It was a hideous type of laughter."

"Were there people trying to help him?"

"No. It was as if he had his own world, and it was of his own making."

. . . "Do you have any special messages for anyone who might read your story?"

"Yes. I want to talk a little about fear. Fear is a blessing."

"How so?"

"Fear is the key to unfolding what is within us. If we didn't have fear there would be nothing to propel us into the next adventure or experience. Without fear we would not be alert to the full measure of the experiences we pass through. Those experiences are vital for our growth. Tears and grief are what carve the opening for us to have joy and love. If we didn't have a cavity carved by fear, pain, and grief, we wouldn't be able to fully appreciate the love and joy that are within our reach.

"The key to growth in the future is to love ourselves and to extend that love to others. The interconnectedness of all living beings, and the love we feel for all life, are gifts from God. The Lord made it possible for us to love as we should, but we often deny ourselves that privilege. When we grieve, we should know that we are grieving tears of precious love—a love for the connectedness of all humans."

"What about injury and illness?"

"That's a difficult question, because I don't like suffering. When I was suffering the most, though, I actually grew closer to those I loved than when I was well. Sometimes trauma and illness occur in order to help those who associate with the one having the trauma. We tend to feel that we come here and live our lives for ourselves—we are very selfish. In my life's review I understood that my life was lived, not just for me, but for others that I interacted with. We are all connected in God's plan. We, and every other living thing, affect everything else.

"It is time for people to wake up and appreciate, from the inside, who they are. You don't have to belong to a religion to do that. Religion was created as a tool so that God could help you to know yourself. There is a *you* inside of you, a soul, that is united with God."

"Are there any final thoughts you would like to express?"

"Just know that life is not a series of circumstances; each of us were given the privilege of creating our life. We even create our own troubles, it's really amusing."

"Do you mean create, or do you mean choose?"

"We chose before we came here certain big events. But all the roads in between, we create."

Theresa's experience included knowledge of several elements of the Plan. She, too, understood that there was a Plan. In addition, she dictated to Carol and me one of the more lucid explanations of the reasons for opposition—a primary element in the Plan—that we had heard outside of LDS scriptures. Let us compare just a portion of what she said with a few lines from the Book of Mormon.

From Theresa:

> Those experiences are vital for our growth. Tears and grief are what carve the opening for us to have joy and love. If we didn't have a cavity carved by fear, pain, and grief, we wouldn't be able to fully appreciate the love and joy that are within our reach.

From the Book of Mormon:

> For it must needs be, that there is an opposition in all things. If not so, my first-born in the wilderness, righteousness could not be brought to pass, neither wickedness, neither holiness nor misery, neither good nor bad. Wherefore, all things must needs be a compound in one; wherefore, if it should be one body it must needs remain as dead, having no life neither death, nor corruption nor incorruption, happiness nor misery, neither sense nor insensibility.[28]

DeLynn—Premortal Life and Choice

Key to understanding the Plan of Salvation in LDS doctrine is the knowledge that we lived before as spiritual sons and daughters of God. Our Heavenly parents set the pattern that we would later follow on earth. In premortal life we advanced to a certain point in our progression, and it was necessary as part of the Plan to continue our growth in a physical earthly environment—an environment where we would have agency. Agency to make choices between good and evil.

My first meeting with DeLynn in 1993 was at the University of Utah Medical Center where he had stopped for a check-up of his cystic fibrosis. When I met him he was in his early forties. Most of his life had been spent in one medical crisis or another. Despite these crises DeLynn had completed his schooling, including college; he had served a two year mission for the LDS Church; he had married, and he had children.

DeLynn attributed his ability to survive his many medical emergencies and to lead a relatively normal life—far beyond what most cystic fibrosis patients do—to a blessing given him by his father when he was a child.

DeLynn's NDE was extensive and the entire experience is too long for inclusion in this chapter. Again, I shall include those portions pertinent to the sub-title subject.[29]

> At this point in my experience I became aware of a voice talking to me. My surroundings, and my analysis of them, had so interested me that I had not paid attention to the voice at first. It was a soft, fatherly voice that kept repeating my name. Facing the light, and then turning 90 degrees to my left and looking up at a slight angle, I looked to see where the voice was coming from. There was no one that I could see— but the voice persisted, not in my ears, but in my mind. I finally responded by asking the voice: "What?"
>
> The voice didn't immediately respond. I wondered how I could hear with my mind and not my ears, and I learned that it wasn't necessary for me to understand the process just then. My mind next thought the questions: "Why am I here? Why me? I'm a good guy—why did I die?"
>
> The voice answered: "You are here because you have earned the right to be here based on what you did on earth. The pain you have suffered qualifies you to be here. You have suffered as much pain in 37 years as a normal person might have suffered in 87 years."
>
> I asked: "It's pain that gets me here?" and the answer was yes.
>
> This still puzzled me so I asked: "But why was it necessary for me to suffer so? I was a worthy member of the Church; I kept all the commandments. Why me?"
>
> Then I received a most startling answer. He said to me: "You chose your disease and the amount of pain you would be willing to suffer before this life—when you were in a premortal state. It was your choice."
>
> While I was hearing this voice, I became aware that it was a familiar voice—it was one that I knew. It was a voice that I had not heard during my mortal lifetime. When it was speaking to me, though, there

was no question but that I knew who it was. There was enormous love for me in the voice.

When He told me that it was my choice, in a premortal environment, to suffer when I came to earth, I was both astonished and incredulous. He must have understood my incredulity, because I was immediately transported to my premortal existence. There was a room that I was viewing from above and to the side, but at the same time I was sitting in it. In a sense I was both an observer and a participant. About thirty people were in the room, both men and women, and we were all dressed in the white jump-suit type of garment.

An instructor was in the front of the room, and he was teaching about accountability and responsibility—and about pain. He was instructing us about things we had to know in order to come to earth and get our bodies. Then he said, and I'll never forget this: "You can learn lessons one of two ways. You can move through life slowly, and have certain experiences, or there are ways that you can learn the lessons very quickly through pain and disease." He wrote on the board the words: Cystic Fibrosis, and he turned and asked for volunteers. I was a volunteer; I saw me raise my hand and offer to take the challenge.

The instructor looked at me and agreed to accept me. That was the end of the scene, and it changed forever my perspective of the disease that I previously felt was a plague on my life. No longer did I consider myself a victim. Rather, I was a privileged participant, by choice, in an eternal plan. That plan, if I measured up to the potential of my choice, would allow me to advance in mortal life in the fastest way possible. True, I would not be able to control the inevitable slow deterioration of my mortal body, but I could control how I chose to handle my illness emotionally and psychologically. The specific choice of cystic fibrosis was to help me learn dignity in suffering. My understanding in the eternal sense was complete—I knew that I was a powerful, spiritual being that chose to have a short, but marvelous, mortal existence.

DeLynn passed away in late 1997. Just prior to his death he had his children gather around him and he gave each one a blessing. The chapel at the funeral was filled to overflowing, and the program followed the agenda previously prepared by DeLynn.

DeLynn's experience illustrated several elements of the Plan. As with the preceding examples, DeLynn understood that there was a Plan. More importantly, he relived portions of his premortal existence, and he saw that in that setting he had made choices that affected his mortal journey.

This was the first person I interviewed—others followed—who saw himself so explicitly in a premortal situation. The idea of a premortal existence comes up implicitly in many NDEs where individuals speak of coming home, of being indestructible, and of understanding that they have always lived.

As noted from what DeLynn said, he also had freedom to make important choices that bore directly on what kind of physical life he would lead. Indeed, DeLynn used to jokingly say, "There are no accidents in this life." I would argue with him and point out that, carried to the extreme, that would mean there are no choices in this life. He would reluctantly agree that some accidents may occur. DeLynn never met Theresa, but I am sure that he would have agreed with her statements in this question and answer dialogue which she and I had:

"Are there any final thoughts you would like to express?"

"Just know that life is not a series of circumstances; each of us were given the privilege of creating our life. We even create our own troubles, it's really amusing."

"Do you mean create, or do you mean choose?"

"We chose before we came here certain big events. But all the roads in between, we create."

These two experiences, and others, convinced me that agency to make free choices—as a part of the Plan—is much broader and extends further back in time than I had initially believed.

Families—Theresa's Experience

Another important element in the Plan, and a fundamental part of LDS doctrine, is the maintenance of earthly family ties after this life. It is the primary reason for the dedicated work of thousands of LDS members trying to establish genealogy links as far back as they can.

This is also one of the most common events in near-death experiences. I have literally talked with dozens of experiencers who have related details of the continuation of these ties. Julie, Joy, and Vern Swanson in Chapter 4; and DeAnne Shelley, Bill English, and Susan in Chapter 5, all saw deceased family members. In addition, we apparently keep association with individuals we had spiritual ties with in our premortal life.

To illustrate an extended, but not atypical example, of this type of event let me again quote from Theresa:

> Looking toward the light, I saw my wonderful great-grandmother, the one who had helped raise me, and the one who offered me most of the love that I got as a child. She had died about seven years before that, and she was more beautiful than I remembered her. She was dressed in a soft white-flowing material. There were no shadows in her face, and she appeared to be about thirty years of age. I remembered her as an old woman. My recognition of her was not from her appearance, I just knew it was her—don't ask me how I knew, I just did.
>
> My great-grandmother put her hand out, as if to point in a direction, and when I looked in that direction I saw so many people that . . . as far as I could see there were people. They were all happy to see me, and I knew each of them just as I knew my great-grandmother. I was over-whelmed by the feelings of love that these people shared with me. I couldn't imagine that I could love that many people—and that they could love me.
>
> Moving toward the people, they sort-of stepped back, and as I got closer to many of them the light got very bright. They formed a circle around me. Allen stayed with me the whole time, but he stayed a little off to the side.
>
> One of the people who came to me from the circle was a little . . . Theresa paused to shed some tears, and then continued, it was a little child. I knew that the child was the little baby girl that I had who died in childbirth. She told me, "I'm here for you. I will never leave you."

Knowledge—DeLynn, Rivers and Sylvia

From the Plan we know that we lived as premortal spirits with our Heavenly Parents and our elder brother, Jesus Christ. We also know that we agreed, as part of the Plan, to come to the earth with a loss of the memory and much of the knowledge that we had before this life—in order to enhance our agency during earthly existence. When we return to our previous home, depending upon our choices here, we shall ben-efit by what we learned in this life—and regain the knowledge we had in our previous existence. From the Doctrine and Covenants we read: "And if a person gains more knowledge and intelligence in this life through his diligence and obedience than another, he will have so much the advantage in the world to come."[30]

Common in the NDE research community are recorded stories of those who had a restoration of prior knowledge of why the world is as it is. I interviewed many such individuals. Stephanie LaRue in Chapter 5 regained such an understanding. Another who exhibited it in a remarkable way was DeLynn:

> At this point I realized that I had come home. Everything was familiar—especially God's love. His voice was a familiar voice of unlimited and unconditional love.
>
> The knowledge I was obtaining, too, was knowledge that I had held before. The events in my experience merely reawakened in me a dormant part of my memory, and it was wonderful. I no longer felt picked on because of my pain and illness. I understood the choices I had made and the reasons for them. And I understood the tremendous love that God had for me to allow me to make those choices—and to suffer pain. . . .
>
> It was astonishing, the speed with which I was learning. Knowledge that had somehow slumbered deep in my soul was released, and I was extremely exhilarated by this reawakened knowledge. Light and knowledge were flowing into me from every direction. I could feel it. Every part of my body was reverberating with the light gushing in. Even my fingertips were receptors of light and knowledge. It was as if I were drinking from a fully engaged fire hydrant. I was excited with the thought of going further into this wonderful world of knowledge and love.[31]

And from the extensive NDE of Virginia Rivers reported by Kenneth Ring:

> . . . My mind felt like a sponge, growing and expanding in size with each addition. The knowledge came in single words and in whole idea blocks. I just seemed to understand everything as it was being soaked up or absorbed. I could feel my mind expanding and absorbing and each new piece of information somehow seemed to belong. It was as if I had known already but forgotten or mislaid it, as if it were waiting here for me to pick up on my way by.[32]

Of particular interest was Sylvia's experience (*Chapter 1*) where she explained: "I came back feeling that I had to learn, that I had to absorb like a sponge as much as I could. It was as though I was charged with a duty to learn." Her statement may be compared with the well-known LDS scripture from the Doctrine and Covenants repeated in the first paragraph of this section.

Karen—A Suicide Attempt

In order to maximize our agency to choose, the Plan provided that Satan and his followers would have limited ability to influence us. In the extreme, we could completely reject God and all that he stands for and become a disciple of Satan. Most of us, fortunately, make choices that fall somewhere between perfection and complete evil. Under these circumstances the Plan accords us a means of recovery through repentance and the atonement of Jesus Christ.

A number of those that Carol and I interviewed had NDEs which had unpleasant or frightening events in them. A portion of Dee's horrifying experience is given in Chapter 5. The literature is replete with frightening NDEs.

Karen, a shy, blond lady with a graceful, feminine manner visited with us in 1993. She described how, in 1976, because of a divorce and other traumatic events she was contemplating suicide. Her account follows:

> One night as I was lying in bed, asleep, I was awakened by a male voice saying: "I'm going to get you. Sooner or later, I'm going to get you." The event frightened me and I sat up, wide awake. I told my roommate, and she said it was just a dream, and not to worry about it.
>
> About a week later, everything seemed so hopeless that I took the bottle of tranquilizers. My full intention was to kill me. It seemed the best way to handle my problems, just go to sleep.
>
> It didn't work out the way I wanted, though, because I fell out of bed and woke my roommate. She called the ambulance at about one o'clock in the morning. At the hospital, I found out later, they pumped my stomach and put charcoal in it. They didn't think I was going to make it. My heart had stopped, and they used defibrillator paddles to restart it.
>
> During this period I became aware that I was conscious, but I was enveloped in total darkness. It was pitch-black all around, yet there was a feeling of movement. My conscious self assured me that I was in the form of a spiritual body.

A male voice spoke to me, a different voice than the one I heard a week before. This voice said: "You have a choice. You can stay here, or you can go back. If you stay here, your punishment will be just as it is, right now. You will not have a body, you will not be able to see, touch, or have other sensations. You will only have this darkness and your thoughts, for eternity."

Terrified because of the experience, and because of what I had heard, I understood that this would be my private hell. There would be no contact with other life or with the sensations of life, for eternity. Yet I would remain conscious with my thoughts in total blackness.

Frantically scared, I knew immediately that I had made a terrible mistake. Telling the voice that I had made a mistake, I asked to go back, to return to life. The voice said, "All right, you may return."

Suddenly I felt myself being pulled back. It's hard to explain. There was total darkness, yet I had the feeling of movement as I was pulled back.

Next, I found myself in the hospital room, in an elevated position, looking down. I could see the doctor, I could see my roommate, I could see my body in the bed. My roommate was crying, and the doctor was explaining something to her. It was clear that they thought I was gone.

While I was watching this scene, I felt myself slowly descending. Then, suddenly, I was sucked into my body. It was fast.

My next conscious act was to open my eyes and see my doctor looking down on me. Surprise and a relieved smile showed on his face. He asked me if I could squeeze his hand. With great effort I was able to do a feeble squeeze, and I knew that I was back by the grace of God.[33]

Karen's story illustrates both the freedom to choose, and the consequences associated with those choices—and it shows the existence of evil beings. There is one aspect of Karen's experience which needs explanation. Karen's understanding that she would be trapped in Hell for eternity was not quite correct according to LDS doctrine. She would be left in that state for a long time, but at the resurrection she would be freed from that Spirit Prison. Joseph Smith put it this way:

> Let your hearts rejoice, and be exceedingly glad. Let the earth break forth into singing. Let the dead speak forth anthems of eternal praise to the King Immanuel, who hath ordained, before the world was, that

which would enable us to redeem them out of their prison; for the prisoners shall go free.[34]

The Life Review

More on John Stirling

In Chapter 3 John Stirling's NDE and his life review were described. In a follow-up interview with John I asked him some further questions about his life review. He said:

"The life's review came as a shock. When I heard the voice say: 'Well, let's see your life,' I didn't know how it would happen. It was totally unexpected, and it was right there in my view. It was as if both the voice and I were viewing it—and both of us could feel it as well as visually see it."

"Was there judgment in the voice?"

"Not at all. It was the same feeling you would get in a heart-to-heart conversation with a loving father about anything that concerned you. Not that judgment would be involved, but that you would both view the circumstances, see the way things were, and go on from there."

"So it was a teaching experience more than a judgmental experience?"

"It wasn't judgmental. I didn't know that I was coming back so I didn't realize, at the time, that it was a teaching experience."

"You mentioned that when you saw different events from your life you could also feel the emotions associated with those events. Did you understand that the voice also felt those emotions?"

"I felt, inside, that we both felt the emotions. As I recall, the life review started when I was two or three years old. The review, starting from that time, showed all the daily events, all the people involved, as I lived through the events. There were the funny times, the sad times, and my concerns at the time—for my age."

Theresa

I previously mentioned Theresa's extensive NDE. She also had a life's review and that portion of our interview follows:

"Drawing me close to Him, everything got very quiet, and He asked me to look at my life. In an instant, everyone, all the people in that room—no, it wasn't a room—everyone in that space saw and felt and truly experienced my whole life. Just like I did.

"It all happened so quick, and they saw and felt everything from the moment I was born. They saw and felt the agony of my pre-birth when there was an unsuccessful attempt to abort me. From my early birth, it was such a struggle to live, but I knew that I was supposed to live.

"I felt and relived the pain as they separated me from my birth-mother in the hospital. I so much wanted her to hold me. My despair—as an infant—was felt again as I cried from behind the screen where they put me, away from the other babies.

"In my growing years, I saw that I was a trusting little child. I also saw that I desperately wanted love, but I didn't know how to get it. Other children were often cruel because of my dark complexion, and because I was adopted.

"Every moment of my life was displayed before me, and I felt the emotions again—and everyone else in that large group also saw and felt what I did. It was so difficult for me."

"Why was it difficult?" I asked.

"Because I knew that these people were also experiencing what I was. Their emotions were my emotions, and I didn't want them to have to relive the misery or agony that I felt as a child, and later. But they saw my good and my bad and my everything else—and they loved me."

"As the last scene of my life that I saw, I witnessed myself leaving my body in the hospital. My spirit lifted up from the neck portion as I left. That was the last event of my life that I witnessed. Then Jesus looked at me and said something to the effect: 'How would you surmise your life? What was your experience of life?' Those weren't the exact words, but that was the sense of it."

An LDS Perspective on the Life's Review

From the Plan of Salvation we learn that at death our body and spirit separates and the spirit passes to another sphere until the resurrection. From the Book of Mormon we read:

> Now, concerning the state of the soul between death and the resurrection—Behold, it has been made known unto me by an angel, that the spirits of all men, as soon as they are departed from this mortal body, yea, the spirits of all men, whether they be good or evil, are taken home

to that God who gave them life. And then shall it come to pass, that the spirits of those who are righteous are received into a state of happiness, which is called paradise, a state of rest, a state of peace, where they shall rest from all their troubles and from all care, and sorrow.

And then shall it come to pass, that the spirits of the wicked, yea, who are evil—for behold, they have no part nor portion of the Spirit of the Lord; for behold, they chose evil works rather than good; therefore the spirit of the devil did enter into them, and take possession of their house—and these shall be cast out into outer darkness; there shall be weeping, and wailing, and gnashing of teeth, and this because of their own iniquity, being led captive by the will of the devil.[35]

From this scripture it is apparent that at death the spirits of all individuals, good or bad, return to that God who gave them life. There is, at that time, an initial judgment—which lasts until the resurrection—to select the domain where the spirit being will dwell. For the righteous spirits it is a domain of love and peace, Paradise; for the unrighteous it is a domain of pain and despair, Hell. For those who have never heard the glad tiding of the gospel of Jesus Christ, a separate spirit area exists, much like earth-life, where they are taught and given opportunity to accept Christ and receive his forgiveness and saving grace.

The question is, Who makes the selection and how is it made? From the Plan of Salvation it is apparent that the one who earned the right to make judgments on all humans is that being who sacrificed Himself and suffered at Gethsemane to atone for the sins of each of us. The question remains, How does He make such judgments? Again, the Book of Mormon gives us a clue concerning how the judgment is made.

... Then will ye longer deny the Christ, or can ye behold the Lamb of God? Do ye suppose that ye shall dwell with him under a consciousness of your guilt? Do ye suppose that ye could be happy to dwell with that holy Being, when your souls are racked with a consciousness of guilt that ye have ever abused his laws?

Behold, I say unto you that ye would be more miserable to dwell with a holy and just God, under a consciousness of your filthiness before him, than ye would to dwell with the damned souls in hell. For behold, when ye shall be brought to see your nakedness before God, and also the glory of God, and the holiness of Jesus Christ, it will kindle a flame of unquenchable fire upon you.[36]

From this scripture it seems clear that individuals who have lived unrighteously could not stand to be in the presence of God and Jesus Christ after they die. Given the choice, therefore, they would undoubtedly prefer to reside with like beings. Joseph Smith in explaining the judgment of unrighteous spirits put it this way: "The great misery of departed spirits in the world of spirits, where they go after death, is to know that they come short of the glory that others enjoy and that they might have enjoyed themselves, and they are their own accusers."[37]

These scriptures and teachings agree remarkably with the understanding of those who have life reviews. Kenneth Ring in his book *Lessons from the Light* had this to say about it:

> But, again, we must remind ourselves there is a balance here: There may be no blame, but there is certainly self-examination in the life review. The being of Light holds you, as it were, in arms of unconditional love in order to allow you to see yourself truly—without guilt, and objectively—so that you can become a *clear-eyed judge of yourself.* For make no mistake about it, you still have to face yourself and learn from your actions. The life review does not let you off the hook, but merely suspends you from it so that you can see and understand your life as a totality.
>
> And NDErs, of course, understand this—and are plain to say that while the being of Light never judges, *they themselves do.*[38]

Referring back to the Plan of Salvation, it is clear that the judgment made immediately at death is not the judgment which occurs at the Resurrection. It is only then that a final judgment and determination will be made—based upon an equal opportunity for *all* who have lived to achieve full growth—as to where the resurrected souls of individuals will dwell. It is beyond the scope of this book to expand into this area, but based upon the Plan, except for a very few called the *Sons of Perdition,* all will reside in a realm of glory suitable to their life and choices. Even the least of the glories will be beyond anything now seen on this earth.

Some Interesting Patterns[39]

As Carol and I watched those we were interviewing, in addition to the emotional involvement they had as they relived their stories, it became obvious that certain patterns of word usage were developing.

The patterns in some instances were astonishing. And they came from individuals with different educational, cultural, and religious backgrounds.

Most often they were not aware that they were exposing a pattern of thought or behavior that someone else had also exposed. As these repeated patterns of thought or words became evident, it was almost as if some other power were directing their words, thoughts, and actions.

One word showed up so often that it almost seemed that the people were under compulsion to use it. That word was: *peace* and its synonyms.

Karl Muecke said: "It was all around me, the most peaceful, the most beautiful feeling . . . ." Ann said: "Suddenly I felt this tremendously powerful . . . it's beyond words of powerful, it's . . . I was suddenly enveloped in this deep, deep peace." Jennete described it this way: "The serenity . . . there are no words that can explain . . . the peace, the calm." Pauline recalled: "And then, the peace, the unbelievable peace," while she was drowning.

By the time we interviewed fifteen-year-old Tracie who left her body during a diabetic coma, I was prepared. Therefore, when she said: "It was very peaceful and I felt safe," I asked her why she used the word peaceful. Her reply was, "I don't know, it just seems like the right word."

Jesus, when he was nearing the end of his ministry and was trying to prepare his disciples for that event, told them that they would receive the Holy Ghost. And then he said:

> Peace I leave with you, my peace I give unto you: Not as the world giveth, give I unto you. Let not your heart be troubled, neither let it be afraid.[40]

And from Phillipians 4:7:

> And the peace of God, which passeth all understanding . . .

This was the sense of the word being used by the many experiencers that we interviewed. Another word that had repeated usage was *Love,* and it, too, appeared to be used in a scriptural sense. Other words which seemed to emerge more often than one would normally expect, and which had a more ethereal meaning were: *soft, warm, joy, color, energy, brightness* and *music.* People using the word warm and its derivatives, when asked if they meant that things were hot would stumble as they tried to tell Carol and me what they intended. Usually they would mumble something like, "It was more inside of me, a warm, peaceful feeling. It wasn't hot or unpleasant at all."

The Church of Jesus Christ of Latter-day Saints

Which Church to Join?

One of the questions frequently asked me, especially by Latter-day Saints, is: "When people have these experiences why doesn't the Lord tell them to join the Church of Jesus Christ of Latter-day Saints—after all, it is His Church isn't it?"

My response to that question is, yes it is His Church, but if he told people to join it, then he would be abrogating their freedom of choice. The follow-on question to that answer is: "But that's what the Lord did when Joseph Smith asked the question. Why shouldn't he do as he did with the Prophet?"

And that's just the point. Joseph *was* the Prophet, and his mission was to restore the pristine church. Those who have NDEs are participants of a singular experience for their benefit. If everyone who lived were told by God what church they should join then there would be no freedom of choice. God inspires, entreats and occasionally grants a marvelous vision or experience to fortunate individuals, but He never forces His will on anyone.

Another perspective is also worthy of consideration. There are six billion people living on this planet. The Latter-day Saints, at 10 million, constitute less than 0.2 percent of all the sons and daughters of God living today. Surely many of those other 99.8 percent will also find their way home to God. Indeed, that is one of the main purposes of LDS Temples.

Howard Storm was an atheistic professor of Art on a trip to Europe with some of his students when he developed a bleeding ulcer. Due to improper care in a French hospital he had an extensive NDE. During that NDE, after an unpleasant encounter with evil spirits, he was rescued by a radiant being in the Light. After his rescue other brilliantly illuminated beings appeared and he had a life's review in their presence. He called these beings his "friends." Upon completion of the review

Howard was permitted to ask many questions, which were instantly answered. One of the questions had to do with what church to join.

> My friends answered lots of questions in funny ways. They really knew the whole tone of what I asked them, even before I got the questions out. When I thought of questions in my head, they really understood them. I asked them, for example, which was the best religion. I was looking for an answer which was like: "Presbyterians." I figured these guys were all Christians. The answer I got was: "The best religion is the religion that brings you closest to God." [41]

That answer seems to me to be most appropriate. Howard, today, is the pastor of a congregation of the United Church of Christ, and he is doing a marvelous job of spreading the Word and doing the work of the Lord.

Gary Gillum—A Conversion Experience

In 1962 Gary was attending St. John's College in Winfield, Kansas. St John's was a Lutheran institution and Gary was studying to be a Lutheran minister. He was studying hard to accomplish his goal, but he was troubled by some points of Lutheran doctrine. He couldn't believe, for example, that there was only heaven and hell, and if you weren't baptized you were consigned to hell. So he made it a matter of personal prayer and asked Heavenly Father to give him an experience that would head him in a direction so that he could find the truth.

Shortly after this prayer he went home to California for Christmas vacation. After the holidays, on the return trip in a friend's automobile, they had a head-on collision with another car. Both Gary and his friend were severely injured. Later, in the hospital he had an NDE.

In his NDE Gary saw the Light, and his deceased paternal grandfather.

> Basically, I was given a choice to stay or to return to this life. Having prayed for some kind of experience, I sort of felt the question and the answer. It was: "If I don't go back to earth and to my body, what am I going to miss out on?" And the answer was: "If you go back, some day you will find the truth. Also, you have a lot of experiences still to have on the earth. If you stay here, you will have at least what you now see and feel, but if you go back to your body and come here later, and if you are faithful, then you will have much more than this."

While I was in this state, I learned—I probably learned much more than this—but I learned that the important things in life are service, love, and knowledge. I also had an inkling, because I now had an absolute knowledge that there was a life after death, that life would be more difficult for me than it otherwise would have been.[42]

Following this basic experience Gary was still in terrible shape physically and he kept going in and out of his body. He said this about the next episode:

It was even more strange than the first experience. I saw a building with tall spires, and I saw people in a room dressed in white clothing. The people were involved in a strange ceremony. I didn't understand any of it. It was totally foreign to my experience, and I didn't know what it symbolized, if anything.[43]

When Gary recovered sufficiently from his injuries he resumed his studies at the Lutheran college. He was still puzzled about finding the truth, but he diligently working to achieve his goal. Then, in 1969, six years after the accident, Gary began dating a girl who was LDS. She asked him if he would be interested in having missionaries meet with him to teach him about the Mormon Church. Gary thought that was a great idea since it would make him a better Lutheran minister. Gary told me what happened next as follows:

As the missionaries taught me, there was no contest when it came to reviewing the scriptures from the Bible. I could read them in the original Greek and Hebrew. But I was impressed by the individual testimonies of the missionaries. I had no similar experience from my Lutheran background. Lutherans are outwardly very unemotional about their religion. They would find it objectionable to view an emotional testimony meeting.

The missionaries also told me about the promise in the Book of Mormon given by Moroni to know if the book was true—that I could know the truth by the power of the Holy Ghost. I took that promise seriously. I prayed about what I was reading in the Book of Mormon. As I did, I again experienced the light which I had previously seen during my accident. I didn't see any personage, but everything brightened up in the room. It was a personal testimony given to me to help me recognize the truth.[44]

Gary joined the Church and married Lyn. Then, a couple of years later as they traveled to Manti to be sealed in the temple, Gary had a startling experience.

> That morning, when we were 17 miles from Manti, I recognized the spires of the temple which I had seen, years earlier, in my experience after the accident. I looked at Lyn, and I said: "I've seen those spires before." (I had never been to Manti in my life.) And when I got inside and saw the people dressed in white—bingo! I recognized the whole scene from my previous experience. In fact, after going through the temple I later wrote a short story, never published, entitled: "With Him We Walk in White."[45]

This story of Gary's conversion to the LDS Church is similar to several people that Carol and I interviewed. In no case were these individuals *told* which church to join. They found their own way to the truth—often helped by what they had experienced in their NDE—but always as a result of further effort on their part.

Final Thoughts on this Chapter

These case studies have been presented to allow the reader to draw their own conclusions about the evidence presented. Admittedly, the evidence is incomplete, but it should provide a picture where similarities and parallels between LDS doctrine and NDE events can be considered.

8

The Evidence

What Evidence?

God! His fingerprints are everywhere we look. Yet many of us stumble through life blindly groping for some meaning in what we see. And when the evidence displays itself and cries for our recognition the scales on our eyes further blind us to the truth. We ask again, Pilate's question of Christ, "What is Truth?" And since our anchors for truth have long since been discarded in the name of "Science," we drift aimlessly through a morass of ever changing relativism.

In our frantic attempts to explain what we see—yet deny the truth that underlies the Godly exhibit—we invent new theories and speculations about how it might have happened. To make the proposed ideas and guesses more acceptable we dress them up with fancy names such as "a new scientific paradigm." Then we speculate that: given enough time, or, with an infinity of tries, or possibly by some law not yet fully understood we could, for example, have an anthropic universe.

When we have arrived at enough postulates of the type: *it could have,* . . . *it might have,* . . . *it probably was,* and cloaked them in the respectability of science, then we congratulate ourselves for our wisdom. What folly! Our educated arrogance stands in the way of our education. It is no wonder that the scriptures tell us that we and our wisdom shall perish. Isaiah in the Old Testament, and again in the Book of Mormon, warns us of this hazard. From 2 Nephi 9:28 we read:

> O that cunning plan of the evil one! O the vainness, and the frailties, and the foolishness of men! When they are learned they think they are wise, and they hearken not unto the counsel of God, for they set it aside,

supposing they know of themselves, wherefore, their wisdom is foolishness and it profiteth them not. And they shall perish.

The Fingerprints of God

NDEs—A Clear Fingerprint

I mentioned the fingerprints of God. Where might we find such fingerprints? Let us start with near-death experiences. In my opinion they represent one of the clearest fingerprints of God. Alternative attempts at explaining how NDEs happen are nearing exhaustion. Corroborative NDEs, where the individual left his or her body and saw things—later verified by other witnesses—which could not have been seen by the disabled person are becoming more numerous in the literature. Kenneth Ring's work with blind people who have had NDEs is a striking example of current research where alternative explanations to a spiritual or other-worldly explanation become difficult.

Perhaps another example of a corroborative type NDE would be helpful. Elane Durham had an extensive NDE in 1976 as the result of a brain tumor which precipitated a stroke. Although unconscious, she watched herself being transferred by ambulance to Mercy Hospital in Chicago. After arrival at the hospital Elane was wheeled into the emergency room where she left her body for a meadow in a more beautiful world. She was torn from that world by defibrillator paddles slamming her painfully back into her body. Then, for a time, she was aware of mass confusion by medical personnel as they struggled to save her. She became aware of a nurse in the room praying for her. Then her condition deteriorated until she heard the doctor say: "It doesn't matter about her. She's flat. Get her out of the way."

Before the doctor gave up, he had ordered that a Catholic priest be summoned for the last rites. The priest arrived just after someone gave orders to have Elane's body prepared for the morgue.

The priest began to give her a blessing, which she could hear. As he was praying Elane said that she felt, "an incredible rush of energy, a strong spiritual power that went from my head to my toes in warm, surging waves." Immediately thereafter she left her body again and saw the priest as she rose upward.[1]

In 1998, Elane's book, *I Stand All Amazed,* described her NDEs in detail and included a written statement from the priest who had administered last rites to her twenty-two years earlier; he confirmed what she said had happened to her. When he arrived he was told she had been dead for fifteen to twenty minutes. Upon reaching her body he found no signs of life so he administered the ordinance and left.

He returned to the hospital a week or two later, and when he looked in one of the beds and saw, to his complete amazement, Elane, he said: "Elane Durham, What happened to you? You were dead!"

Elane then assured him that she wasn't dead, and he responded that she was. He was shocked to find her still alive.[2]

Although Elane's experience is dramatic and worth studying, the corroborative portion is particularly interesting, for she included the testimonies of witnesses who wrote their recollections of what happened from their perspectives. I have seen the scars on Elane's head where the operation for removal of the tumor occurred.

Researchers continue to discover more of these corroborative types of NDEs. Other researchers frantically attempt to explain how the events might have happened without relying on other-worldly or Godly explanations. To me, their attempts have long since proved futile, including such comments as the late Carl Sagan's explanation that the NDE is merely the result of the individual, under stress, reliving the birth experience.[3] No doubt Carl now has a different explanation for the NDE.

The Anthropic Universe

The Anthropic Universe is another example of the fingerprints of God. From previous chapters it is apparent that there are an inordinately large number of natural constants and physical laws which seem precisely tuned so that life can exist.

Examples of a finely tuned universe—and earth—could be expanded almost indefinitely. If the earth were a little closer to the sun it would scorch all life, if it were a little farther away it would freeze all life. The earth's orbit around the sun is nearly circular, unlike that of Mars which is elliptical. The annual variation of the earth's distance from the sun is only three percent of the total distance—hence stability of temperature. The resulting modest temperature variation, further moderated by the

23 degree tilt of the earth in its rotation, is just right to keep water liquid under most conditions required for life. Much of our earth's iron core is molten due to pressure and radioactivity. This molten iron core produces our magnetic field which deflects otherwise harmful radiation from the sun. The internal heat is also just right for periodic volcanoes which were essential for the release of trapped subterranean water. Gravity is properly tuned so that atmospheric oxygen and nitrogen do not escape into space. If the ratio of nitrogen to oxygen in our atmosphere were significantly less, then most lightning strikes would result in essentially unstoppable conflagrations. If the ratio were significantly greater, then life as we know it would not be possible. If the density of ice were greater than water—as happens with most other materials when they change from liquid to solid—then it would sink in water and the oceans would become largely ice. If heavy elements such as carbon, oxygen, iron, and uranium had not been properly distributed by star dust, then . . . If photosynthesis did not work, then . . . If the ratio of water to land were different on our planet, then . . . If the earth were greater or lesser in diameter . . . If the heat of vaporization of water were different . . . If . . .

It is true, as shown in Appendix D and as John Leslie argues, that one can make a case for an infinite variety of universes based on a probabilistic creation phenomenon. The question is, when all of the other fingerprints of God are examined, what is the most likely answer to the reasons for an anthropic universe?

Spontaneous Creation of Life

This is one of the clearest of God's fingerprints. When considering how such life might have developed by *chance* one has no choice but to use the tools of probabilistic mathematics. And when these tools are applied according to the rules of science, the chances of spontaneous creation are outrageously small—much smaller than what mathematicians would call impossible. Similarly, the time available for any chance combination of chemicals in a prebiotic soup for even the simplest of life forms exceeds even the life of the universe, never mind the much smaller life of the earth.

This situation creates an especially difficult dilemma for those who do not recognize God's fingerprints. Either the tools of science work or they do not. One cannot argue that they may be applied in one situation but not another. When Morowitz calculated the probability of broken chemical bonds in a single celled bacterium reassembling under ideal chemical conditions, he said this about his calculated enormously small odds:

> . . . no amount of ordinary manipulation or arguing about the age of the universe or the size of the system can suffice to make it plausible that such a fluctuation would have occurred in an equilibrium system. It is always possible to argue that any unique event would have occurred. This is outside the range of probabilistic considerations, and really, outside of science. We may sum up by stating that on energy considerations alone, the possibility of a living cell occurring in an equilibrium ensemble is vanishingly small.[4]

Origin of the Big Bang

This is an interesting fingerprint which is seldom discussed. The issue is, what or who initiated the big bang? Before the big bang commenced the situation is described by physicists as a singularity—where the laws of physics do not apply. In other words, they haven't the foggiest idea as to what is going on.

Stephen Hawking recognized the God dilemma posed by a big bang model with an implied beginning. In the singularity time has no meaning, and one cannot logically speak of the singularity being a beginning. All one can say is that suddenly, at Planck time, the big bang was happening and the laws of physics applied. Time then had meaning. But if it wasn't God who initiated the event, what was it?

To avoid ascribing the initial cause or beginning of the big bang to God, Hawking postulated a space-time universe with no boundary. In this postulation he used the mathematics of imaginary numbers (such as the square root of negative numbers) to suggest that time could move either forward or backward. Such a universe might have an expansionary mode where life could exist—such as we are now in—followed by a contracting mode where life could not exist. In a non-boundary universe there would be no singularity.[5]

The implication of Hawking's postulate of a non-boundary universe is that by repeated expansion and contraction cycles the universe could exist in this mode for an infinity of time. There would be no beginning or end, and therefore no need for an initial cause—or God.

Hawking never proposed this idea as a theory. Merely as an idea that other physicists might think about and work on. Since Hawking is such a bright fellow, other physicists did think about it. Dean Overman summarized some of the arguments against Hawking's idea.[6]

There is not room in this chapter to discuss all of the arguments pro and con for a non-boundary universe. The principal problem with the postulate derives from the second law of thermodynamics—the heat death law. That law states that entropy must always increase in any actual thermodynamic process. Mathematically it is given as: $S = \int dQ/T$, where S is Entropy, $\int dQ$ is the integrated change in heat during the process, and T is the temperature. For any non-reversible thermodynamic process, which includes all real processes, dQ/T must always be positive.

In simpler terms the second law means that anything that happens in the universe must proceed from a state of order to a state of increased disorder. Thus, for example, when you blow up a balloon by expending energy through the huff and puff of your lungs, and your four-year-old pops it, no amount of crying on his part will restore the escaped gas from the balloon. The energy is lost forever in a state of greater entropy and greater disorder. Even if you have another empty balloon, you must expend more energy by again huffing and puffing to satisfy your crying youngster.

For Hawking's non-boundary universe this means that whether the universe is expanding or contracting, in any real (not imaginary) system, things are progressing from an organized state to a more disorganized state. We cannot proceed indefinitely in an alternately expanding and contracting universe since ultimately things will reach a state of infinite disorder (the heat death of the universe). At this point the universe would have reached an end. To say that it reached an end implies that it had a beginning. Increasing entropy in any thermodynamic process inevitably implies a beginning where entropy was lower.

So, we are brought back to the initial fingerprint. There obviously was a beginning. And in the beginning, who or what wound up the universe (created the state of high order or low entropy), and who or what caused the big bang to be initiated? Could it have been God?

Matter and Antimatter, Gravity and Light

In Chapter 3 under the subtitle "Serendipity" I observed that current theory holds that early in the big bang matter and antimatter existed in about equal quantities, and when they interacted with each other they destroyed themselves. Why matter survived and antimatter did not—indeed, why our universe in this early period did not destroy itself is a quandary. Numerous theories have been advanced in an attempt to explain the surplus of matter over antimatter, but there is no definitive answer. Gerald Schroeder wrote, in his book *The Science of God:*

> For an exotic, still uncertain reason, infinitesimally more matter than antimatter was produced. We and all the material universe are testimony to that primordial inequality. The difference in paring was small, one part in ten billion. That is, for each 10,000,000,000 antiparticles, 10,000,000,001 particles were formed. As the particles and antiparticles annihilated, that one extra particle in ten billion remained. From those rare "extras," every galaxy, star, and human is composed.[7]

Consider gravity for a moment. Scientists can describe in detail, with great mathematical precision, gravity's effect. It is clear that objects are attracted to each other in proportion to their mass. Individuals weigh less on the moon than on earth, for example. But why is this so; what is the cause of this attraction? Ask a scientist to explain what gravity is and he will quickly describe its effect, but he will also admit to not knowing why it works as it does. He may even mumble something about space, time and gravity all being interrelated, but he will not give you a definitive answer concerning its nature or cause.

A similar situation exists for light. Scientists will describe light as a form of electromagnetic radiation, but from that point their explanation gets fuzzy. They will be able to show you—again with mathematical precision—how under certain conditions light behaves as a particle, and under other conditions it behaves as a wave. But ask them to explain why this different behavior, or what exactly is light, and they will again confess ignorance.

These are a few more examples of how nature works extremely well for the benefit of all life. Although these fingerprints are not clearly identifiable with God, they surely seem to point to him. Other explanations stretch or exceed the limits of known science.

Spacetime and Speed of Travel—An Interesting Fingerprint

In the Appendix I discuss some of the strange happenings to space, time and space travelers when relativity and quantum effects are considered. Even though those effects may seem strange to those of us living in a world where we can normally only travel slightly faster than the speed of sound, still, they obey laws which are predictable. And scientists are able to verify that time does indeed stretch or shrink—depending upon the state of the observer—when we begin to approach the speed of light.

The troubling aspect occurs when we get evidence from a relatively recent and different type of scientific finding that there might exist a different dimension in which time, space and speed of travel are different than in our four dimensional universe. Those who have NDEs frequently speak of time having no meaning where they were, and of traveling between the stars at immense speeds—seemingly faster than the speed of light. A few examples may be useful. First, I shall include some comments from NDEs concerning time:

> I don't know. I didn't really have a sense of time.[8]
>
> You could say it [NDE] lasted one second or that it lasted ten thousand years and it wouldn't make any difference how you put it.[9]
>
> It was a different sphere . . . one in which the concept of time is meaningless.[10]
>
> For what seemed to be endless time, . . .[11]
>
> I found myself in a space, in a period of time, I would say, where all space and time was negated.[12]

Next, are illustrations of some of those who said they traveled great distance at enormous speeds:

> We left the hospital room by rising straight up through the roof and then we headed over the surface of the Earth at a very rapid speed.[13]
>
> My speed was tremendous—indescribable. Nothing on earth has ever gone that fast, nothing could.[14]
>
> I felt as if I was being propelled forward at the speed of light or faster.[15]
>
> We started off on our journey through space, seemingly with the rapidity of lightning (for I can make no other comparison).[16]

Gradually, you realize . . . you're going [at] at least the speed of light. It might possibly be the speed of light or possibly even faster than the speed of light. You realize that you're going just so fast and you're covering vast, vast distances in just hundredths of a second. . . .[17]

In these instances the fingerprint of God is blurred. The NDEs do show evidence of individuals existing in some other dimension, or in some other form (or both), where time does not work the same as here and where enormous speeds are possible. Assuming that NDEs represent reality (discussed below), this may be evidence that such things are possible, and that God is the enabler, but at least at this point the case is not compelling. The fingerprint is blurred.

But what if we compare these NDE events with some LDS teachings and scriptures? First, considering time, from the Doctrine and Covenants we read:

And so on, until the seventh angel shall sound his trump; and he shall stand forth upon the land and upon the sea, and swear in the name of him who sitteth upon the throne, *that there shall be time no longer;* and Satan shall be bound, that old serpent, who is called the devil, and shall not be loosed for the space of a thousand years.[18] (Italics, mine.)

And from a recent writing of Elder Neal A. Maxwell of the Quorum of Twelve Apostles in The Church of Jesus Christ of Latter-day Saints:

Eventually, the veil that now encloses us will be no more. Neither will time (D&C 84:100). Time is clearly not our natural dimension. Thus it is that we are never really at home in time. Alternately, we find ourselves wishing to hasten the passage of time or to hold back the dawn. We can do neither, of course, but whereas the fish is at home in water, we are clearly not at home in time—because we belong to eternity. Time, as much as any one thing, whispers to us that we are strangers here.[19]

Now, as to the speed with which spiritual beings may travel, Brigham Young said:

As quickly as the spirit is unlocked from this house of clay, it is free to travel with lightning speed to any planet, or fixed star, or to the uttermost part of the earth, or to the depths of the sea, according to the will of Him who dictates.[20]

When the NDE descriptions of time and speed of travel are compared to these LDS teachings and scriptures, the fingerprint becomes less obscure. Indeed, close examination begins to illuminate the individual whorls of the fingerprint.

Quantum Quandaries

Quantum teleportation is a peculiar state in which one atomic particle can transmit information to another over immense distances instantly (see Appendix D for a more detailed explanation). Another kind of "spooky action," as Einstein called it, is illustrated in experiments which demonstrate the dual nature of light—that of particles (photons) and that of waves.

It has long been known that the wave characteristics of light can be shown by placing a light behind a barrier with two vertical slits in it. If a screen is placed on the other side of the barrier an image will appear on the screen which is a series of alternating bands of dark and light vertical stripes. This is the famous experiment carried out in the early 1800s by the Englishman Thomas Young[21] which demonstrated interference of light waves after passing through the slits. The dark lines corresponded to the areas where the waves from the two slits were interfering (canceling) each other, and the bright lines correlated with the areas where the waves reinforced each other. This is analogous to dropping two stones in a pond and watching the waves from the two stones interfere with one another.

A single slit does not produce this effect but instead shows a pattern of photons of light passing through the slit and striking the screen in a single vertical bright line. The question as to why light acts in one case as waves with typical patterns characteristic of waves interfering with one another, and in the other case acts like particles—which can be affected by gravity (see Appendix D)—is puzzling enough. But the real quandary came when physicists working in the field of quantum mechanics began to extend Young's experiment.

Imagine the two slit experiment, but instead of a beam as the source of light consider it to be a particle emitter which can spit out one photon at a time. Now, believe it or not, as we shoot single photons through one of the two open slits it hits the screen but it scrupulously avoids places where the dark lines would normally appear if there were wave interference. As more and more single photons are sent through the same slit, the familiar pattern of dark and light stripes begins to appear. How can this be, since we are not sending photons through the other slit? There should not be wave interference patterns since there are not waves from the other slit to interfere with those of the first slit.

To make matters worse, let us close the second slit. This time the single photons being shot through the first slit behave as they should, as normal particles striking the screen and developing a bright line where they hit. Let us now open the second slit and continue to shoot single photons through the first slit. Now, suddenly, the photons seem to "know" that the second slit is open. They behave as if they were again in wave interference patterns. They avoid the spaces where dark lines should appear on the screen and arrange themselves neatly in locations where the bright stripes would appear if there were wave reinforcements. Brian Silver, in his book *The Ascent of Science,* said:

> Photons spreading out from a particular slit apparently "know" that they must not travel in the direction of the dark stripes. There is something distinctly weird going on here. Imagine that you are a photon passing through a slit. How on earth do you know not to go toward the location of a dark line? . . .
>
> If a photon "knows" that it can't go to a dark line *because it interacts with the slit as it goes through,* then shutting the other slit shouldn't make any difference. How can a photon possibly "know" that the other slit is closed or open?[22]

These quantum quandaries concerning particles light-years from each other which seem to instantly sense what their partner is doing, and photons of light which know what they shouldn't know—no one told them that the other slit was open or closed—are simply unexplainable. Physicists acknowledge the weirdness of these quantum effects, but they can do little other than shrug their shoulders when asked what is going on.

Although this is not a clear fingerprint of God, it does seem that he was in the area. There appears to be something about his laws which are unfathomable to present day science.

The Scriptures

The scriptures have ever been a witness of God. In the LDS perspective those scriptures include, but are not limited to: the Old and New Testaments of the Bible, the Book of Mormon, the Doctrine and Covenants and the Pearl of Great Price. They also include the teachings of modern day prophets—which appear in the monthly Church publication, Ensign.

Because it is so important to the LDS Church, and because the veracity of the Book of Mormon also tends to verify the Bible, I shall first comment on it.

The Book of Mormon

Attempts to Discredit Translation or Witnesses

This book has been studied extensively by believers and non-believers alike. Indeed, the strength of the LDS Church is largely dependent upon individual members who bear witness that after reading and praying about the book they have received an absolute assurance of the book's truth. I shall further discuss that method of finding the truth in a moment. For the present let me consider other means of verifying the authenticity of the book.

In Chapter Five I reviewed important elements in early Church history. Two of those elements were: (1) the method of translating the book, and (2) the witnesses to the Book of Mormon. Concerning the method of translating the book, consider for a moment the poorly educated twenty-three year old farm boy who dictated the book in an elapsed time of approximately ninety days. He did this with no reference materials and under extremely difficult conditions. The resulting 531 page book has remained essentially unchanged—except for grammar, spelling, verse designations and a few other minor changes. The patent absurdity of one uneducated young man accomplishing this has sent droves of critics searching for some other explanation. None has been found.

Similarly concerning the witnesses, although some fell away from the Church, none ever denied their testimony throughout their lives. David Whitmer, one of the three witnesses, was born in 1805 in Pennsylvania. After becoming disenchanted he left the Church and spent much of the latter part of his life in Richmond, Missouri, where he died in 1888. Throughout his life, but especially in later years, he was often visited by newspaper reporters and other interested persons asking him if his testimony in the front of the Book of Mormon were really true. Several individuals tried to get him to change his story. He never did. Many if not most of his interviews with others, particularly with reporters, were recorded. Lyndon W. Cook accumulated those records and included them in a book—*David Whitmer Interviews*—published in 1991.

The book, *David Whitmer Interviews*, chronicles David's last words in this manner:

> On Sunday evening before his death he called the family and his attending physician, Dr. George W. Buchanan, to his bedside, and said, "Doctor, do you consider that I am in my right mind?" to which the Doctor replied, "Yes, you are in your right mind, I have just had a conversation with you." He [David] then addressed himself to all present and said: "I want to give my dying testimony. You must be faithful in Christ. I want to say to you all that the Bible and the record of the Nephites [The Book of Mormon] are true, so you can say that you have heard me bear my testimony on my death bed. . . ."[23]

Scholarly Studies of The Book of Mormon

There have been scholarly studies in almost every conceivable area, and volumes have been published concerning those studies. In the archaeological area a recent book is: *An Ancient American Setting for the Book of Mormon* by John L. Sorensen.[24] Another book in this category is *Exploring the Lands of the Book of Mormon* by Joseph L. Allen.[25] Both books explore archaeological evidences and both identify the probable lands of the Book of Mormon as extending from Southern Mexico to Honduras or Nicaragua.

The Book of Mormon covers three groups of settlers who were led to this continent by God. One group, the Jaredites, came from the Tower of Babel from 2900 to 2500 b.c.e. Two groups, the Mulekites and the Nephites, left Israel about 600 b.c.e. The book chronicles their activities until they finally destroyed most of their civilization in about 420 a.c.e. Since the book claims ancient Hebrew roots, and since it states that it was written in "reformed Egyptian," many studies have been conducted to establish whether or not it fits into those milieus. A recent book in that regard is: *Book of Mormon Authorship Revisited—The Evidence for Ancient Origins* which includes chapters by numerous eminent scholars.[26]

A fascinating article by two non-Mormon scholars was published in 1998 in the "Trinity Journal," a publication of the Trinity Evangelical Divinity School in Deerfield, Illinois. The article is entitled, *Mormon Scholarship, Apologetics and Evangelical Neglect: Losing the Battle and Not Knowing It*, authored by Carl Mosser and Paul Owen. Mosser graduated from the Talbot School of Theology with a masters degree, and Owen is a Ph.D. candidate at the University of Edinburgh, Scotland where he is studying theology. The basic thrust of their article is that in the religious war of scholarly ideas, the Mormons are winning. A couple of quotations from the article will illustrate their point.

> We realize that what we say will not be welcomed by all. Some may criticize us for giving the Mormons too much credit and for being too harsh on fellow evangelicals. However, much like testifying against a loved one in court, we cannot hide the facts of the matter. In this battle the Mormons are fighting valiantly. And the evangelicals? It appears that we may be losing the battle and not knowing it.[27]

> The evangelical world needs to wake up and respond to contemporary Mormon scholarship. . . . Our suggestions are as follows: First, evangelicals need to overcome inaccurate presuppositions about Mormonism. Second, evangelical counter-cultists need to refer to qualified persons LDS scholarship that is beyond their ability to rebut. Third, evangelical academicians need to make Mormonism, or some aspects of it, an area of professional interest. Fourth, evangelical publishers need to cease publishing works that are uninformed, misleading, or otherwise inadequate.

> . . . The fact is that the growth of Mormonism is outpacing even the highest predictions of professional sociologists of religion, and is on its way, within eighty years, to becoming the first world-religion since Islam in the seventh century.[28]

Chiasmus

It would not, of course, be practical in this book to list, much less reproduce, many of the studies pro and con about the Book of Mormon.

For those having such interest they are encouraged to contact the Foundation for Ancient Research and Mormon Studies (FARMS) in Provo, Utah. In order to illustrate the type of studies carried out and/or published by FARMS, however, I shall include portions of some work concerning chiasmus carried out by John W. Welch.[29]

Chiasmus is a structured rhetorical device that has been used in prose and poetry for nearly three thousand years. The form has been used extensively in the Bible, although it was relegated to intellectual obscurity in Western civilization until the mid-nineteenth century. There is no evidence that anyone in America understood chiasmus in 1830 when the Book of Mormon was published.

In 1967 John Welch first discovered chiasmus in the Book of Mormon. Since then he has done an intensive study of examples of this literary form in the Bible and the Book of Mormon.

Chiasmus, as used in the Bible, is a form of Hebrew poetry that employs reverse parallelisms. It was used in olden times because it helped people to remember passages that they could quote. It is best understood by illustrating some examples. The first example is from Genesis 7:21-23.

a. And all flesh died that moved upon the earth,
  b. Both birds,
    c. And cattle,
      d. and beasts,
        e. And every creeping thing that creepeth upon the earth,
          f. And every man:
            g. All in whose nostrils was the breath of the spirit of life
              h. Of all that was on the dry land
                I. Died
                I. And was destroyed;
              h. Every living thing
            g. That was upon the face of the ground,
          f. Both man,
        e. And creeping things,
      d. (And beasts),
    c. And cattle,
  b. And birds of the heavens;
a. And they were destroyed from the earth.

As can be seen from the example, thoughts expressed in *a* from the beginning of the passage are repeated in *a* from the end of the passage. Similarly for *b, c, d, ...*

When reading the Bible or the Book of Mormon in English, and with chapter and verse formats, it is not immediately obvious that this poetic form exists. The text must be carefully studied before it becomes readily accessible to the reader. In the ancient form, however, it must have been a powerful tool for remembering and understanding passages of scripture.

The next two examples are from the Book of Mormon.

Chiasmus from Mosiah 5:10-12:
a. Whosoever shall not take upon him the name of Christ
  b. must be called by some other name;
    c. therefore, he findeth himself on the left hand of God.
      d. And I would that ye should remember also,
      that is the name . . .
        e. that never should be blotted out,
          f. except it be through transgression; therefore,
          f. take heed that ye do not transgress,
        e. That the name be not blotted out of your hearts . . .
      d. I would that ye should remember to retain the name . . .
    c. that ye are not found on the left hand of God
  b. but that ye hear and know the voice by which ye shall be called,
a. and also, the name by which he shall call you.

Chiasmus from Mosiah 3:1-3:
a. for behold, I have things to tell you concerning
  b. That which is to come.
    c. And the things which I shall tell you
      d. Are made known unto me by an angel from God.
        e. And he said unto me: Awake;
          f. and I awoke, and . . . he stood before me.
        e. And he said unto me: Awake,
      d. and hear the words
    c. Which I shall tell thee;
  b. For behold, I am come
a. to declare unto you the glad tidings of great joy.

These examples from the Bible and the Book of Mormon could be expanded many times. The entire thirty-sixth chapter of Alma in the Book of Mormon is written in the form of a chiasmus. It is a classic of its type. The question, then, is: How was Joseph Smith able to construct large portions of the Book of Mormon in this form of ancient poetry when twentieth century scholars just began to research the form in recent times? Since he dictated the Book of Mormon without notes or without pausing to research how the parallel phrases met the criteria of a chiasmus, how did he do it? Is this another fingerprint of God?

The Bible

Conservative and Liberal Views of the Bible

I shall not attempt to review the almost infinite number and variety of studies conducted on the Bible. Suffice it to say, there are believers and non-believers, with every possible shade in between. Evangelical/Fundamental Christians tend to be believers in the Bible as the inerrant word of God.[30] To these more conservative Christians, the Bible is the ultimate authority, and its interpretation is a matter of individual conscience—which leads to some interesting conflicts when discrepancies in the text of the Bible are noted.[31]

On the other hand, liberal Christians find their conservative brethren and sisters completely in error concerning the more literal interpretation of the Bible. After reading Bruce Bawer's *Stealing Jesus*,[32] I wrote these comments to a friend:

> To get around the Biblical injunctions for repentance, baptism and other sacramental ordinances, Bawer adopts the liberal Protestant point of view—to agree with all "higher criticism" of the Bible. Indeed, Bawer even goes further. He essentially dismisses the Old Testament as irrelevant, and he selectively agrees with portions of the New Testament. Paul's writings are, to him, suspect. He is especially fond of the Gospels—Matthew, Mark, Luke, and John—except he would like to eliminate much of John.
>
> In order to avoid recognizing the ten commandments and other Biblical strictures, he—and other liberal Protestants—dismiss them as irrelevant to today's culture. He also agrees with the "higher criticism" which removes the miracles that Christ and others performed in the Bible. They are merely poetic allegories which are not intended to be interpreted literally in today's more enlightened scientific world.

Although he does not overtly reject the resurrection of Jesus Christ, he comes close to it, and he certainly does reject the virgin birth of Christ. In fact he devotes considerable material to showing how, historically, many pagan groups have created mythical heroes who were born of a virgin. Satan and hell are dismissed as pure fiction.

An Angelic Response About the Bible

With these many differing voices speaking about the Bible, how are we to accept it as the word of the Lord? Howard Storm, whose extensive NDE is recorded in *Journeys Beyond Life* asked his angelic "friends" about the Bible. Howard was an atheist before his experience, and so he wondered about the truth of the Bible. The record of that portion of his experience is instructive:[33]

When the review was finished they asked: "Do you want to ask any questions?" and I had a million questions. I asked, for example, "What about the Bible?" They responded: "What about it?" I asked if it was true, and they said that it was. Asking them why it was that when I tried to read it all I saw were contradictions, they took me back to my life's review again—something that I had overlooked. They showed me, for the few times I had opened the Bible, that I had read it with the idea of finding contradictions and problems. I was trying to prove to myself that it wasn't worth reading.

I observed to them that the Bible wasn't clear to me. It didn't make sense. They told me that it contained spiritual truth, and that I had to read it spiritually in order to understand it. It should be read prayerfully. My friends informed me that it was not like other books. They also told me, and I later found out this was true, that when you read it prayerfully it talks to you. It reveals itself to you. And you don't have to work at it anymore.

The LDS Position on the Bible

The eighth Article of Faith of The Church of Jesus Christ of Latter-day Saints is: "We believe the Bible to be the word of God as far as it is translated correctly; we also believe the Book of Mormon to be the word of God."[34] Equally important to this statement of Faith is the fact that the Book of Mormon quotes many portions of the Old and New Testaments—just as the New Testament frequently references passages in the Old Testament. Entire portions of Isaiah are included in the Book of Mormon. When Christ appears to the Nephites in the Book of Mormon, he repeats the Sermon on the Mount. Thus, if one accepts that the Book of Mormon is the word of God, then one must also accept that the Bible is the word of God. Moreover, referring back to Chapter 5 on the history of the LDS Church, it is obvious that prophets from the Old Testament appeared to Joseph Smith, and the angel Moroni quoted from many sections of the Bible.

So from an LDS perspective, Moses was a real prophet of God, and he did lead the Children of Israel from bondage; the Ten Commandments have not been rescinded; Jesus Christ is the literal Son of God, was born of the virgin Mary, was physically resurrected, and makes possible our restitution through the Atonement.

Freedom of Choice and the Heisenberg Uncertainty Principle

In Chapter 6 the importance of agency, or freedom of choice, to LDS philosophy was outlined. It is fundamental to the Faith that individuals are granted a brief period in mortality in which they can learn the consequences of their freely chosen actions. That freedom is only constrained by the physical limits of their existence and by the political and social environment that they live under, and within those constraints they are held accountable to God for their choices.

Near-death experiences universally support this theological position as illustrated by some of the examples given in Chapter 6. Many more such examples could have been used.

But what of Science, what does it have to say about freedom of choice? Prior to the advent of quantum mechanics in the early 1900s scientists and philosophers struggled with the idea of free choice. Newtonian science showed a marvelous predictability about cause and effect. It was possible using the laws of motion developed by Newton, for example, to calculate with precision the trajectory of an artillery shell. Nature, under these rules, seemed certain to always respond in a deterministic and predictable way.

From these observations concerning science it was natural that philosophers would extend the idea of predictability to suggest that the future was predetermined. Since all acts in heaven and the earth were governed by deterministic laws of physics and chemistry, there would be no free choice—or so they thought.

Quantum mechanics and the Heisenberg uncertainty principle as developed by Max Planck, Werner Heisenberg and Niels Bohr changed this deterministic view of the world and the universe (see Appendix D). Gerald Schroeder explained what happened:

> In 1927 a revolutionary concept pulled the rug from beneath the logic of . . . Determinism. In that year, Werner Karl Heisenberg published his principle of indeterminacy, the uncertainty principle. This defined a limit to the precision by which the position and momentum (mass times velocity) of any particle could be measured. The more closely one determined the momentum of an object, the less precisely one could measure the object's position. The exact value of both can never be measured. . . .
>
> For the first time, the scientific community admitted that there was a limit to scientific knowledge. Not being able to know the present exactly obviously meant that the future could not be foretold.[35]

Here, then, is an example of how Mormonism, near-death research and science have all reached the same conclusion. Again, the evidence seems to suggest another fingerprint of God.

Joe Swick's NDE and Conversion[36]

I interviewed Joe on the campus of Brigham Young University where he was a graduate student who also taught Japanese. Joe had served a mission for the LDS Church in Japan. He was 32 years of age when I interviewed him.

When Joe was nine years old, he was crossing the street with a bicycle when he was hit by a car. His NDE occurred as follows:

> I felt myself separated from my body—I didn't see my body, and it was black. But I remember being conscious and thinking about what was happening. And . . . and I had a feeling—not just my mind—that there was something to me. There was something tangible to me.
>
> After awhile I recalled a sense of motion, or a feeling that I was moving. And it was like . . . it was like there were walls, or there was something confining me. I recalled moving, at first not very fast, but then the speed began to increase. I saw a light, a very bright

light; I could feel a very strong and powerful love that was coming towards me—filling me, from this light.

The light, or the love, or something, was speaking to me with a very comforting voice. I was drawn closer and closer to it. Although I could sense this really compassionate feeling coming from the light, I realized that if I arrived at where the light was there was a point at which I would not be able to come back. And I wouldn't be with my family or my friends. That thought frightened me.

I remember that the light was speaking to me, and I don't recall the exact words. It wasn't like a voice that you hear, it was more like . . . it was like speaking to my heart. And it was telling me that there were still things in life for me to experience.

I grew very close to the light, and I could feel that power, and the love flowing through me. I don't have a recollection of going back. It was black, and at some point I opened my eyes and there was a paramedic and some other people standing over me.

When Joe was fifteen years old he began to listen to LDS missionaries because he saw how joining the Mormon Church had helped his father—who had previously divorced Joe's mother. At the time Joe was living with his mother and stepfather. Portions of our interview proceeded as follows:

"As the missionaries taught me, I was not impressed—to say the least, I was not impressed." Joe laughed as he thought back.

"What was it that caused you not to be impressed?"

"Well, the idea that some farm boy in upstate New York had been visited by God and his son Jesus Christ did not impress me as something that I could believe. I also didn't think that The Book of Mormon had much to give me in the way of instruction over the Bible."

"Did you tell the missionaries what you thought?"

"Oh yes, they knew how I felt. I don't know why they continued to come out, but they did. And they challenged me to be baptized on January 15, if I knew that the Church was true by that date. I told them: 'Sure, if I know it's true—but there's a fat chance of that happening.'

"By the fourteenth when the missionaries were to visit me I had decided that I wasn't going to be baptized. I told my mother and my step-father that I didn't know that the Church was true, and I didn't want to be involved with it. I felt that this would be the final meeting with the missionaries.

"They had someone with them to interview me. He had the regular flip charts and he showed me a picture of Joseph Smith. He asked me if I believed Joseph Smith was a prophet, and I told him no, I thought he was a fraud. He asked me if I thought The Book of Mormon was the word of God, and I told him no, I thought it was bogus. He showed me a picture of Spencer W. Kimball and asked if I thought he was a prophet of God. I told him that the man had a kindly face, but I didn't believe he was a prophet of God.

"The missionary then asked me if I wanted to know if these things were true—if I really wanted to know. And it wasn't what he said, it was the way he said it. I felt something inside of me that said: *Yes, that is why you have been speaking with the missionaries. That is why you have had them come.* I found myself saying: 'Yes, of course I want to know if it's really true.'

"He asked if I would like to pray about it right then. I responded: 'Certainly.' I had prayed before, but I hadn't been very serious—it had seemed so obviously fraudulent.

"We went into my room, this young missionary and I, and as I got on my knees, it was not a vocal prayer, I began to pray. I felt the Holy Ghost wash over me. It was a very powerful feeling.

"At that time I didn't know it was the Holy Ghost. The missionary opened his eyes and said to me: 'That feeling that you are feeling now is the Holy Ghost. If you ask the question you are going to ask, you will get an answer.'

"I was surprised that he knew what I felt. I closed my eyes and . . . and at that point it was as though the walls fell away from my room, and the floor fell from beneath me. I was just there. And it was that same intensely bright light. There was that same powerful feeling of love that I had known when I was hit by the car." Joe had difficulty holding back the tears as he remembered the event. He continued with some difficulty.

"It was more than viewing the light. It was like being totally enveloped. And it was reassuring me—again not with an audible voice—but it was speaking very powerfully to my heart, that the step I was about to take, I needed to do; that it was important for me to do that.

"I don't know how long that continued, but after awhile it was done. I became aware of my surroundings. The missionary was still praying beside me. Then he opened his eyes, and we went into the other room. He never asked me what I experienced, and I don't know what he saw or felt. But that was my experience.

"The other two missionaries were sitting at the kitchen table. They looked up, and I told them I was going to join the Church. I thought they were going to fall out of their seats."

Personal Revelation

In the Introduction to this book I mentioned that there were other, spiritual, forms of evidence which are every bit as valid as are the evidences of science for finding truth. In point of fact, if one accepts the proposition that there is a God who plays a role in the life of his children, then that form of truth is more dependable. As previously cited scriptures show, God is the light and the truth.

There is nothing more fundamental to the teachings of the Church of Jesus Christ of Latter-day Saints than is the idea that each individual may receive personal revelation from God. Indeed, each individual has a responsibility to seek such revelation concerning his or her responsibilities, problems, challenges, needs, and, most importantly, concerning their understanding of the Gospel. Upon receiving such revelation, the individual is under obligation to bear testimony of the truthfulness of what he or she knows—particularly concerning the fact that Jesus is the Christ, the living son of God.

The necessity to seek revelation from God is illustrated well in the Book of Mormon. Moroni, the last chronicler of the book, and the individual who later appeared to Joseph Smith as an angel, gave this challenge to those who would read the Book of Mormon:[37]

> Behold, I would exhort you that when ye shall read these things, if it be wisdom in God that ye should read them, that ye would remember how merciful the Lord hath been unto the children of men, from the creation of Adam even down unto the time that ye shall receive these things, and ponder it in your hearts.
>
> And when ye shall receive these things, I would exhort you that ye would ask God, the Eternal Father, in the name of Christ, if these things are not true; and if ye shall ask with a sincere heart, with real

intent, having faith in Christ, he will manifest the truth of it unto you, by the power of the Holy Ghost.

And by the power of the Holy Ghost ye may know the truth of all things.

Arguably, the strength of the LDS Church is in the individual testimonies of the members—those that testify that they know, through revelation from God, that the Church teachings are true and that Jesus is the Christ. In this, as well as in other aspects, the Church is similar to the primitive church established by Christ during his earthly ministry. The early Christian church grew rapidly because there were numerous individuals who claimed, through personal knowledge, that Jesus was the son of God, had been resurrected, and lived again.

Joe Swick had a personal revelation which led him to the truth—and the evidence for that truth was stronger than evidence generated by any other means. Upon completion of describing his NDE I asked him if there were any final comments he would like to make. With tears in his eyes, he said:

> I haven't shared this experience with many people. It is too sacred to me. But whenever I have shared it, I have always told people that the experience has taught me that God is willing to reach out and talk with us. I'm nobody special, I don't have a . . . all I do is translate languages. Nobody knows my name—but I do know that God knows my name. And that he was willing to reach out and talk with me. If he would talk to somebody like me, then he would do it for anybody.
>
> That was a realization that profoundly influenced my joining the Church. God didn't just talk to Joseph Smith, a farm boy in New York. He talked to me too. And he would talk to anybody, it seems to me, if he would talk to somebody like me.[38]

Conclusions

The following conclusions are mine, and you may or may not agree with them. Nevertheless, I present them as my deductions from evidence gathered over a marvelously varied lifetime. It has been a lifetime filled with the excitement of discovery.

Basic Conclusions from Identifying Certain Fingerprints

Based upon the fingerprints of God which were outlined above I came to certain basic conclusions. My first conclusion is that the evidence for a universe and world created by God is overwhelming. Simply asking the questions, What is a singularity? or, What causes quantum weirdness? leads to God. While one can make a case for chance creation of an anthropic Universe in an infinity of non-anthropic universes, when one considers the other evidences presented in this book, all other answers than a God created Universe disappear.

My second conclusion is that evolution by natural selection is a reality, but it cannot be extrapolated to answer many of the complexities of life. In no way can it respond to the question: How did life begin on the earth? From probability considerations, alone, there is only one rational answer as to how life began—God.

Another conclusion is that near-death experiences cannot be explained as anything other than an existence in another spiritual realm. A realm which includes both ethereal and frightening possibilities. Within its ethereal boundaries it is a realm governed by truth, light, love and knowledge—God's realm.

The scriptures, I have concluded, are the Word of God and of his son, Jesus Christ. When prayerfully considered and studied, they can reveal truths about life and how to live that can be obtained in no other way.

A very personal conclusion is that the Book of Mormon is true, and Joseph Smith was a prophet of God who restored the original Church of Christ. As part of that conclusion, a corollary conclusion is that God has over the ages, and continues to this day, to reveal his Word through his servants, the Prophets. And, the Church of Jesus Christ of Latter-day Saints is true, and it is led by a modern prophet of God.

Some Interrelated Conclusions

In the Introduction of this book I observed that my intellectual and spiritual journey traveled on three different paths: *the creation* as understood by science, *near-death studies*, and *Mormonism*. In the beginning I did not see how these paths could cross. I was wrong! As my journey progressed I was inevitably brought back to the same point—a path which led to God.

It was almost as if there were a signpost at the intersection of the three paths which read "God, this way." And the conclusion which followed from that knowledge was that each of the different paths were supportive of the other. All were seeking to find the truth—by their own methods—and the three truths merged into one truth.

The scientists' emerging understanding of the creation, although couched in terms such as: *anthropic universe, properly tuned constants, omega equal to unity* and *improbability of spontaneous life formation,* has increasingly included the idea of a Creator as a scientifically acceptable postulate. Frank J. Tipler, for example, is Professor of Mathematical Physics at Tulane University. In his book, *The Physics of Immortality,* he develops a theory of universal resurrection based on the principles of physics. Without commenting on his particular theory some of his conclusions are particularly pertinent to the changing perspective of many scientists. He writes:

> . . . Physics has now absorbed theology; the divorce between science and religion, between reason and emotion, is over. . . . Science can now offer precisely the consolations in facing death that religion once offered. Religion is now a part of science.[39]

Equally important is the evolving science of near-death research and its finding that corroborative NDEs cannot logically be explained as anything other than a duality of human nature. At death the spiritual entity-consciousness separates and enters a different dimension or realm—one governed by the Light/God. In Chapter 2 some of the research concerning corroborative NDEs by Michael Sabom, a cardiologist, was discussed. Dr Sabom has continued to research near-death and related experiences, and he has elaborated on some of that work in his book, *Light and Death.* He comments about some of his discoveries in this manner:

> Scientists have typically avoided dealing with the nonmaterial world and have preferred to operate in the more comfortable world of the physical, which is amenable to examination and measurement. Any study of the NDE, however, brings these two worlds [the spiritual-nonmaterial world and the physical world] face-to-face and prevents the comfortable partitioning of them. So what we engage in here is in many

respects new ground, and I seek to tread carefully in this territory where science and theology intersect.[40]

In Chapter 7 of this book I correlated some of the LDS theology with various near-death research findings. Because NDE research also calls upon the tools of modern science for its explanations—albeit different tools from the physicists and cosmologists—it acts as a bridge between the two sciences and religion.

Thus the creation scientists in the fields of astronomy, mathematics, cosmology, physics, geophysics, chemistry, anthropology, biology and microbiology can speak to the emerging NDE scientists in the fields of physiology, psychology, chemistry, biology, microbiology, sociology and pharmacology about their common findings which point to a Creator. Moreover, the intersection of the two scientific fields with that of religion could lead to greater understanding between religionists and scientists.

There was one other astonishing conclusion which belatedly became obvious to me. It was that of the three paths which I followed there was only one path which had the constancy and the power to have yielded the truth in the beginning and throughout my journey. And that was the path which in my youth I partially denied—the path grounded in my Mormon heritage.

Recalling that my search began in the 1950s, science was still discovering many of the factors that would lead to the idea of an Anthropic Universe, which name was only coined by Brandon Carter in 1974. Similarly with near-death research; the term near-death experience was invented by Raymond Moody in his book *Life After Life* in 1975. So neither of these paths had the capacity early in my journey to divulge the fingerprints of God as they later did.

But the fingerprints of God—and his power—were always discernable by simply following the beckoning path which my parents had so lovingly pointed me towards. That I stumbled badly early in my journey is undeniable. For the Plan of Salvation, as delineated in LDS scriptures, clearly provided a road map of the path to truth. Moreover, that road map overlaid all of the paths by explicitly defining the ultimate destiny of humankind.

In summary, the three paths which I traveled ultimately offered me the same truth: namely, that all paths lead to God. In the process they reinforced each other concerning that very truth.

Implications

What are the implications of these conclusions? They are enormous. Instead of mankind being swallowed up by the things which matter least, mankind is the thing that matters most. It means that there is a God and that life does continue after mortality. Instead of life being a chance event destined to be obliterated in future stellar explosions, life becomes the purpose behind cosmic eruptions. Instead of a meaningless drift through a mortality characterized by comic-tragic absurdities—which end with the greatest absurdity of all, extinction—mortality becomes a purposeful mission commissioned by the Truth and the Light: God.

From the LDS scriptures we read, " . . . men are that they might have joy,"[41] and, ". . . this is my work and my glory—to bring to pass the immortality and eternal life of man."[42] We, as sons and daughters of God, are bound in an eternal journey of growth. We have lived forever and we shall continue to live forever. All of us are guaranteed, through the atoning blood of Jesus Christ, to be resurrected at some future time with a combined spiritual and perfected physical body, never again to die. Before we reach that final state, immediately after death, we shall leave our physical body and continue life as individual spirit beings. Ultimately, depending upon how we lived in this probationary life, we can become as God, joining with him in his work and his glory.

This perspective on our future also impacts on our present. Just as those who have NDEs return to life with a sense of mission and an overwhelming desire to adjust their lives so as to conform to a more helpful, a more spiritual, and a more loving existence, so too will we adjust our lives if we truly believe the Godly evidence presented to us. We left our former home in the heavenly cosmos for a brief testing period in the school of mortality. When we left we shouted for joy for the opportunities granted us by our Heavenly Parents. When we return, and if we have measured up to our heavenly potential, our joy will be complete.

If you were to ask most of those who have had a near-death experience to describe their experience in a single word, almost certainly, it would be *love*. When Christ was asked by the Pharisees, "Which is the great commandment in the law?" he answered: "Thou shalt love the Lord thy God with all thy heart, and with all thy soul, and with all thy mind. This is the first and great commandment. And the second is like unto it, Thou shalt love thy neighbour as thyself. On these two commandments hang all the law and the prophets."[43]

C.S. Lewis, the great Christian apologist, said this about God's love:

God, who needs nothing, loves into existence wholly superfluous creatures in order that He may love and perfect them. He creates the universe, already foreseeing—or should we say "seeing?" there are no tenses in God—the buzzing cloud of flies about the cross, the flayed back pressed against the uneven stake, the nails driven through the mesial nerves, the repeated incipient suffocation as the body droops, the repeated torture of back and arms as it is time after time, for breath's sake, hitched up. . . .

Herein is love. This is the diagram of Love Himself, the inventor of all loves.[44]

For those privileged individuals who get a glimpse of the Master's realm they are overcome by the love that they feel. That love permeates their very being and they come back wishing to share what they have found. Another of my conclusions, therefore, is that lying deep within each of us is the power to call upon the love of God and to change the world by exercising that power.

Who Are We?

I restate the final and most important finding from my life's intellectual and spiritual odyssey. It is that we are, each of us, sons and daughters of God commissioned by him to come to earth for further growth and development. We are spiritual beings enjoying a temporary, but critically important, physical schooling. Our physical bodies are made of star dust, but our spiritual bodies are the stuff of eternity organized by God. Our destiny, should we so choose, is to become one with the Light, and to share in the glory and power of God. And though we now see through a glass darkly, then we shall see and know, and be seen and be known, in the eternal light and glory that was and is our rightful home.

How Great Thou Art

I cannot think of a better way to end this book than to quote the text from the hymn *How Great Thou Art* by Stuart K. Hine.[45]

> O Lord my God, When I in awesome wonder
> Consider all the worlds thy hands have made,
> I see the stars, I hear the rolling thunder,
> Thy pow'r thru-out the universe displayed;
>
> When thru the woods and forest glades I wander,
> And hear the birds sing sweetly in the trees,
> When I look down from lofty mountain grandeur
> And hear the brook and feel the gentle breeze,
>
> And when I think that God, his Son not sparing,
> Sent him to die, I scarce can take it in,
> That on the cross my burden gladly bearing
> He bled and died to take away my sin,
>
> When Christ shall come, with shout of acclamation,
> And take me home, what joy shall fill my heart!
> Then I shall bow in humble adoration
> And there proclaim, "My God, how great thou art!"
>
> Then sings my soul, my Savior God, to thee,
> How great thou art! How great thou art!
> Then sings my soul, my Savior God, to thee,
> How great thou art! How great thou art!

Appendix A

Other Attempts to Explain the NDE

A Variety of Failed Explanations

As I explained in Chapter 2, in 1998 Craig Lundahl and I submitted the paper "Near-Death Studies and Modern Physics" for publication in the *Journal of Near-Death Studies*. In the paper Lundahl performed a comprehensive review of the many attempts to explain what was happening in an NDE. Much of what was reported in that paper is repeated below.

Efforts to explain the near-death experience have tended to focus on theories to explain the NDE as a biological, mental, psychological or social phenomena and theories that explain it as a real occurrence. These attempts have been proposed by researchers and theorists from a number of different fields. They tend to fall into a number of categories of explanation that include cultural, pharmacological, physiological, neurological, psychological, and religious.

These many attempts at explanation include such factors as prior social or cultural conditioning by Rodin in 1980;[1] drugs and sensory deprivation by Grof and Halifax in 1977,[2] Palmer in 1978[3] and Siegel in 1980;[4] cerebral anoxia or hypoxia, temporal lobe seizures, and altered states of consciousness by McHarg, in 1978,[5] Blacher in 1979[6] and Schnaper in 1980;[7] temporal lobe dysfunction, hypoxia/ischemia, stress, and neuropeptide/neurotransmitter imbalance by Saavedra-Aguilar and Gomez-Jeria in 1989;[8] sigma receptors and excitatory amino acid receptors by Saavedra-Aguilar and Gomez-Jeria in 1989;[9] NMDA-PCP receptor, the sigma receptor, and the endopsychosins by Jansen in 1989[10] and 1990;[11] serotonergic mechanisms by Morse,

Venecia, and Milstein in 1989;[12] brain-stem function by Cook in 1989;[13] endorphin release by Thomas in 1976[14] and Blackmore in 1993;[15] stress-induced limbic lobe dysfunction by Carr in 1982;[16] autoscopic hallucinations by Lukianowicz in 1958;[17] the replay of the birth experience by Sagan in 1979;[18] the depersonalization syndrome occurring in the face of life-threatening danger by Noyes and Kletti in 1976;[19] altered state triggered by the threat of imminent physical death by Quimby in 1989;[20] protective functions to conserve energy and provide necessary brain stimuli by Krishnan in 1981;[21] hallucinations by Siegal in 1980,[22] Menz, 1984[23] and Gibbs in 1987;[24] the denial of death by Ehrenwald in 1978;[25] regression in the face of death by Lowental in 1981;[26] stress induced psychological phenomena by Appleby in 1989;[27] fulfillment of prior personal expectations of death by Schnaper in 1980;[28] multiple personality disorder by Serdahely in 1992;[29] psychological transition by Tien in 1988;[30] hypnagogic sleep by Counts in 1983;[31] and religious expectations by Palmer in 1978,[32] . . . to name a few.

These attempts to explain the NDE as a biological, mental, psychological or social phenomena have failed to do so. The explanations either fit only a minute proportion of the reported near-death experiences or else they describe experiences other than true NDEs (Moody, 1975;[33] Osis and Haraldsson, 1977;[34] Sabom and Kreutziger, 1978;[35] Ring, 1980;[36] Grosso, 1981;[37] Becker, 1982;[38] Sabom, 1982;[39] Woodhouse, 1983;[40] Gabbard and Twemlow, 1986[41]). In particular, the explanations fail to account for the corroborative type of NDE described in Chapter 1.

Another Study of Corroborative Experiences

In Chapter Two I suggested that as the cumulative evidence becomes more obvious corroborative NDEs will receive increased research effort from various groups. An interesting case in point is provided in the Summer 1998 edition of the *Journal of Near-Death Studies* in an article entitled: "Physically Transcendent Awareness: A Comparison of the Phenomenology of Consciousness Before Birth and After Death," by Jenny Wade, Ph.D.

In her study Dr. Wade reviewed the extensive case literature on human experiences at the extremes of life span when central nervous system functioning is compromised; namely, before birth, when neurological processes are demonstrably immature, and after death, when the brain has ceased measurable activity. Her study was restricted to veridical cases, that is, cases in which there was information which could be independently verified by third parties. Validation was provided by records and personal accounts of medical personnel, relatives and other witnesses—in other words, she used only corroborative experiences.

Wade's study is of particular interest since this book presents evidence for the existence of human consciousness both in a premortal and in postmortal state, and her work also addresses those subjects. In the premortal case she relates numerous instances where very young children have memories of birth or pre-birth situations in which the children describe details of their circumstances and that of the mother prior to or during birth. In most of these cases the neurological state of the child was such that it would have been impossible for the child to have seen, heard or understood what was happening to him or her, yet the details were later verified by adults who were present during the experience.

In the case of near-death experiences, Wade examined many of the corroborative kinds of situations that are illustrated in this book. She also considered many of the explanations, such as those discussed in the previous Section, which attempt to provide answers on how such events could have happened to the individuals. Her conclusions mirror those of this book; namely that these many attempted explanations fall short in their ability to account for corroborative types of NDEs.

She explains her findings this way:

> To summarize all of the above, none of the psychologically or physiologically based arguments holds up well for the out-of-body phase of near-death phenomena, primarily because they are conclusions extrapolated from research on other states: their parallels with near-death conditions are tenuous at best; and none explains all the data. . . .
>
> The traditional positions are inadequate to account for the data, and in the aggregate, the findings suggest that some unknown source of awareness transcends the physical limits of the body, as currently understood, at the extremes of human life.[42]

In other words, as Dr. Wade says in the abstract of her article, ". . . some form of personhood can exist independently of known cellular processes associated with the body." As the readers of this book are by now aware, the author believes that the independent personhood is the spirit of the individual which exists in a premortal sphere before this life, joins the physical body during life on this earth, and separates from the body at physical death to live eternally in another realm.

New Age Explanations

Scientific attempts at explaining the NDE are not the only approaches used. The wide publicity given the subject has attracted New Age adherents, talk show hosts, followers of Eastern religions, UFO believers, and a host of other hangers-on, most of whom have their own prescriptions as to why and how NDEs occur. The majority of these explanations have been dismissed by scientists as without merit. During my initial NDE research effort I read and listened to much of what these groups had to say and, in general, I agree with the scientists' view of their explanations.

Reincarnation[43]

Why Reincarnation Interest by NDE Researchers?

The following discussion of reincarnation is provided because the subject often arises when NDEs are discussed. In many cases it has been used to explain events that persons having the near-death experience underwent.

The Buddhist, Hindu, Sikh and Jain religions in the East account for the reincarnation interest in that area of the world, but why such continued interest in the West? There is a certain glamour, of course, when Shirley MacLaine describes her previous existences (much of which Ian Wilson has shown to be a confused dialogue).[44] But the persistence of the attraction goes beyond the glamour of Shirley MacLaine.

Many reputable researchers of the near-death experience report that those they interviewed mentioned the possibility of reincarnation. Kenneth Ring shows that numerous of his subjects reported being more inclined to a reincarnation perspective following their near-death experience than before.[45] Of all those Carol and I interviewed, two or three indicated that they thought reincarnation might be possible—one of those was quite certain about it.

I believe there are two reasons for this continued belief in the possibility of reincarnation. The first reason has to do with a feeling by many undergoing an NDE that they lived before this life, and that they will continue to live in some other type of future life. The idea that they existed prior to this life was new to them, and some of them considered their feelings as evidence of a cyclic life phenomenon. Researchers, themselves, are confused by these discussions of a previous life, and they sometimes succumb to the same type of thinking.

Hypnotic Regression Therapy

The second reason for the tenacity of reincarnation belief may have to do with a different type of research; namely, research associated with hypnosis. Psychologists have, for some years used hypnosis for different therapeutic and experimental purposes.[46]

Psychotherapists using hypnotism have "regressed" patients into previous lives. This is particularly true of "New Age" therapists. Recent work by others in this field has proved interesting. Raymond Moody, Jr., in his book *Coming Back—A Psychiatrist Explores Past-Life Journeys*[47] describes how he allowed himself to be hypnotized and regressed into nine previous lives. After that personal experience he conducted almost two hundred hypnotic regressions on other willing subjects.

As a result of Raymond Moody's work he neither argues for the reality of reincarnation nor against it.[48] He found regressive hypnotism to be useful as a method for revealing deep-seated psychological problems in patients, but he was uncertain as to its usefulness as a method for discovering historically correct facts. He pointed out that "the mind likes to please and for that reason it is highly suggestible. When given the opportunity, it will fill in gaps with great aplomb. And when given the focused leisure time that hypnotism presents, it will often occupy itself with self-made fantasies."[49]

Different Beliefs Concerning Reincarnation

One view of human destiny is that our Karma is to have repeated existences (reincarnation) on this planet until we get it right—when we reach a state of Nirvana, which is a state of perfect peace or blessedness. After nirvana is achieved a hazy sort of life continuation occurs, but not as individual beings. Rather, we become part of an overall life force. Buddhists, Hindus, Sikhs and Jains (approximately one-third of the world's population) believe in reincarnation.

The Western concept of reincarnation (and that of most New Age writers) is one which normally restricts the repeated lives of an individual to existences in human form. In Eastern belief the soul of an individual can be reincarnated in plant or animal form—until the soul learns from its previous lives how to improve so as to warrant being reborn into a higher level of existence. Shirley MacLaine's different incarnations, for example, never included her as a snake, or, say, a banana. Perhaps Westerners just have a higher Karma than do the Easterners.

One of the leading investigators of reincarnation is Ian Stevenson, born in 1918, and a psychiatrist at the University of Virginia. He began his investigations in 1958 and he has been widely quoted as providing substantial evidence on the validity of reincarnation. His writings are the basis for "scientific" discussions of reincarnation.[50]

Ian Wilson, a British historian and author, in writing on the near-death phenomenon investigated many of the widely known cases of reincarnation.[51] He showed that many of the cases which Stevenson cited as showing evidence of reincarnation were suspect. Wilson tabulated, for example, Stevenson's data on the most publicized Indian and Sri Lankan cases. In every case the child claiming to have been reincarnated from a particular family was born into a poor family—but the child was alleged to have reincarnated from a nearby rich family. The implications are, of course, that the poor family with the supposedly reincarnated child made a conscious effort to select a wealthy family as the origin of the child from a previous incarnation. They could thereby enhance their own societal position and wealth.

Bridey Murphy and Jane Evans—Publicized Cases

Numerous publicized cases of claimed reincarnation have resulted from the use of hypnotism on people who regressed to former lives, in some cases even speaking in a foreign tongue, or describing detailed experiences in a different era and culture. The most publicized event in the United States was that of "Bridey Murphy" in 1952. Her story was essentially discounted in subsequent investigations.[52]

A similar but more complex case occurred in England in 1976. It was the case of "Jane Evans," and it was featured on BBC television. Upon being hypnotized, the 30 year old housewife regressed into six previous existences. Regressed back to Roman times, she recalled a life as "Livonia," wife of a tutor to the family of a Roman legate, Constantius, in the fourth century AD.

Jane knew substantial details of each life, but the most puzzling was her Roman experience. She gave details of individuals who could be, and were, checked historically for accuracy. She also named other Roman citizens who could not be found in historic documents of the period, but it was assumed these were lesser known figures who didn't make the history books.

One of those checking on the historic accuracy of Jane's story was Melvin Harris, a compulsive browser in second-hand bookstores. He stumbled upon Louis de Wohl's historical novel *The Living Wood*, published in 1947. The novel was devoted to the lives of Constantine, Constantius and Helena who lived in fourth century Rome. Moreover, he found the names of fictitious individuals whom Jane had named as being among her acquaintances in her previous life.[53]

Jane's story collapsed after these and other discoveries. It appeared that she had read and forgotten the novel some years before. It is interesting that under hypnosis she could withdraw from her subconscious memory the details of the story.

Hazards of Hypnosis for Retrieving Historic Facts

Numerous scholarly studies have verified the danger of using hypnotism as a tool for reconstructing memories, either memories of this life or memories of a presumed previous incarnation. The unreliability of such hypnotically derived memories is sufficiently great that "the AMA [American Medical Association] has indicated that previously hypnotized witnesses should not give testimony in court concerning the matters about which they have been hypnotized."[54]

One of the reasons hypnotic subjects are not reliable purveyors of historic facts is because "the inclination to confabulate [make up information] and to draw inferences to fill in missing information is apparently greater in hypnosis, and, as a consequence, can render the memory reports of hypnotized individuals deceptively more believable than normal recall."[55] This enhanced believability of the hypnotized subject can confuse even the therapist.

In addition to confabulating information under hypnosis, "there is evidence . . . that other exogenous sources such as books, movies, or special childhood and adult relationships may provide material that can be assimilated in a dissociated state and later be recalled under hypnosis as original material believed by the subject to be personal experience. The most publicized examples of this have been reincarnation stories elicited during hypnotic age regressions."[56]

Controlled Hypnotic Regression Experiments

Marian Bergin is a clinical social worker who has engaged in hypnotherapy in her own practice. She is convinced that work which reveals previous lives in hypnotized subjects is false. She has given me a number of papers, of the type discussed below, in which researchers show the extreme culpability of the patients to suggestions by the hypnotherapists. Hypnotherapy may be used, with care, for treatment of specific psychic disorders, but not for accurately reclaiming historic information.

Marian sent me the paper: *Secondary Identity Enactments During Hypnotic Past Life Regression: A Sociocognitive Perspective*. Despite its ponderous title, it is an excellent work. It relates to the reincarnation hypothesis that is so popular among New Age adherents and some near-death researchers.

Researchers for this study, led by Nicholas Spanos of Carleton University in Ottawa, Canada, conducted a series of controlled experiments on 175 subjects at the university. The subjects were selected for their hypnotizability and separated into three control groups. The groups differed in the specificity of suggestions made before and during hypnosis by the hypnotist. Individuals in all groups were led by the hypnotist back in time to presumably earlier lives.

Results of the study showed that subjects in all three groups were significantly affected by what they thought was wanted of them by the hypnotist. The more information that was transmitted to them by the hypnotist, the more detailed their past life regressions became. The researchers also showed that the subjects confabulated, or made-up, their previous lives' histories from books they had read, plays they had seen, newspapers they had read, or travels they had taken. Where information was lacking about a topic the researcher was asking about, the subjects' imagined fictitious stories and represented them as real. Some of the subjects were, in fact, convinced that their stories were real.

The researchers deliberately led the subjects into increasing detail about the geopolitical history from their so-called previous lives. These histories were checked later and found, universally, to be faulty.[57]

230

Appendix B

Basic Facts About the Universe

Fundamental Forces

There are four fundamental forces of nature and they govern the interaction of energy and matter—and all of the forces are the result of distortions in spacetime as described by the general and special laws of relativity developed by Einstein.[1] Newton formulated the first of the fundamental forces, *gravity*, and it describes the attraction of matter to matter. It is effective across the vast reaches of space and holds the solar system together and prevents the explosion of stars. Gravity keeps planets in their orbits and controls the movement of galaxies. It is also the prime mover in the creation of black holes. Gravity is the weakest of the four forces, but unlike the others, its reach extends throughout space.

The *electromagnetic force* is 10^{38} times stronger than the gravitation force but is effective over only a limited range.[2] It holds electrons in fixed and discrete atomic orbits, and it competes with the strong nuclear force in determining the structure of the nucleus. Without the electromagnetic force there would be no chemistry as we understand it. Photons of light carry the electromagnetic force.

The *strong nuclear force* binds quarks together and holds neutrons and protons to their atomic nuclei with the specific and regular structures of the naturally occurring elements of our universe. The strong nuclear force is the strongest of the forces, being 10^2 stronger than the electromagnetic force.[3] The strong force prevents the repulsive positive force of protons from tearing the nucleus apart. The strong force is carried by gluons. The strong force makes a star bright, and as the star burns its nuclear fuel, energy from the strong force is released in the form of radiation and light.

The **weak nuclear force**—being about 10^{-7} of the strong force—acts over a very limited range (smaller than an atom's nucleus), and it causes certain types of nuclei to break apart spontaneously.[4] This force controls the decay of a neutron into an electron, a proton and an anti-neutrino. The force also controls proton-proton fusion in stars. It is not a significant factor in the binding of nuclei.

The Big Bang—Evidence For

The evidences for the big bang are three-fold. The first evidence was provided by Edwin Hubble (after whom the Hubble space telescope is named), who, in 1929 made the landmark observation that wherever you look, distant galaxies are moving away from us.[5] In other words, the universe is expanding. If we think in reverse, it also means that at earlier times the universe would have been more compact. In fact, from these observations physicists deduced that at some point, 10 to 20 billion years back in time, the universe must have existed as an infinitely dense point of matter and energy. Numerous other scientists have since confirmed that the universe is expanding. Indeed, recent observations by astronomers led to this headline in the *New York Times:* "Shocked Cosmologists Find Universe Expanding Faster."[6]

The second bit of evidence which confirmed the big bang theory was provided by both theorists and experimentalists. In 1948 Ralph Adler and Robert Herman calculated the background radiation which should exist today as a remnant of the big bang. Their calculations showed that the temperature in space in all directions should be about 5 degrees Kelvin.[7] In 1965 two physicists, Arno Penzias and Robert Wilson working at Bell Laboratories were testing a microwave detector and were concerned because the detector seemed to be picking up radiation no matter where they pointed it. At first they thought it might have been caused by bird droppings. Ultimately they ruled out all extraneous causes and concluded that this must be radiation which was traveling to us from across space from the early moments of the big bang.[8] Later observation from the Cosmic Background Explorer (COBE) satellite have shown a background temperature of 2.726 degrees Kelvin.[9] This corresponds to a background electromagnetic energy level throughout the universe of 411 photons per cubic centimeter.[10]

In addition to this background radiation from the big bang, scientists have also detected an infrared background which does not seem to be coming from the remnants of the big bang, but rather may be coming from dust in the universe or it could be light coming from distant galaxies.[11] This infrared radiation from distant galaxies, if confirmed, is of the type postulated by Olbers's paradox, except, obviously, much smaller in magnitude. The reduction in magnitude from Olbers's postulate is for the reasons explained in that section.

The third evidence for the existence of the big bang is the remarkable correlation between the predicted—from theory—abundances of certain light elements synthesized in the early stages of the big bang compared with the observed abundances of those elements.[12] This is especially true of helium. The only way that helium could appear in the universe as abundantly as it does, instead of hydrogen, is in a big bang expansion starting at billions of degrees Kelvin. Theory—based on mathematical models of expansion from the big bang—predicts about 23% helium in older stars. Observation and spectral measurements have shown between 23 and 24 percent. This is impressive agreement.[13]

Further support for the correlation of the observed cosmic makeup with theoretical expansion models is provided by recent studies of deuterium in distant space gas clouds. In early moments of the big bang deuterium (heavy hydrogen, an isotope of hydrogen consisting of a neutron-proton pair) was abundant. Most of the deuterium combined with other deuterium to form helium, but a small percentage remained unpaired with other deuterium isotopes. Some of this deuterium later got swallowed up in stars to be converted to helium or other heavy elements, but a remnant escaped and floated freely in space. Scientists have recently been able to study the ultraviolet spectrum of light coming from distant gas clouds and thereby determine the amount of deuterium in them. The big bang predicts a certain ratio of deuterium to photons in space, and by knowing the photon density from the COBE measurements scientists are able to calculate this ratio and check it against the theoretical model. Correlation to this point, although somewhat uncertain, has generally confirmed the big bang model.[14]

Star-birth and Star-death

Stars are born when gravity causes the surrounding gases to collapse on themselves and heat up. At a temperature of about 15 million degrees Kelvin, and at enormous pressures, atoms of hydrogen crash together so hard that their protons stick. A series of reactions can fuse four nuclei of hydrogen into one helium nucleus. The helium nucleus weighs 0.7 percent less than the hydrogen that formed it. By Einstein's famous equation, therefore, the energy released by this reaction is $E = 0.007mc^2$, where m is the total mass of the sun and c is the velocity of light. When the total mass of the sun is considered this equation guarantees that there is enough fuel to keep our sun shining for about 10 billion years. The reaction is a controlled reaction—gravity and pressure exactly balance themselves so that the sun burns in a measured way.[15]

Spectral analysis of the oldest stars show that they primarily consist of hydrogen and helium, whereas more recent stars show other heavier elements such as carbon, oxygen, magnesium and silicon. This corresponds with the fact that the universe was essentially only hydrogen and helium when it was first formed. As this hydrogen and helium in early stars fused at high temperatures it began to form the heavier elements. I discussed in Chapter Five how carbon forms, but an example of formation of a heavy element is when helium-4 fuses with carbon-12 to form oxygen-16.

Many stars are larger than our sun. In general larger stars burn their fuel faster than smaller stars, and they burn at higher central temperatures. Some stars have a central temperature of about 100 million degrees, just right for the fusing of carbon from helium. At the higher temperatures of larger stars—up to billions of degrees—heavier elements ranging from carbon to iron are formed.

Early in the universe many large stars became, in effect, atom factories as they lived through their short lives (a billion years or so), burned up their hydrogen and helium and created a rich supply of heavy elements. As their primary fuel was exhausted the outward force of gas and radiation abruptly ceased, and gravity did its job. The star fell in on itself, compressing free neutrons into an incredibly dense interior, and creating a shock wave that blew the remaining materials out in a giant exploding supernova. Depending upon the initial mass of the star the remaining materials wound up as a red giant, a neutron hole, or a black hole[16] (discussed in Appendix D). During the final explosion of a supernova, immensely higher temperatures created even heavier elements such as uranium and thorium. After the universe was formed, and over the next several billion years, stars were born and stars died. The birth and death of stars caused the cyclic reuse of their materials—including in our solar system. We are literally made of the stuff of star dust. And when we use nuclear energy, which burns uranium for fuel, we are extracting energy once created in far away giant stars.

Age of the Earth and the Universe

In the Introduction I stated that the evidence for an extended age—billions of years—of the earth and the universe was overwhelming. Let us consider some of the evidence.

Age of the Earth

Prior to radiometric dating methods geologists attempted to determine time frames for different eras of the earth's existence—which they designated as the Paleozoic, Mesozoic and Cenozoic (most recent) eras—by relatively crude techniques. They estimated times of each of these eras based on different types and thicknesses of rock formations, rates of deposition, rates of erosion, development of life, and concentration of salt in the ocean. Although the techniques yielded time periods in the millions of years, they were subject to error and controversy. That all changed in 1913 when Arthur Holmes published a book entitled *The Age of the Earth*, which established the Phanerozoic Time Scale for the various geologic eras of the earth. This time scale included fourteen periods—compared with the three geologic periods used earlier—with the earliest period being the Cambrian (500-570 million years ago).[17]

In his book Holmes outlined how age determinations based on the principles of radioactive decay, in conjunction with geological data on the maximum known thicknesses of rocks assigned to the various geological periods, could be used to construct a quantitative time scale. The ratios of the daughter products, helium and lead, to the parent uranium, were used to calculate these early radioactivity ages.

Radioactive dating is based on the observed fact that radioactive materials decay at a fixed rate. Radiocarbon dating, for example, works because cosmic radiation entering our atmosphere transforms some of the nitrogen to radioactive carbon with a mass number of 14, represented as C^{14}. The half life of C^{14} is 5,568 years, which means that in that period of time only one half of the original C^{14} will be left; the rest will have decayed into other elements. Over a period of time the carbon-14 in the atmosphere reacts with oxygen to form carbon dioxide, and it reaches a stable concentration in the atmosphere. Assuming that the observed stable concentration has always existed (a somewhat questionable assumption) the carbon dioxide ultimately gets absorbed in rocks, water and living things. Thus, if the bone of an ancient skeleton is subjected to radioactive analysis and it is found that the remaining C^{14} is only one half the concentration of the stable amount in the atmosphere, it may be concluded that the bone is 5,568 years old.

With the development of more sophisticated measuring instruments it has become possible to use other radioactive elements for more precise age determination. U^{238} decays to lead as its final stable element, but in the process it leaves behind eight helium atoms for each atom of uranium-238. Rocks which contain both elements, therefore, can have their age determined by ascertaining the ratio of uranium to helium. Several other decay chains of radioactive elements have also proved useful in accurately calculating age. An even more accurate method has been useful in calculating both fossil and rock ages. Volcanic ash frequently contains minuscule crystals known as zircons, and both radioactive uranium and lead are found in the crystals. By measuring the ratio of the parent uranium to its ultimate element, lead, precise ages can be established where zircon crystals are found. From radioactive dating of zircons found in Siberia scientists now generally agree that the start of the Cambrian period was 543 million years ago.[18]

Returning now to the Phanerozoic time scale, it only proceeded as far back in time as the beginning of the Cambrian era. Using the uranium, helium and lead decay process coupled with spectrographic analysis scientists have been able to date rocks much further back into the pre-Cambrian era. These techniques have successfully established the age of the earth as 4.55 billion years.[19]

Age of the Universe

The age of the universe must, of course, be older than the age of the earth. Numerous indirect methods are used for dating the universe, but the most relied upon method is to use a reverse of the big bang model. I have already discussed the evidence for the big bang. That same evidence is valid for proceeding backward in time from the present to Planck time. Doing that yields a universe age from 10 to 20 billion years. The large span results from the uncertainty in various steps of the method.

Appendix C

Probability, and
Other Attempts to Explain Life

Conditional Probability

Probabilities can rapidly get more complicated as multiple events are considered, and as conditional events are included. Conditional events are those events which can occur, but only if some other event has occurred first. Let us consider a particular example.

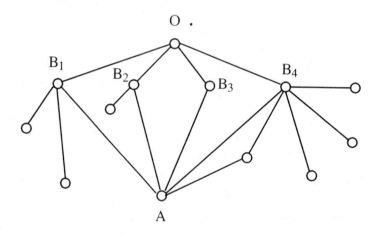

Figure 1

Figure 1 represents a series of trails in Yosemite National Park available to a hiker and his wife. The husband is impatient to get started from point O at the bottom of the canyon in order to reach a peak, designated as point A, near the top of Yosemite Falls, so he doesn't bother to get a map from Park Headquarters. As the hikers leave point O they must choose one of the trails OB_1, OB_2, OB_3, or OB_4. Since the husband did not pick up a map, their choices are in dispute. The wife argues for going back and getting a map, but the husband insists all will be well. They make their choices by drawing straws.

With the various trail choices that they must make, what is the probability that they will reach Point A?

The probability of reaching A is given by the formula:[1]

$$P(A) = \sum_k P(A|B_k) \, P(B_k)$$

Where $P(A)$ is the probability of reaching A, $P(A|B_k)$ is the probability of reaching A under the condition that one of the B_k have been reached. $P(B_k)$ is the probability that any particular B has been reached, and the summation indicates that the products of the various $P(B_k)$ and $P(A|B_k)$ must be summed.

Since the husband and wife have chosen their initial trails at random, the probability of reaching any particular B_k is $P(B_k) = 1/4$ where $k = 1, 2, 3, 4$. The probability of reaching B_1 therefore is one chance in 4. Once having arrived at B_1, the husband and wife again argue since there are three trails which seem equally likely, but only one of which leads to A. Hence the conditional probability of arriving at A starting from B_1 is just $1/3$. Thus $P(A|B_1) = 1/3$, $P(A|B_2) = 1/2$, $P(A|B_3) = 1$, and $P(A|B_4) = 2/5$. Inserting all of these values into the formula at the top of the page, we get:

$$P(A) = 1/4 \times 1/3 + 1/4 \times 1/2 + 1/4 \times 1 + 1/4 \times 2/5 =$$
$$1/4(1/3 + 1/2 + 1 + 2/5) = 67/120 = .5583$$

From this we determine that the husband and wife, starting at point O, had a 55.83 percent chance of reaching point A or a 44.17 percent of not reaching it. Unfortunately, they fell in the 44.17 percent region and returned to the lodge in Yosemite valley exhausted. The husband sulked as he read a Tom Clancy novel, and the wife called her mother.

As with the previous example with the tossing of the die, we could also have assigned times for the various trails that the husband and wife might take, and thereby determine the probable time for traveling from point O to point B.

This example should be sufficient to illustrate some of the rudimentary principles of probability analysis. Some of the arguments in Chapter 4 are based on conditional probabilities. In that chapter we also presented the arguments against a chance universe. Some of the arguments which physicists use for a chance universe shall now be given.

Argument for a Chance Universe

Physicists often speak of symmetry. Symmetry as they use it refers to a mathematical group with a common property that unites its members in a symmetrical way. Many of the properties of ordinary space exhibit symmetry and as a consequence we travel through space with no difficulty and footballs retain their symmetry when they are kicked. If we lived in the intensely curved space near a black hole that would not be true. Because of the asymmetry of the curved space, travel away from the hole would be difficult and travel toward it would be fatal. A kicked football would not maintain its symmetrical shape.

Symmetry also refers to some of the properties of fundamental particles. An electron if transformed into a positron is said to be symmetrical along the axes of mass and spin since these remain the same but asymmetrical with respect to charge, which inverts when the particle is transformed. In this sense, symmetry is defined as a quantity that remains unchanged during a transformation.[2]

Some physicists believe that early in the birth of the universe, when energies and temperatures were enormous, many of the particles which we now find in asymmetrical arrays were originally symmetrical. Fundamental particles, such as quarks, have vastly different masses between the different types. Were symmetry preserved all quarks would be equally massive. The behavior of our universe and its anthropic nature is largely due to symmetries that appear to have been broken some time during the big bang. Why they broke the way they did is the key question.[3]

There are two possible answers to the question of why symmetries broke as they did. One answer, which is anathema to many individuals, is that God preselected the conditions so that broken symmetries would occur in a manner to create the circumstances conducive to life. The other answer is that some type of field, such as the *Higgs field*, named after Peter Higgs of the University of Edinburgh, was the driving force behind broken symmetries which occurred by chance depending upon the Higgs or other randomly occurring field strengths. The transition from a symmetric phase to broken symmetries where tremendous numbers of particles were formed occurred at the critical temperature of 1027 degrees Kelvin.[4] If the fall of the universe from a state of early perfect symmetry is true, then it could mean that things are the way they are from chance instead of necessity.[5]

This second argument about broken symmetries happening by chance is believed by John Leslie to be the strongest argument for multiple universes. He says this about it:

> Probabilistic symmetry breaking provides, . . . a particularly plausible way almost the only way which physicists have taken much beyond off-the-cuff remarks and hand-waving of giving widely varying characters to different universes. . . .
>
> Given many scalar fields each affecting different particles in different ways during symmetry breaking, and given that the intensities of those fields were settled randomly, we could have a mechanism making it likely that there would exist, somewhere or other within a huge set of universes, a universe whose force strengths and particle masses were tuned to Life's needs with enormous accuracy.[6]

Summary of Arguments
For and Against a Chance Universe

From the preceding material and from the information contained in Chapter 4 it appears that there are reasonable arguments for both a God designed universe, and, if one accepts the multiple universe theory, for an anthropic universe which was created by happenstance. To that end, John Leslie said this:

> The conclusion to this argument from probabilities could be that it is altogether likely that either there exist many universes or God has ensured that our universe is just right for Life, *or both.* . . .
>
> My argument has been that the fine tuning is evidence, genuine evidence, of the following fact: that *God is real, and/or there are many and varied universes.* And it could be tempting to call the fact an observed one. Observed indirectly, but observed none the less.[7]

Sample Calculations of the Probability of Chance Life Formation

Calculation of a Specific Protein

This calculation is presented as representative of some of the computations performed to determine the probability of life developing by chance. The outcome of such computations is, to a large extent, governed by the assumptions which establish the framework for the succeeding arithmetic. That being so, it is incumbent upon the originator of the calculation to choose suitably conservative parameters.

The following work is based upon the framework used by Gerald Schroeder in his book *The Science of God*.[8]

There are thirty-four phyla which define the structure of all animal life, and within those phyla there are approximately thirty million (30×10^6) species. A typical bacterial cell contains thousands of genes, and a typical mammalian cell contains tens of thousands.[9] For our model let us select a representative cell as one which contains 60,000 (60×10^3) genes.

If no proteins were common among species, then all life forms would be constructed of the number of different proteins as follows:

$(30 \times 10^6) \times (60 \times 10^3) = 1{,}800 \times 10^9 = 1.8 \times 10^{12}$

There are 20 different amino acids, and a typical protein chain contains from 50 to 1,000 amino acid links.[10] For our model let us use a protein with 300 amino acids in length.

Consider first the twenty different kinds of amino acids. Biochemists often refer to each acid by a single letter abbreviation. G for glycine, S for serine, H for histidine, etc. In a protein chain of three hundred links the possible combinations are manifold. There might be a chain that contains links to ARSEHG . . . and another chain IGRAAG . . . and so forth. With a total protein chain of 300 amino acids and with twenty different kinds of acids the total possible combinations is given numerically as:

$20^{300} = 2^{300} \times 10^{300} = (2 \times 10^{90}) \times 10^{300} = 2 \times 10^{390}$
or approximately 10^{390}

Now, remembering from this last calculation, that we were looking for just one model protein, the result of the calculation means that there is only one chance in 10^{390} tries of finding our model protein. Just for a moment, however, pretend that there were 100, or 10^2 model proteins that we were looking for. In that instance we would have 10^2 chances out of 10^{390} tries to find our model. This would be the same $10^2/10^{390}$ = $1/10^{388}$, or one chance out of 10^{388} tries.

But we saw from the first calculation that observed life actually existed in 1.8×10^{12} different proteins. We may, therefore, consider them as the model proteins that we are looking for. Under those circumstances we would have 1.8×10^{12} chances out of 10^{390} tries to find any one of our known proteins of life. Mathematically that can be represented as:

$$(1.8 \times 10^{12})/10^{390} = 1.8/10^{378}$$

or, for all intents when considering such large numbers, $1/10^{378}$.

What this is saying is that there is only one chance in 10^{378} tries to have random processes which would generate a single life producing protein from the available pool of 1.8×10^{12} proteins. This compares with the calculations of Bradley and Thaxton referred to on page 58 where, with a model protein of 100 amino acids, they calculated that for a single protein there would be one chance in 10^{191} tries to get it by random selection.

When it is remembered that impossibility is defined as one chance in 10^{50} tries it is clear that the above numbers correspond to impossible situations. Actually the situation would be worse than that shown if a less simplified model were used.

Calculation of Random Creation
of a Blood Clotting Protein

This particular calculation is based upon data provided by Michael Behe in his book *Darwin's Black Box*.[11]

Animals with blood-clotting cascades have approximately 10,000 genes, and each is divided into an average of three pieces. There are thus 30,000 gene pieces. Tissue Plasminogen Activator (TPA), which is one of the special proteins needed in the clotting process, has four different types of domains. The odds of getting the four domains together as required for the necessary chemical action for clotting is given as one chance in:

$$30,000^4 = (3 \times 10^4)^4 = 3^4 \times 10^{16} = 81 \times 10^{16} = 8.1 \times 10^{17}$$

or approximately 10^{18} tries.

Now let us look at how much time it might take for us to go through these various combinations. Let us assume that the four TPA domains are somehow shuffled around so that they come together with the 30,000 gene parts in their random maneuvering, and that they make such a shuffle once each tenth of a second.

Under these conditions, the total time elapsed to shuffle through the total number of tries in order to get the proper arrangement would be:

$$\{(0.1 \text{ sec./try}) \times (10^{18} \text{ tries})\}/\{(8760 \text{ hours/year}) \times (3600 \text{ sec./hour})\} =$$
$$10^{17} / \{0.876 \times (3.6 \times 10^7)\} = 0.317 \times 10^{10} = 3.17 \times 10^9 \text{ years.}$$

In other words, under these conditions, it would take three billion years for the chance development of just one part of the blood clotting mechanism in animals. But the earth is only 4.6 billion years old, and the actual probabilities and time requirements would be much worse if the total blood coagulation process were considered.

Summary Concerning
Calculations of Chance Life Formation

These two simplified calculations show that when multiple permutations occur in a process the number of combinations rapidly reach enormous values. When applied to life processes, because of the many functions involved in these processes, they demonstrate the impossibly low probability that desired goals could have been reached by chance.

Life From Meteorites
or From the Cosmos

The Mars Meteorite

Meteorite ALH84001 is believed by scientists to have originated in the Martian crust which solidified about the same time that the earth's crust solidified, four and a half billion years ago. They theorize that an asteroid or a comet smashed into Mars about 15 million years ago, casting the meteorite into space, where it wandered for 13,000 years until it was captured by earth's gravity and landed on the Antarctic ice sheet. It was recovered with other meteorites by geologists in 1980.

Examination of this meteorite showed carbonate globules and peculiar cylindrical forms that showed some resemblance to microbial bacteria fossils from earth. It was also found that iron sulfate particles in the meteorite showed no uniformity of magnetic polarity as would have been the case if high temperatures had been reached when it entered the earth's atmosphere.

It was therefore concluded that any fossil replication on the falling meteorite would not have been destroyed by searing heat when it fell to earth.[12]

Some scientists are fairly sure that the carbonate structures in the meteorite are representative of fossil life forms found on earth. One NASA group of scientists in a *Scientific American* article wrote this:

> Close-up SEM [Scanning Electron Microscopy] views show that the carbonate globules contain ovoid and tube-shaped bodies. The objects are around 380 nanometers long, which means they could very well be the fossilized remains of bacteria.[13]

Other scientists aren't so sure. Dr. John W. Valley, one of the geochemists who helped with the analysis said: "Everything we see is consistent with biological activity, but I still wouldn't rule out low-temperature inorganic processes as an alternative explanation. We have not proven that this represents life on Mars. . . ."[12]

The question as to whether or not there was rudimentary life on Mars must await more Mars probes. Even if the life hypotheses proves to be true, the life forms would be of the elementary bacterial phyla found in the earliest earth records. The same probabilistic arguments against chance development of fossils on earth would be true for Martian fossils.

Life From the Cosmos

John Gribbin, an astrophysicist at the University of Cambridge in England, and now a full-time science writer, wrote the book, *In the Beginning—The Birth of the Living Universe*. His book postulates some fascinating theories about life and evolution on earth and in the universe. It is clear from reading his book that he is just as convinced that creation of the universe, the earth, and life on the earth happened by chance as I am that it did not.

Being a smart man, and recognizing the dilemma posed by the time requirements for probability to work its way through an evolutionary spawning of life, he suggested a creative way to overcome the time dilemma.

What if, he asked, the millions or billions of years required for chance development of life were accomplished in the cosmos instead of solely on earth?

Gribbin pointed out that in the 1960s and 1970s, by using microwave analysis of particular inorganic and organic compounds and comparing the resulting microwave signature of the chemicals with the microwave radiation from distant gas clouds in space, it became possible to determine the chemical makeup of these clouds. The resulting effort by scientists showed that ammonia (NH_3), water (H_2O), formaldehyde (H_2CO), formic acid ($HCOOH$), and methanimine (H_2CHN) had all been found in dense space clouds.

Since some of the chemicals found in the space clouds were carbon based, and since water was present, Gribbin postulated that, in the gravity-less environment of space, pools of water could have accumulated some of these chemicals in a prebiotic soup. Over the millions or billions of years of time, and with radiation from stars providing the necessary energy, at the very least amino acids would have developed. Gribbin put it this way:

> The notion that life had to start from scratch (which means from methane, ammonia, carbon dioxide and energy) in warm little ponds on the surface of the Earth is now completely outmoded, and those opponents of evolutionary ideas who still, even in this scientific age, argue that life has not had time to evolve on Earth are, along with those misguided scientists who try to defend the position, simply wasting their breath. It is scarcely necessary to go beyond the probable arrival of amino acids and similarly complex molecules in the prebiotic soup in our search for how life got started on Earth.[14]

Gribbin then postulated various ways that this soup with its life-facilitating chemicals might have gotten to earth where evolutionary forces on our planet would have finished the job. He even theorized that rudimentary life forms themselves could have been generated in space and then been deposited on earth, but he admitted that this was speculative.

Between 1977 and 1981, Hoyle and Wickramasinghe wrote a series of articles extending the work of Gribbin. Unfortunately the authors kept changing their minds about the chemicals they found in the dust clouds. This was undoubtedly due to the inaccuracy of their method of using infrared radiation light coming from the clouds. In any event, the entire subject has since fallen into some disrepute.[15]

A variation on the idea of life originating in space was reported by Bernstein, Sandford and Allamandola of Ames Research Center (a part of NASA) in a 1999 Scientific American article.[16] They point out that water, methanol and hydrocarbon ice often found in interstellar dust clouds reacts with silicate particles when ultraviolet radiation from stars strikes them.

Broken molecules from the reaction recombine into more complex hydrocarbon structures such as alcohols, ethers and quinones. The authors demonstrated similar reactions in an experimental cloud chamber in which ice particles were exposed to infrared and ultraviolet radiation. The resultant complex molecules are typical of what is found in many meteorites or in meteorite dust (captured in space vehicles). Quinones, the authors observed, are found ubiquitously in living systems.

From these experiments and observations, the authors speculate that early life on earth may have been given a head start by meteorites and meteorite dust rich in such complex hydrocarbon molecules raining down on the infant earth. They end their article, however, with this cautionary note:

> Of course, a huge gap still yawns between even the most complex organic compounds and the genetic code, metabolism and self-replication that are crucial to the definition of life.[17]

The Probability of Life Originating in Space

It is difficult for me to comment objectively on these ideas concerning life, or the beginnings of life, evolving in space and being transplanted to earth. This represents, to me, another example of scientists frantically trying to describe some otherwise unexplained phenomenon without recognizing the obvious fingerprints of God.

Ignoring all of the problems associated with getting the life-forms or chemicals through space and dropping them unaffected through the earth's atmosphere to a gentle landing on earth, one is still beset by the same probabilistic problems as discussed above and in Chapter 5. Even with the existence of amino acids, the improbability of creating multiple proteins from them becomes astronomical. It is really irrelevant as to where life developed in the universe, there is insufficient time for random evolutionary forces to have completed the task.

It should not be concluded from this discussion that I am arguing against the possibility of life existing elsewhere in the universe. On the contrary, logic and my religious convictions convince me that life exists on countless other planets. But it is life created by God not by happenstance!

Life From the Bottom of the Sea or Deep in the Earth

In his book, *The Fifth Miracle—the Search for the Origin and Meaning of Life*, Paul Davies postulates that life might have originated by a chance combination of the appropriate chemicals spewing from ancient volcanic vents on the sea bottom.[18] He points out that microorganisms have been found under a variety of previously supposed impossible life conditions in the sea and in the rocks beneath the sea. Core samples taken from the Mediterranean Sea and the Atlantic and Pacific Oceans have shown microbial colonies in the seabed to a depth of 750 meters.[19] Other microbes called hyperthermophiles have been found in temperatures around 100-150 degrees Celsius, the temperature range often found near volcanic vents.[20]

In certain locations under the sea, pockets remain where conditions resemble those of very long ago where volcanic vents disgorge a bounty of sulfur, energy and other chemicals. In these locations one still finds organisms retaining a primeval lifestyle. A black smoker, as the vents are called, may be a forbidding spot for most life, but for an organism like Pyrodyctium occultum it is a veritable paradise.[21]

Using this information about bacteria that survive in environments harsh to most forms of life, but rich in chemicals and in thermal energy provided by volcanic activity, Davies says this about how life might have started:

> Though we can't pinpoint where life ultimately began, it seems increasingly likely that, after the bombardment abated [from comets and meteorites striking the earth], life was confined to locations on or beneath the seabed, either near volcanic vents, or inside off-ridge hydrothermal systems. Once life had established itself securely in such a place, the way then lay open for proliferation and diversification.[22]

The problem I have with Davies' hypothesis is that it suffers from the same fatal defect that afflicts the argument about how life started in a pre-biotic soup on the surface of the earth. While it is true that life deep in the sea and feeding on chemicals and energy from volcanic action avoids the need for free oxygen and sunlight, and such life is protected from cataclysmic meteor collisions, still, the atoms and molecules in the chemical stew must somehow be arranged in precisely coded complex forms that constitute life replicating cells.

As shown in Chapter 5, and in the beginning of this appendix, the probability of even the simplest bacterium forming by chance is prohibitively small. Moreover, the time necessary for such formations exceeds even the life of the universe, never mind the much smaller time available on the earth.

Davies admits that his postulate of the chance formation of life under such conditions is purely speculative. Elsewhere in his book he concedes to the improbability of the chance formation of RNA,[23] and he concludes his book by acknowledging that we are left with a mystery which he describes in this way:

> . . . The real problem of biogenesis is clear. Since the heady successes of molecular biology, most investigators have sought the secret of life in the physics and chemistry of molecules. But they will look in vain for conventional physics and chemistry to explain life, for that is a classic case of confusing the medium with the message. The secret of life lies, not in its chemical basis, but in the logical and informational rules it exploits. Life succeeds precisely because it *evades* chemical imperatives.[24]

The failure of conventional physics and chemistry to explain life leads to the mystery of how to explain the fantastic life code locked in the DNA and RNA of each of our cells. Where did that code come from, how was it devised or who devised it? The mystery becomes less mysterious if the other evidences for the fingerprints of God given in this book are considered.

Darwinian Evolution

The biologist Ernest Mayr from Harvard University wrote this about Darwinian evolution:

> Darwinian natural selection is today almost universally accepted by biologists as the mechanism responsible for evolutionary change. It is best visualized as a two-step process: variation and selection proper.
> ... Now there are hundreds, if not thousands, of well-established proofs, including such well-known instances as insecticide resistance of agricultural pest, antibiotic resistance of bacteria, industrial melanism, the attenuation of the myxomatosis virus in Australia, the sickle-cell gene and other blood genes and malaria, to mention only a few spectacular cases.[25]

When Darwin originally proposed his theory, he envisaged it as a gradual process, one that occurred over millennia and hundreds of thousands of generations. Over these generations, the fittest species would survive and the others would die out. One of the major problems with this concept, recognized by Darwin, was that the fossil record did not support it. Professor Mayr had this to say about the biologist's dilemma:

> Most students of macro-evolution were still thinking in terms of transformational evolution, that is, a gradual change of evolutionary lineages toward ever greater specialization or adaptedness. However, they were confronted by Darwin's dilemma that the fossil record did not at all support this concept. On the contrary, long, continued gradual changes of phyletic lineages were rare, if they existed at all. Instead, new species and higher types invariably turned up in the fossil record very suddenly, and most lineages became extinct sooner or later.[26]

Mayr went on to point out that the geneticists, de Vries and Goldschmidt, postulated the sudden evolution by macromutations of what they called "hopeful monsters." To get around the problems of hopeful monsters, Mayr, in 1954, proposed a solution:

That the genetic restructuring takes place during a speciational process in founder populations and that some of the gaps in the fossil record are due to the fact that speciating founder populations, very much restricted in space and time, are most unlikely ever to be found in the fossil record.[27]

Other biologists accepted Mayr's proposal, and in 1972 Eldredge and Gould gave the term "punctuated equilibria" to this kind of speciational evolution. In other words, Mayr's proposed solution to the lack of evidence for the gradual speciation suggested by Darwin's theory was to suggest that species, in fact, developed more rapidly than Darwin had suspected. The lack of evidence for punctuated equilibria evolution was because such fossils are unlikely to be found. Indeed!

In any event most biologists accepted some version of punctuated equilibria. And it is clear that "survival of the fittest" evolutionary forces can explain much of what we see in nature. Anyone who has taken an antibiotic is aware that bacteria are becoming ever more adaptive to medicines that at one time quickly eradicated them.

In the late 1960s approximately sixty thousand fossilized specimens were found in little used cabinets in the Smithsonian Institution. The fossils, which dated into the Cambrian period (about 530 million years ago), had been there since 1909; placed there by Charles Doolittle Walcott who was at that time the director of the Smithsonian.[28]

Walcott had discovered and extracted the fossils from the Burgess Pass area of British Columbia. Although now a part of the Canadian Rockies, anciently it was part of a continental shelf in a tropical sea. Life teemed in the shallows of this sea, and fine sand and mud washing from the adjacent shore trapped many life forms in the accumulating mud. Over the millennia the mud solidified into shale. When continental drift created the Rockies it lifted this shale to an exposed location to be found by Walcott millions of years later. After recovering the fossils and shipping them to the Smithsonian he filed them away to await rediscovery about 50 years later.

The Burgess fossils were rediscovered by three paleontologists Harry Whittington of the University of Cambridge and his two students, Derek Briggs and Simon Conway Morris who embarked on a methodical re-examination of the Burgess fossils.[29] Their detailed studies caused a furor in the scientific community. The reason is that the half-

billion-year old specimens demonstrated features that were not supposed to exist in fossils that old. They included phyla (body plans)
which illustrated eyes, gills, jointed limbs and intestines, sponges and
worms and insects and fish, and they had all appeared simultaneously.
There was none of the gradual evolution of simple phyla such as
sponges into the more complex phyla of worms and then on to the more
complex forms such as insects over millennia of time. Instead, they all
dated to the same early time period.

Gerald Schroeder, in his book The Science of God, wrote this about
Walcott's fossils:

> Rediscovery of Walcott's fossils in the mid-1980s changed the con-
> cept of evolution. Their effect has been so dramatic that the most wide-
> ly read science journal in the world, Scientific American, in its 1992
> issue was moved to question: "Has the mechanism of evolution
> altered?" The same reaction to these fossils appeared in the October
> 1993 issue of National Geographic magazine. The science section of
> the New York Times referred to the fossils as demonstrating "revolu-
> tion more than evolution." and Time magazine featured them in a com-
> prehensive and scientifically accurate cover story titled "Evolution's
> Big Bang."[30]

Schroeder hastened to add that the Burgess fossils did not bring into
question the development of classes of life. Individual phylum or body
plans first appeared as simple aquatic forms and became more complex
with the passage of time. What the new finds did illustrate was that the
previously supposed gradual evolution of new phylum from existing
evolutionary streams was false. The Burgess finds, in conjunction with
other discoveries, indicate that essentially all animal phyla appeared
almost simultaneously 530 million years ago. All further development
was confined to variations within each phylum.[31] Amphibians, insects,
reptiles and mammals later descended from these ancestral phyla. How
and why they appeared as they did is a mystery. Classical natural selection evolutionary theory cannot explain them.

So we are again faced with the question, how did these multitudinous life forms suddenly appear on the scene? If classical natural selection evolutionary theory cannot explain them, what can? What are the
probabilities of all of these life forms suddenly developing by chance?
Is this another of the fingerprints of God?

Appendix D

Cosmic Structure

Why This Subject?[1]

This subject is added for completeness. Much of what science believes about the creation is dependent upon the structure of matter and how matter and energy interact. Although not essential for understanding the basic premise of this book many readers will find it useful to, at least, scan this material in order to have a fuller understanding of why scientists believe as they do.

The Nature of Matter as Defined by Modern Physics.

Physicists have long known that all matter consists of atoms, which in turn consists of neutrons (with no charge), protons (with a positive charge) and electrons (with a negative charge). In stable atoms the neutrons and protons, which constitute the nucleus of an atom, are held together by the strong nuclear force and are difficult to separate. The nearly massless electrons vibrate around the nucleus to which they are held by the electromagnetic force.

With the advent of high energy particle accelerators (atom smashers) it became possible to break the strong nuclear force by accelerating nuclear particles to high energies and forcing them to collide with target atoms. The resulting collision broke the target atoms apart and allowed physicists to study the particles emanating from the parent atom.

In 1960 at Caltech, the physicist Murray Gell-Mann theorized that neutrons and protons are each composed of three particles which he called *quarks*. He theorized the existence of these quarks and other quarks, for a total of six types, as a result of certain symmetries of nature predicted by advanced mathematics. Initially Gell-Mann's theory was viewed with skepticism, but as particle accelerators got more energetic (and more expensive) Leon Lederman and others were able to show that quarks did indeed exist.[2] Protons and neutrons turned out to be made of what was called up and down quarks, with the proton consisting of two up quarks and one down quark, and the neutron consisting of two down and one up quark.

In 1995 the last of the six types of quarks that Gell-Mann's theory predicted to exist was found in an experiment at the Fermilab collider in Illinois.[3]

Quarks reside at different quantum energy levels and can become excited to higher energy levels by eating energy. Quarks are held together by the strong nuclear force, and they belong to the family of hadrons (meaning "bulky" particles). Actually, quarks are held together by what are called gluons, a form of "messenger" particles (gauge bosons) which carry messages regarding the forces of one particle on another.[4] There are also messengers, or gauge bosons, for the weak and electromagnetic forces. The gauge boson for the electromagnetic force is the photon. The weak nuclear force is responsible for causing certain unstable nuclear particles to decay.

The lepton family includes the lighter particles such as muons, electrons, taus, and neutrinos. All particles that are built of quarks belong to one of two families: *mesons* consist of a single quark and a single antiquark; *baryons,* such as protons and neutrons, consist of three quarks.[5]

The special and general theories of relativity—produced by the Swiss patent office clerk Albert Einstein in 1905 and in 1915—treated light as a particle, and as such it would be subject to the influence of gravity. This was later proved to be true by observing the bending of light rays from distant stars as they passed a massive body.[6]

Contemporary with Einstein were other giants of physics including Max Planck who originally proposed that light, X-rays and other waves could only be emitted in packets called quanta, and Werner Heisenberg who formulated the famous uncertainty principle.[7] The combination of Planck's quantum hypothesis and Heisenberg's uncertainty principle led to the conclusion that the more accurately you try to measure the position of a particle, the less accurately you can measure its speed, and vice versa. Heisenberg showed that the uncertainty in the position of the particle times the uncertainty in its velocity times the mass of the particle can never be smaller than a certain quantity, known as the Planck constant.[8]

Niels Bohr generated the mathematics which allowed the development of quantum mechanics.[9] Paul Dirac, in the 1920s, worked out the mathematics for an electron that incorporated both quantum mechanics and special relativity.[10] In recent years Richard Feynman developed a set of computations which simplify the mathematics of quantum mechanics. In the Feynman method of explaining and computing quantum mechanics reactions he schematically showed how, at the subatomic level, the electromagnetic forces between two charged particles can be understood as the exchange or transfer of photons. As two charged electrons approach each other, for example, a photon is discharged from one of the electrons to the other and they scatter apart as a consequence.[11]

From Einstein's model light could be thought of, and predictive computations made, as if it were a particle. From quantum mechanics light could be thought of, and predictive computations made, as if it were a wave. Both situations are true, but under different circumstances. Indeed, quantum theory makes the definition of matter somewhat schizophrenic. Matter behaves like something that has properties that depend in part on the indivisible quantum links with its surroundings. The question of whether a given object, such as an electron, acts more like a wave or more like a particle is therefore not determined entirely by the electron itself but depends partly on the environment of the electron.[12]

Another theory which has recently come into fashion, and which seeks to explain how various fundamental particles interrelate, is known as superstring theory. This theory was invented as a result of computations involving the symmetry of particles and the quantum theory mathematics of particle spin. In the new theory particles are nothing more than infinitesimally small pieces of space vibrating with different frequencies. These strings of space particles interact in various ways forming loops and crosses. The resulting attributes give rise to the characteristics of all known particles (and many currently unknown).

In 1974 John Schwarz of Caltech and Joel Scherk of the Ecole Normale Supéieure in Paris completed some calculations that showed that string theory might be the way to a fully unified account of all particles and forces including a term which linked gravity inextricably to the theory.[13] This was the first hint that a method might be found which included gravity as a part of quantum theory. Edward Witten of the Institute for Advanced Study at Princeton, when he heard of their work, said: "this was the greatest intellectual thrill of my life."[14]

In 1984, at the Aspen Physics Institute in Colorado, Schwarz and Michael Green further advanced the mathematics of strings by using some calculations known as supersymmetry which eliminated many anomalies that had plagued superstring theory to that point. Their work was sufficiently compelling that Witten joined them in their work and they wrote a book, in 1987, entitled *Superstring Theory,* which attracted many other researchers to the work.[15]

Superstring theory comes mainly in two varieties, one with twenty-six dimensions, and one with ten dimensions. The mathematics is very complex, and most scientists work on the ten dimensional variety since its mathematics is simpler. One of the complexities of the theory is that it predicts literally hundreds of particles, most of which have not yet been discovered—and probably will not be for years since the energies required to experimentally find them are enormous. The energies required exceed the capabilities of presently existing particle accelerators. One of the strongest objections to the theory is that we will never be able to demonstrate experimentally whether or not it is true. It is hypothesized that many of the predicted particles are indicative of the universe in its first few microseconds of life, while the energy levels were extremely high—before most of the energy froze into mass of the type we know today. If this is true, then string theory gives us a glimpse of how the universe evolved from the big bang. This is, of course, if the theory of the origin of the universe, as is now widely accepted, originated in a singularity which was followed by the big bang.

One of the major efforts of researchers is to explain how the supposedly ten dimensions (or twenty-six) that superstring theory suggests the universe started out as were compressed down to the four that we now know. Although the mathematics suggests a large number of initial dimensions, it is difficult to describe any physical processes which would reduce them to our present three spatial dimensions and one time dimension. A number of theories have been proposed, but definitive work has yet to be agreed upon in the physics community.

Black Holes

Using Einstein's model for light it is possible to postulate a black hole. As stars burn their fuel—the fusing of hydrogen and later helium—the fuel becomes depleted, over the millennia, and the stars burn less energetically and the temperature drops. As the temperature drops gravity begins to take over and the stars shrink in size. Under certain conditions the star-furnace sputters and gravity causes the remaining mass to collapse on itself in a giant implosion. During the collapse of what was a star, the density of the remaining mass gets ever greater as if it were being squeezed by a giant vise. Depending upon the initial mass of the star the density may become sufficiently great that the speed of light is less than the escape velocity of light from the remaining mass, which by this time would have been squeezed from the size of a sun to essentially a mere point. Under these conditions light could not escape and a black hole would have been created.

These initial ideas on a black hole grew out of the work of many physicists, starting with the work of the Swiss-American astronomer Fritz Zwicky at Caltech in the 1930s and 1943 as he first identified supernovae—exploding stars—and then neutron stars. The hypothetical neutron stars were massive spheres of just neutrons pressed in upon themselves by enormous gravity.[16] Lev Davidovich Landau working in Moscow (between arrests) in 1937 smuggled a paper out of Russia which gave credence to the neutron star theory and started Robert Oppenheimer at the University of California in Berkeley working on it. Oppenheimer showed that stars which began with a mass between 1.5 and 3.0 times the mass of our sun could, as their fuel burned up, collapse and become neutron stars, with a radius of a few miles.[17] In 1956 John Archibald Wheeler of Princeton began work on neutron stars which led ultimately to mathematical proof that for stars that started with a mass much larger than that required for a neutron star, gravity collapse would result in a black hole, a term coined by Wheeler.[18]

Initially it was thought that nothing could escape from a black hole, including light, so it could never be detected, it could only be theorized. In the 1970s Hawking and other scientists showed, through calculations based on the second law of thermodynamics (the so called "heat-death" law), that black holes, in fact, are not totally black.[19] They emit certain forms of radiation such as gamma rays. Unfortunately those emissions are not strong enough to be detected for distant black holes. Black holes might be deduced by observing otherwise unexplained gravitational effects on distant stars, but this was also very speculative.

After Hawking's original computations on the leakiness of black holes, in a brilliant expansion of that idea, he demonstrated that, given enough time, through the loss of radiation the mass of black holes would also gradually decrease. If no further mass were fed into the hole, eventually, the mass would be insufficient to keep space-time wrapped around itself and the hole would explode in a puff of X-rays.[20]

In 1975 Hawking identified a star, Cygnus X-1, which because of its rotational effects seemed to show that it was rotating around a massive object which couldn't be seen.[21] It was also emitting large amounts of X-rays. Both of these phenomena suggested a black hole. Hawking made a bet with Kip Thorne of the California Institute of Technology whether or not it was a black hole. At that time Hawking asserts they were about 75% sure it was a black hole. By the time his book *A Brief History of Time* was written Hawking said that they were about 95% sure it was a black hole.

Black holes, then, which started as a theory are well accepted today in the scientific community, and they appear to be gathering experimental evidence of their existence.

Multiple Universes

To rebut the argument that our universe is so uniquely arranged for life that God must have had a hand in it, the multiple universe theory was developed by physicists. According to this point of view there are an infinite number of universes of which ours is but one. Each of these universes is unique in its own way, having characteristics different from ours. Since there are an infinite number of universes, although most of them would not sustain life a few would, ours being one. Thus, what we see in the way of life in our universe is not the result of design by God, but is merely the result of happenstance. An infinity of universes would, by definition, include one with the characteristics that ours has. Although what we see and know in our universe seems highly selective and unusual, if we could see all of the universes we would recognize that ours is not that unusual, given the many different ones that exist.[22]

A variation on this theme was produced by physicist Hugh Everett in 1957 as a result of his work in quantum physics.[23] He theorized that whenever a quantum transition takes place in the universe, another universe is formed. When uncertainty is involved, for example, and a measurement is performed to determine, say, whether a cat is alive or dead, the universe divides in two, one holding a live cat and the other a dead cat. This occurs throughout the universe countless times each second. Thus there are numerous universes with copies of each of us living in it, each copy of us assuming that he or she is unique.

Another variation came out of Andrei Linde's recent work on quantum genesis. Linde described a process called "chaotic inflation" which suggests that our universe began as a bubble that ballooned out of the space-time of a pre-existing universe.[24]

John Leslie, in his book *Universes* agrees in part with Linde that multiple universes may have come out of "chaotic inflation." He comments:

> Developments in physics and astronomy will strengthen the idea that Reality is split up into very many, very varied parts which might reasonably be called "universes." They will quite probably confirm that Inflation occurred, producing a gigantic Universe; and further, that symmetry breakings could very well have taken place in largely random ways, dividing that Universe into huge domains—domains very different in their force strengths and particle masses. . . . They will very probably confirm the plausibility of at least one of the mechanisms for creating multiple universes [discussed previously].[25]

Since all we can see and make measurements of is our own universe, the multiple universe theory must remain just that, a theory. There may, indeed, be more than one universe, but it can never be proved one way or another. More to the point, it is just as logical to argue that God created other universes which have purpose, order and design—just as ours does—as it is to argue that an infinity of universes were created by happenstance with no input from any creative agency.

Worm Holes

Worm hole theory was built upon the back of black holes and multiple universes. In effect it was speculation built upon speculation. The theory started, almost, as a science fiction writer's dream of connecting two black holes together from different universes (or different space-time bubbles in the same universe). By means of this imagined connection space travelers could travel almost instantly from one universe to another.

In the mid-1980s Thorne proposed that it might be possible to hold worm holes open in such a way as to make them accommodating to travelers.[26] He postulated the existence of "exotic" material that would, his calculations showed, in the worm hole's frame of reference have negative energy which would keep the worm hole dilated.

In early 1988 Thorne further speculated, as the result of a phone call from Carl Sagan, that an advanced civilization might create worm holes through which travelers could travel through both space and time.[27] Working with his student, Mike Morris, and Tom Roman, an assistant professor at Connecticut State University, the trio postulated a worm hole in which people could "travel over interstellar distances far faster than light"[28] This type of thinking leads to a paradox illustrated by Timothy Ferris in this little story:

> A space man could thus enter a worm hole in his living room and return earlier than he had departed. In the process the traveler would have created a copy of himself. In this type of speculation, the copy of the traveler could stop the initial version of the traveler from entering the worm hole, in which case the version of the traveler that stopped the other version would not have shown up to intervene—in which case he would.[29]

Thorne recognized this type of paradox, and he put it this way: "If I have a time machine (worm hole-based or otherwise), I should be able to use it to go back in time and kill my mother before I was conceived, thereby preventing myself from being born and killing my mother."[30]

Despite these paradoxes, Thorne and others (including Stephen Hawking) kept working on the mathematics of worm holes and time machines. The result of that effort may be summarized by a quotation from Hawking:

> Whenever one tries to make a time machine, and no matter what kind of device one uses in one's attempt (a wormhole, a spinning cylinder, a "cosmic ring," or whatever), just before one's device becomes a time machine, a beam of vacuum fluctuations will circulate through the device and destroy it.[31]

In time, Thorne came to agree with Hawking.[32] Most other scientists also reject such versions of time travel. Hawking jokes that evidence of the improbability of time travel is demonstrated by "the fact that we have not been invaded by hordes of tourists from the future."[33]

Universe Expansion, Anti-Gravity and Dark Matter

A Russian scientist, Alexander Friedmann, in 1920, set about explaining Einstein's prediction of a non-static universe. He showed, in a brilliant bit of theoretical work, that the universe looked essentially the same in all directions (far enough away) as to be nearly homogeneous, and that it was expanding and would continue expanding, or it would collapse on itself according to the total mass of the universe.[34]

In 1929 Edwin Hubble established the *Hubble Law* which states that the farther away a star or galaxy is the greater will be the red shift displayed in its spectrum.[35] He also developed the *Hubble Constant* which established the rate of expansion of the universe. Later, the Hubble Constant was combined with the *deceleration parameter* which measures the rate at which cosmic expansion slows down. Combination of these two quantities yields the factor omega (Ω). If omega is less than one the universe is destined to expand forever. If it is more than one it is destined to collapse. If omega is exactly one, the universe is at critical density and will expand forever, at a rate that approaches but never quite reaches zero.[36] Also, if the universe has an omega of one it is said to be *flat;* if it has an omega greater than one, it is very dense, and it is said to be *closed,* and it is analogous to a sphere; if it has an omega less than one it is *open* and will expand forever.

Hubble's findings led to the desire to measure the rate of expansion of the universe and attempt to determine omega. This proved to be very difficult, among other reasons, because it required a reasonably accurate account of the total mass in the universe. Cosmologists, therefore, took upon themselves the formidable task of estimating the total mass of the universe.[37] This they did by adding up the masses of all the stars we can see in our galaxy and other galaxies. Simultaneous with this work, other scientists were measuring the rate of expansion by the red shift and brightness of stars. Still others were measuring gravitational effects that stars had on each other by observing their orbits in the galaxies. The gravitational effects turned out to be greater than expected from the calculated masses of the observed stars, and the total estimated mass of the visible universe turned out to be much less than required to agree with the estimated value of omega. As the result of such observations, and similar ones concerning galaxies themselves, it was concluded that there must be a large amount of matter in the universe that cannot be observed directly. Calculations showed that the visible universe contained only about ten percent of that required to reach an omega approaching the critical value of unity—estimated at that time to be the case by many physicists.[38]

In 1933, Zwicky discovered that the outlying galaxies in the Coma cluster were moving much faster than they would be if its mass were limited to that of the visible galaxies in it. From these gravitational effects Zwicky calculated that Coma would need ten times the matter than that which was observed. To account for this anomaly he coined the term *dark matter*.[39] In the late 1950s Vera Rubin decided to study the rotational and gravity effects of large spiral galaxies. Working with colleagues at Carnegie Institution she found that stars near the outer disks of galaxies were traveling faster than the gravitational effects of the visible mass would allow.[40] The only way to account for this faster than expected rotation was if unseen mass were included in the galaxy. Many other similar findings followed Zwicky's and Rubin's initial work, and physicists then estimated that the universe must be 90 percent dark matter.[41]

Recent work by two teams of astronomers working separately at the Lawrence Berkeley Laboratory in California and at the Harvard- Smithsonian Center for Astrophysics in Cambridge, Mass. concluded that dark matter may be much less than 90 percent. They made this determination from observations of a certain class of distant exploding stars, or supernovas, which showed that galaxies about halfway back in cosmic time were receding at velocities comparable to, or slower than, objects of more recent epochs. This led to the conclusion that the universe is not slowing its expansion as would be the case if it contained enough mass to have an omega of one or greater. Based on these findings, some estimates placed the mass of the universe as only 20 to 30 percent of the amount required for an omega of one. Saul Perlmutter of the Berkeley Laboratory said, "Apparently there isn't enough mass in the universe for its gravity to slow the expansion, which started with the Big Bang, to a halt." These results also meant that the universe, instead of being about eight billion years old, might be as old as fifteen billion years. The findings were reported in a January, 1998 meeting of the American Astronomical Society.[42] The findings even led to the speculation that some type of a cosmological constant, such as that which Einstein originally proposed and later rejected, was acting on the universe to create a negative gravity and thus speed up expansion.

In an attempt to improve on the earlier findings of the COBE satellite concerning microwave background radiation from the remnants of the big bang, in 1996 the QMAP team of de Oliveira-Costa, Tegmark and five colleagues from the Institute for Advanced Study at Princeton flew instruments on a balloon 100,000 feet above Texas and New Mexico. Their measurements were more precise than previous measurements, and they confirmed the idea of a flat universe (omega=1). Combined with other observations, including those of distant supernova, the QMAP results corroborated the prevailing theory of inflation— with the twist that the universe was only one third matter (both ordinary and dark) and two thirds quintessence, a bizarre form of energy, possible inherent in empty space.[43]

These recent findings from various astronomical effects and from observation of supernovae (exploding stars) have convinced cosmologists that the universe is actually accelerating in its expansion with time.[44]

To account for the apparent flatness of the universe with its accelerating expansion—and inadequate matter to account for a flat universe— the anti-gravity theory once proposed by Einstein has been reinstated as a possible answer. Einstein called his anti-gravity effect the "Cosmological Constant." The more recent term is "Quintessence" which is similar to the cosmological constant except that it varies with time.

Like many of the finely tuned constants of nature discussed in the last chapter, the cosmological constant (or quintessence) has a unique value which is very puzzling to cosmologists. In the January 1999 issue of *Scientific American*, Lawrence M. Krauss said:

> . . . Weinberg and others have arrived at a result that is compatible with the apparent magnitude of the cosmological constant today.
>
> Most theorists, however, do not find these notions convincing, as they imply that there is no reason for the constant to take on a particular value: *it just does*.[45] (Italics, mine.)

It just does, indeed. Could it be that this is one of the fingerprints of God?

The next question after determining that the universe contained dark matter was, what is dark matter made of? The only dark matter of significance that physicists had confidence in were black holes and neutron stars, but these did not seem sufficient to add up to the amount needed. Postulated candidates included baryonic matter (neutrons and protons) and massive cold gas clouds. In addition, physicists speculated that non-baryonic matter such as leptons might be dark matter.[46] The problem with leptons (such as electrons and neutrinos) is that they were supposed to have little or no mass. Electrons were known to have little mass, but recent measurements have shown that even the ghostly neutrinos probably do have some mass.

To further define what constitutes dark matter physicists have speculated that there may be hot dark matter and cold dark matter. The hot matter are particles that at the time of the big bang were moving at velocities close to the speed of light, and the cold matter are particles which were moving more slowly. The leading hot dark matter candidate is the neutrino. One group of physicists has proposed that the universe might contain a mixture of 30 percent hot and 70 percent cold dark matter.[47] These estimates and theories about the types and mixtures of dark matter will undoubtedly change as the result of the new astronomical findings concerning the rate of expansion of the universe.

One interesting method of searching for the missing matter in the universe are the High Energy Astronomical Observatories (HEAO) which are a set of satellites scanning the universe for particles and radiation that we cannot detect down here on earth. Satellites of this sort have detected intense emission of X-rays from clusters of galaxies, from intergalactic spaces where there was hitherto no hint of any matter.[48]

To put the subject of dark matter in perspective, a quote from Longair is useful:

> . . . Most of the matter in the universe is probably in form of dark matter and thus this matter is likely to have a profound impact upon the formation of galaxies.
>
> . . . I would caution, [however], that the whole story must be regarded as provisional because the basic physics is far from secure.[49]

Spacetime and Speed of Travel

Let us consider the physicists' understanding of space-time and speed of travel. According to relativity, nothing can exceed the speed of light. Imagine, for example, a spaceship traveling ever faster. As it approaches the speed of light its mass increases and its length, measured along the axis of its direction of travel, shrinks. The passage of time on board slows. The amount of energy required increases enormously, approaching infinity as it gets nearer to the speed of light. Meanwhile the mass of the ship approaches infinity, its length shrinks to zero, and time on board comes to a stop.[50] For a space-man leaving the earth, as the traveler approaches the speed of light, time passes slower than for those remaining on earth.

Einstein demonstrated that time is, in fact, elastic and can be stretched and shrunk by motion. Each observer carries around his own personal scale of time, and it does not generally agree with anybody else's. In our own frame, time never appears distorted, but relative to another observer who is moving differently, our time can be wrenched out of step with his time.[51]

Equally extraordinary effects afflict space, which is also elastic. When time is stretched, space is shrunk. The mutual distortions of space and time can be regarded as a conversion of space—which shrinks—into time— which stretches, and vice versa.[52]

Just as time scales change from place to place in a gravitational field, so do the length scales. Rulers change lengths as you move around. It is impossible with space and time so intimately mixed to have something happen with time that isn't in some way reflected in space.[53]

The above discussion should be sufficient to demonstrate that as very high speeds are realized (approaching the speed of light) time does not behave in the same manner as we usually think of it behaving. It is stretchable, depending upon where it is observed, as is space.

One could argue, therefore, that some future traveler to a distant location in space could do so with very little time as observed by himself. There are two difficulties with this argument. The first is that when the traveler returned to earth, everyone with whom he came in contact would be very much older. The second difficulty has to do with the distance traveled. The nearest star to us, Proxima Centauri, is about four light-years away. To an observer on earth, therefore, the astronaut traveler must have taken a minimum of four years to travel to the closest star. Many stars, of course, are thousands, or millions of light years distant.

There are at least two peculiar circumstances where science recognizes velocities in excess of the speed of light. One circumstance has to do with the space of the universe which has been expanding since the big bang. In static space it is true that nothing can exceed the speed of light. In the cosmological model that many physicists accept—a vast inflationary universe of critical (omega=1) density—the universe began its expansion with a velocity much greater than that of light.[54] The recent astronomical findings concerning the expansion of the universe may change this model, but the possibility of a velocity greater than light is, at least in some models, an acceptable theory.

A second peculiar situation derives from some of the characteristics of quantum theory and the uncertainty principle. It can be illustrated by a hypothetical experiment in which one particle decays into two particles. Of the remaining two particles, one has a spin of +1 and the other has a spin of -1. Let us remove one particle far away, say two light-years. A physicist measures the spin of the particle near him and finds that it is -1 and he knows, therefore, that the distant particle has a spin of +1. If, somehow the near particle has its spin reversed to +1, then the distant particle *instantly* has a spin of -1. For that to occur logic would demand that some sort of signal be exchanged, traveling with *instant* speed from the distant point to the near point, so that the far particle *knows* that it must reverse its spin. It is one of the paradoxes of science.[55] Einstein called it "spooky action at a distance."

A striking example of the experimental verification of this remote spooky action was reported in the 11 December 1997 issue of *Nature*. It occurred when scientists working separately in Austria and Italy had similar results. Their experiments were called *quantum teleportation*. Teleportation is a way of transferring the state of one particle to a second using "entanglement"—a mysterious connection between objects separated by arbitrary distances. The Austrian group succeeded in teleporting photons of light.[56] The Italian group teleported the photons' polarization states.[57]

The state of an object—atom, electron, photon, etc.—is defined by both its quantum characteristics and its classical characteristics. In order to replicate the object both sets of characteristics are needed. The problem in the past, concerning determining the quantum characteristics, was that the measurement itself, by the uncertainty principle, changed the characteristics of the particle.

In the Austrian laboratory, bits of light in one place were destroyed and duplicated in a perfect replica some distance away. This was done by using "entangled" photons with one photon at the point of origin and the other entangled photon at a distance. A "message" photon was used to transfer information about a crucial physical characteristic of the original light bits or photons. The necessary quantum information was picked up instantly by other, distant entangled photons. The classical information required to complete the necessary data for duplication was transferred by a classical channel at the speed of light. Thus, the distant light photons took upon themselves the identical characteristics of the original photons and they became perfect replicas.

These are the first clearly demonstrated experiments which show the distant spooky action predicted by quantum mechanics. A possible practical application will be in future generations of even faster computers.

Despite these strange instances of something exceeding the speed of light, scientists still insist that in general nothing can travel faster than the speed of light. To do so would violate the principles of relativity. In the above experiments the distant replica cannot be created faster than the speed of light since the required classical information travels at that speed, even though quantum information is communicated instantly. Scientists are still at a loss to explain how entanglement works. Nevertheless they do accept that in some magic way quantum information is being transmitted instantly over arbitrary, and in theory enormous, distances—clearly in excess of the speed of light. In wrestling with the quantum theory paradoxes, Ferris postulated that if some of the physicists' theories are true, then:

> We live in a universe that presents two complementary aspects. One obeys locality and is large, old, expanding, and in some sense mechanical. The other is non-local, is built on forms of space and time unfamiliar to us and is everywhere interconnected. We peer through the keyhole of quantum weirdness and see a little of this ancient, original side of the cosmos.[58]

Endnotes

Introduction—From Skeptic to Believer

1. Du Noüy, Lecomte, *Human Destiny*. New York, London, Toronto: Longmans, Green and Co., 1947.
2. Du Noüy, *op. cit.,* pp. 33-34.
3. Du Noüy, *op. cit.,* p. 34.
4. Du Noüy, *op. cit.,* p. 202.
5. Moody, Raymond A., Jr., *Life After Life*. New York, N.Y.: Bantam Books, 1988.
6. Ritchie, George G. with Sherrill, Elizabeth, *Return from Tomorrow*. Old Tappan, New Jersey: Spire Books, Fleming H. Revell Co., 1978.
7. Ring, Kenneth, *Life at Death. A scientific investigation of the near-death experience*. New York, N.Y.: Coward, McCann and Geoghegan, 1980.
8. Ring, Kenneth, *Heading Toward Omega*. New York, N.Y.: William Morrow, Inc., 1984-1985.
9. Carter, Brandon, "Large Number Coincidences and the Anthropic Principle in Cosmology." In M.S. Longair, ed., *Confrontation of Cosmological Theories with Observational Data*. Dordrecht: D. Reidel, 1974, pp. 219-298.
10. Overman, Dean L., *A Case Against Accident and Self-organization*. New York, Oxford: Rowman & Littlefield, p. 173.
11. Leslie, John, *Universes*. London and New York: Routledge, p. 198.
12. Gibson, Arvin S., *Glimpses of Eternity*. Bountiful, Utah: Horizon Publishers and Distributors, Inc., 1992.
13. Gibson, Arvin S., *Echoes From Eternity*. Bountiful, Utah: Horizon Publishers and Distributors, Inc., 1993.
14. Browne, Malcolm W., "Age of Universe is Now Settled, Astronomer Says." New York, N.Y.: *The New York Times* (web edition), March 5, 1996.
15. Johnson, George, *Fire in the Mind—Science, Faith, and the Search for Order*. New York, N.Y.: Vintage Books, 1996, pp. 34-35.

16. Easterbrook, Gregg, *Beside Still Waters—Searching for Meaning in an Age of Doubt.* New York, N.Y.: William Morrow and Co., 1998, pp. 74-75.
17. Madsen, Truman G., *Eternal Man.* Salt Lake City, Utah: Deseret Book Company, 1966, p. 30.

1
Near-Death Experiences—A Different Reality

1. Davies, Paul, *The Fifth Miracle—The Search for the Origin and the Meaning of Life.* New York, N.Y.: Simon & Schuster, 1999, p. 260.
2. Gibson, Arvin S., *Journeys Beyond Life--True Accounts of Next-world Experiences.* Bountiful, Utah: Horizon Publishers & Distributors, Inc., 1994, p. 218.
3. Gibson, *Glimpses of Eternity, op. cit.,* pp. 114-119.
4. Gibson, *Glimpses of Eternity, op. cit.,* pp. 44-47.
5. Gibson, *Echoes From Eternity, op. cit.,* pp. 77-93.
6. *IANDS of Utah Newsletter,* August, 1994, and personal communication with Susan in 1998.
7. Sharp, Kimberly Clark, *After the Light—What I Discovered on the Other Side of Life That Can Change Your World.* New York: William Morrow and Company, Inc., 1995, pp. 7-14.
8. Wordsworth, William, *Ode, Intimations of Immortality from Recollections of Early Childhood.* 1807, st. 5.

2
Near-Death Experiences—Research

1. Moody, *op. cit.,* pp. 14-18.
2. Kubler-Ross, Elisabeth, *On Life After Dying.* Berkeley, California: Celestial Arts, 1982, pp. 9-10.
3. Crowther, Duane S., *Life Everlasting—A Definitive Study of Life After Death.* Bountiful, Utah: Horizon Publishers & Distributors, Inc., 1997.
4. Zaleski, Carol, *Otherworld Journeys—Accounts of Near-Death Experience in Medieval and Modern Times.* New York, Oxford, Toronto: Oxford University Press, 1987, p. 19, 28-31.
5. Wilson, Ian, *The After Death Experience—The Physical of the Non-Physical.* New York: William Morrow and Company, Inc., 1987, pp. 7-15.
6. Swedenborg, Emanuel, *A Scientist Explores Spirit.* West Chester, Pennsylvania: Chrysalis Books, 1997, p. 39.

7. Swedenborg, Emanuel, *Heaven & Hell—The reason we are united in spirit to both Heaven and Hell is to keep us in freedom.* West Chester, Pennsylvania: Swedenborg Foundation, Inc., 1976, 1979.

8. *The Bible.* Acts 9:1-22.

9. *The Book of Mormon.* Alma 36:6-24.

10. Rawlings, Maurice, *Beyond Death's Door.* New York, Toronto, London, Sydney, Auckland: Bantam Books, 1979.

11. Sabom, Michael, *Recollections of Death.* New York: Harper & Row, 1982.

12. Morse, Melvin with Perry, Paul, *Closer to the Light.* New York, N.Y.: Villard Books, 1990.

13. Atwater, P. M. H., *Coming Back to Life—The After-Effects of the Near-Death Experience.* New York, Toronto: Ballantine Books, 1988.

14. Sutherland, Cherie, *Reborn in the Light--Life After Near-Death Experiences.* Australia, New Zealand: Bantam Books, 1995. (First published as *Transformed By the Light.* Australia, New Zealand: Bantam Books, 1992.)

15. Sutherland, Cherie, *Within the Light.* Australia, New Zealand: Bantam Books, 1993.

16. Sharp, Kimberly Clark, *After the Light—What I Discovered on the Other Side of Life That Can Change Your World.* New York: William Morrow and Company, Inc., 1995.

17. Ring, K. and Cooper, S. "Near-death and out-of-body experiences in the blind: a study of apparent eyeless vision." *Journal of Near-Death Studies,* 16,1997, pp. 141-147.
Ring, K. and Cooper, S. (1999). *Mindsight: Near-death and out-of-body experiences in the blind.* Palo Alto, California: William James Center for Consciousness Studies, Institute of Transpersonal Psychology.

18. Atwater, P. M. H., *Beyond the Light—What Isn't Being Said About Near-Death Experience.* New Jersey: A Birch Lane Press Book, 1994.

19. Lundahl, Craig R. & Widdison, Harold A., *The Eternal Journey—How Near- Death Experiences Illuminate Our Earthly Lives.* New York: Warner Books, Inc., 1997.

20. Valarino, Evelyn Elsaesser, *On the Other Side of Life—Exploring the Phenomenon of the Near-Death Experience.* New York, London: Insight Books, 1984.

21. Ring, Kenneth, *Lessons from the Light—What We Can Learn from the Near-Death Experience.* New York, N.Y.: Plenum Publishing, 1998.

22. Top, Brent L. And Wendy C., *Beyond Death's Door—Understanding Near-Death Experiences in Light of the Restored Gospel.* Salt Lake City, Utah: Bookcraft, 1993.
23. Lundahl, Craig and Widdison, Harold, "The Mormon explanation of near- death experiences." *Journal of Near-Death Studies,* 3, 1983, pp. 97-106.
24. Jansen, K.L.R., "The Ketamine Model of the Near-Death Experience: A Central Role for the N-Methyl-D-Aspartate Receptor." *Journal of Near-Death Studies,* 16, 1997, pp.5-26.
25. Jansen, K.L.R., " Response to commentaries on 'The ketamine model of the near-death experience.'" *Journal of Near-Death Studies,* 16, 1997, pp.79-95.
26. Morse, Melvin. Letter dated July 14, 1998, to "Vital Signs," International Association for Near Death Studies, Vol XVII, No. 3, 1998.
27. Gibson, *Echoes From Eternity, op. cit.,* pp. 50-52.
28. Gibson, *Glimpses of Eternity, op. cit.,* pp. 150-157.
29. Gibson, *Glimpses of Eternity, op. cit.,* pp. 121-125.
30. Gibson, *Echoes From Eternity, op. cit.,* pp. 44-49.
31. Gibson, *Glimpses of Eternity, op. cit.,* pp. 137-139.
32. Arnette, J. Kenneth, "On the Mind/Body Problem: The Theory of Essence." *Journal of Near-Death Studies,* 11, 1992, pp. 5-18; and, "The Theory of Essence, II: An Electromagnetic-Quantum Mechanical Model of Interactionism." Journal of Near-Death Studies, 14, 1995, pp. 77-99.
33. Gibson, *Echoes From Eternity, op. cit.,* p. 88.
34. Morse, Melvin with Perry, Paul, Parting *Visions—Uses and Meanings of Pre- Death, Psychic, and Spiritual Experiences.* New York, N.Y.:Villard Books, 1994, p. 6.

3
Questions About NDEs

1. Ring, Kenneth, and Cooper, Sharon, "Near-Death and Out-of-Body Experiences in the Blind: A Study of Apparent Eyeless Vision." *Journal of Near-Death Studies,* 16, 1997, p. l03.
2. Ring, Kenneth, *Heading Toward Omega: In search of the meaning of the near-death experience.* New York, N.Y.: William Morrow, Inc.,1985, p. 35, plus personal communication.
3. Ring, *op. cit.,* 1985, pp. 45-46.
4. Gibson, Arvin S., *Journeys Beyond Life—True Accounts of Next-world Experiences.* Bountiful, Utah: Horizon publishers & Distributors, Inc., 1994, p. 224.

5. Ring, Kenneth, Personal communication with author, Nov. 1998.

6. Gibson, *Glimpses of Eternity, op. cit.*, p. 76.

7. Atwater, P. M. H., *Coming Back to Life-The After-Effects of the Near-Death Experience.* New York, Toronto: Ballantine Books, 1988, pp. 45-47.

8. Ritchie, George G. with Sherrill, Elizabeth, *Return from Tomorrow.* Old Tappan, New Jersey: Spire Books, Fleming H. Revell Co., 1978.

9. Gibson, Arvin S., *Journeys Beyond Life--True Accounts of Next-world Experiences.* Bountiful, Utah: Horizon Publishers & Distributors, Inc., 1994, p. 216.

10. Gibson, *Echoes From Eternity, op. cit.*, p. 122.

11. Gibson, *Glimpses of Eternity, op. cit.*, p. 74.

12. Atwater, P. M. H., *Coming Back to Life, op. cit.*, p. 37.

I 3. Atwater, P.M.H., *Coming Back to Life, op. cit.*, p. 34.

14. Rawlings, Maurice, *Beyond Death's Door.* New York, N.Y.: Bantam Books, 1979.

15. Atwater, P.M.H., "Is There a Hell? Surprising Observations About the Near-Death Experience." *Journal of Near-Death Studies,* 10, 1992, pp. 149- 160.

16. Gibson, *Glimpses of Eternity, op. cit.*, pp. 154-155.

17. Gibson, *Glimpses of Eternity, op. cit.*, pp. 181-185.

18. Gibson, *Glimpses of Eternity, op. cit.*, pp. 52-55.

19. *The Bible.* Exodus 33:20.

20. *The Bible.* Exodus 33: 11.

21. *The Doctrine and Covenants.* 67: 11.

22. Ring, K. and Coopers, S., *Mindsight: Near-death and out-of-body experiences in the blind.* Palo Alto, California: William James Center for Consciousness Studies, Institute of Transpersonal Psychology, 1999, p. 58.

23. Gibson, *Echoes From Eternity, op. cit.*, pp. 173- 174.

24. Gibson, *Echoes From Eternity, op. cit.*, pp. 156- 157.

4
The Creation

1. *The Bible.* Genesis 1: 1 -5.

2. *Pearl of Great Price.* Moses 1: 1-4, 8, 27-28.

3. *The Bible.* Acts 7:22.

4. Schroeder, Gerald L., *Genesis and the Big Bang-The Discovery of Harmony Between Modern Science and the Bible.* New York, London, Toronto: Bantam Books, 1990, p. 32. It is noted that b.c.e. and a.c.e. in

this book refer to "before common era," and "after common era" rather than the earlier designations of B C. and A.D

5. Schroeder, Gerald L., *Genesis and the Big Bang-The Discovery of Harmony Between Modern Science and the Bible.* New York, London, Toronto: Bantam Books, 1990, and *The Science of God-The Convergence of Scientific and Biblical Wisdom.* New York: Broadway Books, 1998.

6. Leslie, John, *Universes.* London and New York: Routledge, p. 32.

7. *The Bible.* Genesis 1:14, 16.

8. Leslie, *op. cit.,* p. 34.

9. Leslie, *op. cit.,* p. 35.

10. Leslie, *op. cit.,* p. 35-36.

11. Overman, Dean L., *A Case Against Accident and Self-organization.* New York, Oxford: Rowman & Littlefield, pp. 134-135.

12. Davies, Paul, *God & The New Physics.* New York, London, Tokyo, Sydney, Toronto: Touchstone, 1984, p. 179.

13. Ferris, Timothy, *The Whole Shebang-A State of the Universe Report.* New York, N.Y.: Simon and Schuster, 1997, p. 200.

14. Davies, Paul, *The Fifth Miracle—The Search for the Origin and the Meaning of Life.* New York, N.Y.: Simon and Schuster, 1999, p. 95.

15. Ferris, *op. cit.,* pp. 102-103.

16. Schroeder, *op. cit.,* p. 65.

17. Overman, *op. cit.,* p. 125.

18. Guth, Alan and Steinhardt, Paul. "The inflationary universe," *The New Physics.* Cambridge CB2 IRP, United Kingdom, Cambridge University Press 1989, pp. 43-47.

19. Overman, *op. cit.,* p. 125.

20. Overman, *op. cit.,* pp. 125-126

21. Overman, *op. cit.,* p. 126.

22. Overman, *op. cit.,* p. 126.

23. Overman, *op. cit.,* p. 126.

24. Schroeder, *op. cit.,* p. 112.

25. Behe, Michael J., *Darwin's Black Box-The Biochemical Challenge to Evolution.* New York, London, Toronto, Sydney: The Free Press,1996, p. 27.

26. *The Bible.* Genesis I :31; 2: 1-3.

27. *The Bible.* Psalms 8: 1, 3-5.

5
The Probability of Life

1. Davies, Paul, *God and the New Physics.* New York, London, Tokyo, Sydney, Toronto: Touchstone, 1984, p. 178.
2. Davies, *op. cit.,* p. 179.
3. Video of Carl Sagan's science series in possession of Dr. Tim Hunt, Biology Teacher.
4. Behe, Michael J., *Darwin's Black Box-The Biochemical Challenge to Evolution.* New York, London, Toronto, Sydney, Singapore: The Free Press, 1996, p. 260.
5. Silver, Brian L., *The Ascent of Science.* Oxford, New York:: Oxford University Press, 1998, pp. 292-293.
6. Silver, *op. cit.,* pp. 326-327.
7. Silver, *op. cit.,* pp. 296-297.
8. Silver, *op. cit.,* pp. 297-300.
9. Silver, *op. cit.,* p. 300.
10. Silver, *op. cit.,* p. 301.
11. Silver, *op. cit.,* p. 347.
12. Nash, J. Madeleine, "When Life Exploded," *Time,* December 4, 1995, p. 70.
13. Behe, *op. cit.,* p. 39.
14. Overman, Dean L., *A Case Against Accident and Self-organization.* New York, Oxford: Rowman & Littlefield, p. 50.
15. Schroeder, *The Science of God, op. cit.,* p. 68.
16. Nash, J. Madeleine, "When Life Exploded," *Time,* December 4, 1995, p. 72.
17. Mayr, Ernst, *This is Biology-The Science of the Living World.* Cambridge, Massachusetts, London: The Belknap Press of Harvard University Press, 1997, p. 179.
18. Schroeder, *Genesis and the Big Bang, op. cit.,* p. 163.
19. Mayr, *op. cit.,* p. 149.
20. Nash, J. Madeleine, "When Life Exploded," *Time,* December 4,1995, p. 70, 72.
21. Schroeder, *Genesis and the Big Bang, op. cit.,* p. 145.
22. Nash, J. Madeleine, "When Life Exploded," *Time,* December 4, 1995, pp. 70, 71.
23. Bernstein, Max, Sandford, Scott, and Allamandola, Louis, "Life's Far-Flung Materials," *Scientific American,* July, 1999, pp. 42-49.
24. Schroeder, *Genesis and the Big Bang, op. cit.,* p. 111.

25. Overman, *op. cit.,* pp. 58-60.
26. Overman, *op. cit.,* pp. 60-62.
27. Overman, *op. cit.,* p. 62.
28. Behe, *op. cit.,* pp. 232-233.
29. Ring, Kenneth, *Lessons from the Light-What We Can Learn from the Near Death Experience.* New York, N.Y.: Plenum Publishing, 1998, p. 298.
30. Gibson, *Glimpses of Eternity, op. cit.,* pp. 65-66.

6
Mormonism-The History

1. Crowther, Duane S., *Life Everlasting-A Definitive Study of Life After Death.* Bountiful, Utah: Horizon Publishers & Distributors, Inc., 1997.
2. Barrett, Ivan J., *Joseph Smith and the Restoration.* Provo, Utah: Brigham Young University Press, 1973, p. 33.
3. *Pearl of Great Price.* Joseph Smith History 1:12-20.
4. Barrett, *op. cit.,* p. 61.
5. *Pearl of Great Price.* Joseph Smith History I :29-34.
6. *Pearl of Great Price.* Joseph Smith History I :43-45.
7. Barrett, *op. cit.,* pp. 64-65.
8. Barrett, *op. cit.,* pp. 66-67.
9. Barrett, *op. cit.,* p. 75.
10. Barrett, *op. cit.,* pp. 77-78.
11. Barrett, *op. cit.,* p. 78.
12. Barrett, *op. cit.,* pp. 76-100.
13. Reynolds, Noel B. (Edited by), *Book of Mormon Authorship Revisited-The Evidence for Ancient Origins.* Provo, Utah: Foundation for Ancient Research and Mormon Studies, 1997, Skousen, Royal, Chap. 4.
14. Barrett, *op. cit.,* pp. 101-102.
15. Barrett, *op. cit.,* p. 103.
16. Barrett, *op. cit.,* pp. 100-116.
17. Barrett, *op. cit.,* p. 121.
18. *Pearl of Great Price.* Joseph Smith History 2: Note at end.
19. *Doctrine and Covenants.* 27:12-13.
20. Barrett, *op. cit.,* pp. 129- 130.
21. *Doctrine and Covenants.* 76:58-59.
22. *Doctrine and Covenants.* 96:2.
23. Barrett, *op. cit.,* p. 226.
24. Barrett, *op. cit.,* pp. 322.
25. *Doctrine and Covenants.* 110: 1-7

26. Doctrine and Covenants. 110: 11-15.
27. Barrett, *op. cit.,* pp. 399-401.
28. Barrett, *op. cit.,* p. 396.
29. Barrett, *op. cit.,* p. 437.
30. Barrett, *op. cit.,* p. 587.
31. Barrett, *op. cit.,* pp. 593, 601.
32. Barrett, *op. cit.,* p. 603.
33. Barrett, *op. cit.,* pp. 614-616.
34. Barrett, *op. cit.,* p. 449.
35. Grant, Richard G. *Understanding These Other Christians-An LDS Intro-duction to Evangelical Christianity.* Sandy, Utah: Distr. By Sounds of Zion, Inc., 1998, p. 138.
36. Bloom, Harold, *The American Religion-The Emergence of the Post-Christian Nation.* New York, London, Toronto, Sydney, Tokyo, Singapore, Simon & Schuster, 1993, pp. 124- 125.
37. Bloom, *op. cit.,* p. 94.
38. Bloom, *op. cit.,* p. 95.
39. Bloom, *op. cit.,* p. 99.
40. Bloom, *op. cit.,* p. 113.

7

Mormonism-The Doctrine

1. Ludlow, Daniel H., Editor, *Encyclopedia of Mormonism.* Vols. 1-4, New York: Macmillan Publishing Company, 1992.
2. Gibson, *Glimpses of Eternity, op. cit.,* pp. 205-207.
3. *The Bible.* I John I :5.
4. *The Bible.* James 1:17.
5. *The Bible.* John 1 :6-9.
6. *Doctrine and Covenants.* 88:6- 13.
7. *Pearl of Great Price.* Abraham, 3:24, 25.
8. *The Book of Mormon.* 2 Nephi, 2:25.
9. *Pearl of Great Price.* Moses, 3:26-28; The Book of Mormon. Ether 3: 15-17.
10. *Doctrine and Covenants,* 68:25-28; 88:4.
11. *The Book of Mormon.* Alma, 42:7-10.
12. *The Book of Mormon.* 2 Nephi, 2:27.
13. *The Book of Mormon.* 2 Nephi, 2: 11 - 16.
14. *Doctrine and Covenants,* 59:6.
15. *The Book of Mormon.* I Nephi, 22:1,2. The Bible. Amos, 3:7.
16. *The Book of Mormon.* 3 Nephi, 18: 17-20.

17. *Doctrine and Covenants.* 130:18,19.
18. *The Book of Mormon.* Alma, 22: 14.
19. *The Book of Mormon.* 2 Nephi, 9:21, 22.
20. *The Book of Mormon.* Ether, 4: 18. Doctrine and Covenants. 128: 1-5.
21. *Doctrine and Covenants,* 138: 1 -36; The Book of Mormon. Alma 40: 11-13.
22. *The Book of Mormon.* Mormon, 9: 13.
23. *The Book of Mormon.* Alma, 41: 1-7; 3 Nephi, 26:4-5.
24. *Doctrine and Covenants.* 76:54-70.
25. *Doctrine and Covenants.* 76:81-90.
26. Zaleski, Carol, *Otherworld Journeys-Accounts of Near-Death Experience in Medieval and Modern Times.* New York, Oxford, Toronto: Oxford University Press, 1987, p. 125.
27. Ring, Kenneth, *Lessons from the Light-What We Can Learn from the Near-Death Experience.* New York, N.Y.: Plenum Publishing, 1998, p. 298.
28. *The Book of Mormon.* 2 Nephi, 2: 11
29. Gibson, *Echoes From Eternity, op. cit.,* pp. 123-124.
30. *Doctrine and Covenants.* 130: 19.
31. Gibson, *Echoes From Eternity, op. cit.,* pp. 124- 126.
32. Ring, Kenneth, *Lessons from the Light-What We Can Learn from the Near-Death Experience.* New York, N.Y.: Plenum Publishing, 1998, p. 295.
33. Gibson, *Echoes From Eternity, op. cit.,* pp. 133-134.
34. *Doctrine and Covenants.* 128:22.
35. *The Book of Mormon.* Alma 40: 11-13.
36. *The Book of Mormon.* Mormon 9:3-5.
37. *Encyclopedia of Mormonism, op. cit.,* Spirit World, p. 1409.
38. Ring, *Lessons from the Light, op. cit.,* p. 167.
39. Gibson, *Glimpses of Eternity, op. cit.,* pp. 264-267.
40. *The Bible.* John 14:27.
41. Gibson, Arvin S., *Journeys Beyond Life--True Accounts of Next-world Experiences.* Bountiful, Utah: Horizon Publishers & Distributors, Inc., 1994, p. 221.
42. Gibson, *Glimpses of Eternity, op. cit.,* p. 193.
43. Gibson, *Glimpses of Eternity, op. cit.,* p. 195.
44. Gibson, *Glimpses of Eternity, op. cit.,* pp. 195-196.
45. Gibson, *Glimpses of Eternity, op. cit.,* pp. 196-197.

8
The Evidence

1. Durham, Elane, *I Stand All Amazed—Love and Healing from Higher Realms*. Orem, Utah: Granite Publishing, 1998, pp. 15-26.
2. Durham, *op. cit.*, pp. 96-97.
3. Sagan, C. *Broca's brain*. New York, NY: Random House, 1979.
4. Overman, Dean L., *A Case Against Accident and Self-organization*. New York, Oxford: Rowman & Littlefield, p. 61.
5. Hawking, Stephen W., *A Brief History of Time-From the Big Band to Black Holes*. New York, London, Toronto, Sydney: Bantam Books, 1988, pp. 136-153.
6. Overman, Dean L., *A Case Against Accident and Self-organization*. New York, Oxford: Rowman & Littlefield, pp. 160-172.
7. Schroeder, Gerald L., *The Science of God-The Convergence of Scientific and Biblical Wisdom*. New York: Broadway Books, 1998, p. 161.
8. Gibson, *Echoes From Eternity, op. cit.*, p. 274.
9. Moody, R.. and Perry, P. *The light beyond*. New York, NY: Bantam Books, 1988, p. 14.
10. Brown, J.H. *Heavenly answers for earthly challenges*. Pasadena, CA: Jemstar Press, 1997, p. 202.
11. Ring, K. *Life after Death*. New York, NY: Quill, 1982, p. 98.
12. Ring, 1982, op. cit., p. 98.
13. Ritchie, G.G., Jr. *My life after Dying. Becoming alive to universal love*. Norfolk, VA: Hampton Roads Publishing Company, 1991, p. 21.
14. Wallace, R. and Taylor, C. *The Burning Within*. Carson City, NV: Gold Leaf Press, 1994, p. 91.
15. Grey, M. *Return from death*. London, England: Arkana, 1987, p. 43.
16. Heinerman J. *Spirit world manifestations*. Salt Lake City, UT: Magazine Printing and Publishing, 1978, p. 109.
17. Ring, Kenneth, *Heading Toward Omega: In search of the meaning of the near-death experience*. New York, N.Y.:Quill, 1985, p. 57.
18. *Doctrine and Covenants*. 88:110.
19. Maxwell, Neal A., *All These Things Shall Give Thee Experience*. Salt Lake City, Utah: Deseret Book Company, 1979, p. 11.
20. *Journal of Discourses*. The Church of Jesus Christ of Latter-day Saints.13 :77.
21. Silver, Brian L., The Ascent of Science. Oxford, New York: Oxford University Press, 1998, p. 191.
22. Silver, *op. cit.*, p. 394.

23. Cook, Lyndon W., Editor. David Whitmer Interviews-A Restoration Witness, Orem, Utah: Grandin Book Co., 1991, p. 226
24. Sorenson, John L. *An Ancient American Setting for the Book of Mormon,* Salt Lake City, Utah: Deseret Book Co., 1985, 1996.
25. Allen, Joseph, L. *Exploring the Lands of the Book of Mormon,* Orem, Utah: S. A. Publishers, Inc., 1989.
26. Reynolds, Noel B., Editor. *Book of Mormon Authorship Revisited-The Evidence for Ancient Origins.* Provo, Utah: Foundation for Ancient Research and Mormon Studies, 1997.
27. Mosser, Carl and Owen, Paul. "Mormon Scholarship, Apologetics, and Evangelical Neglect: Losing the Battle and Not Knowing It?" *Trinity Journal,* 2065 Half Day Road, Deerfield, Illinois: TRINJ 19NS, 1998, pp.179-180.
28. Mosser and Owen, *op. cit.,* p. 204.
29. Welch, John W., "Chiasmus in the Book of Mormon," *Book of Mormon Authorship-New Light on Ancient Origins.* Reynolds, Noel B., Editor. Provo, Utah: Foundation for Ancient Research and Mormon Studies, 1982, pp. 33-52.
30. Grant, Richard G. *Understanding These Other Christians-An LDS Introduction to Evangelical Christianity.* Sandy, Utah: Distr. By Sounds of Zion, Inc., 1998, pp. 77-88.
31. Grant, *op. cit.,* p. 64.
32. Bawer, Bruce. *Stealing Jesus-How Fundamentalism Betrays Christianity.* New York: Crown Publishers, 1997.
33. Gibson, *Journeys Beyond Life, op. cit.,* p. 220.
34. *Pearl of Great Price.* Articles of Faith: 8.
35. Schroeder, Gerald L., *The Science of God-The Convergence of Scientific and Biblical Wisdom.* New York: Broadway Books, 1998, p. 148.
36. Gibson, Glimpses of Eternity, *op. cit.,* pp. 197-201.
37. *The Book of Mormon.* Moroni 10:3-5.
38. Gibson, *Glimpses of Eternity, op. cit.,* p. 288.
39. Tipler, Frank J. *The Physics of Immortality.* New York, London, Toronto, Sydney, Auckland: Anchor Books-Doubleday, 1994, pp. 338-339.
40. Sabom, Michael. *Light & Death-One Doctor's Fascinating Account of Near-Death Experiences.* Grand Rapids, Michigan: Zondervan Publishing House, 1998, pp. 199-200.
41. *The Book of Mormon.* 2 Nephi 2:25.
42. *Pearl of Great Price.* Moses 1:39.
43. *The Bible.* Matthew 22:37-40.

44. Lewis, C.S., *The Four Loves.* San Diego, New York, London: A Harvest Book, Harcourt Brace & Company, 1988, p. 127.

45. *Hymns of the Church of Jesus Christ of Latter-day Saints.* Salt Lake City, Utah: The Church of Jesus Christ of Latter-day Saints, 1985, p. 86.

Appendix A
Other Attempts to Explain the NDE

1. Rodin. E.A., "The reality of death experiences: a personal perspective." *Journal of Nervous and Mental Disease,* 168, 1980, pp.259-263.

2. Grof, S. and Halifax, J., *The human encounter with death.* New York, NY: Dutton, 1977.

3. Palmer, J., "Correspondence: Deathbed apparitions and the survival hypothesis." *Journal of the American Society for Psychical Research,* 72, 1978, pp. 392-395.

4. Siegel, R.K., "The psychology of life after death." *American Psychologist,* 35, 1980, pp. 911-931.

5. McHarg, J.F., "Review of At the Hour of Death," by K. Oasis and E. Haraldsson. *Journal of the Society for Psychical Research,* 49, 1978, pp.885-887.

6. Blacher, R.S., "To sleep, perchance to dream . . ." *JAMA,* 242,1979, p. 2291.

7. Schnaper, N., "Comments germane to the paper entitled 'the reality of death experiences' by Ernst Rodin." *The Journal of Nervous and Mental Disease,* 168,] 980, p. 269.

8. Saavedra-Aguilar, J.C. and Gomez-Jeria, J.S., "A neurobiological model for near-death experiences." *Journal of Near-Death Studies,* 7, 1989, pp. 205-222.

9. Saavedra-Aguilar, J.C. and Gomez-Jeria, J.S., "Response to commentaries on 'A neurobiological model for near-death experiences.'" *Journal of Near-Death Studies,* 7, 1989, pp. 265-272.

10. Jansen, K.L.R., "Neuroscience and the near-death experience: Roles for the NMDA-PCP receptor, the sigma receptor and the endopsychosins." *Medical Hypotheses,* 31,1990, pp. 25-29.

11. Jansen, K.L.R., "The Ketamine Model of the Near-Death Experience: A Central Role for the N-Methyl-D-Aspartate Receptor." *Journal of Near-Death Studies,* 16, 1997, pp.5-26.

12. Morse, M.L., Venecia, D., Jr., and Milstein, J., "Near-death experiences: A neurophysiological explanatory model." *Journal of Near-Death Studies,* 8, 1989, pp. 45-53.

13. Cook, R.B., "Guest editorial: A theory of death." *Journal of Near-Death Studies,* 8,1989, pp. 5-14.
14. Thomas, L., "A meliorist view of disease and dying." *Journal of Medical Philosophy,* 1, 1976, p.212.
15. Blackmore, S., *Dying to live: Science and near-death experience.* London, England: Grafton, 1993.
16. Carr, D.B., "Pathophysiology of stress-induced limbic lobe dysfunction: A hypothesis for near-death experiences." *Anabiosis,* 2,1982, pp. 75-89.
17. Carr, D.B., "Pathophysiology of stress-induced limbic lobe dysfunction: A hypothesis for near-death experiences." *Anabiosis,* 2, 1982, pp. 75-89.
18. Sagan, Carl, *op. cit.*
19. Noyes, R. and Kletti, R., "Depersonalization in the face of life-threatening danger: A description." *Psychiatry,* 39, 1976, pp. 19-27.
20. Quimby, S.L., "The near-death experience as an event in consciousness." *Journal of Humanistic Psychology,* 29, 1989, pp. 87-108.
21. Krishnan, V., "Near-death experiences: Reassessment urged." *Parapsychology Review,* 1 2, 1981, pp . 10- 11.
22. Siegel, R.K., "The psychology of life after death." *American Psychologist,* 35, 1980, pp. 911-931.
23. Menz, R.L., "The denial of death and the out-of-body experience." *Journal of Religion and Health,* 23, 1984, pp.317-329.
24. Gibbs, J.C., "Moody's versus Siegel's interpretation of the near-death experience: An evaluation based on recent research." *Anabiosis,* 5, 1987, pp. 67-82.
25. Ehrenwald, J., *The ESP experience.* New York, NY: Basic Books, 1978.
26. Lowental, U., "Dying, regression, and the death instinct." *Psychoanalytic Review,* 68, 1981, pp. 363-370.
27. Appleby, L., "Near-death experience: Analogous to other stress induced psychological phenomena." *British Medical Journal,* 298,1989, pp.976-977.
28. Schnaper, N., "Comments germane to the paper entitled 'the reality of death experiences' by Ernst Rodin." *The Journal of Nervous and Mental Disease,* 168, 1980, p. 269.
29. Serdahely, W.J., "Similarities between near-death experiences and multiple personality disorder." *Journal of Near-Death Studies,* 11, 1992, pp. 19-38.
30. Tien, S.S., " Thanatoperience." *Journal of Near-Death Studies,* 7, 1988, pp. 32-27.
31. Counts, D.A., "Near-death and out-of-body experiences in a Melanesian society." *Anabiosis,* 3, 1983, pp. 115- 135.

32. Palmer, J., "Correspondence: Deathbed apparitions and the survival hypothesis." *Journal of the American Society for Psychical Research,* 72, 1978, pp.392-395.
33. Moody, R.A., *Life after life.* Atlanta, GA: Mockingbird Books, 1975.
34. Osis, K. and Haraldsson, E., *At the hour of death.* New York, NY: Avon, 1977.
35. Sabom, M.B. and Kreutziger, S.A., "Physicians evaluate the near-death experience." *Theta,* 6, 1978, pp.]-6.
36. Ring, K., *Life at death: A scientific investigation of the near-death experience.* New York, NY: Coward, McCann and Geoghegan, 1980.
37. Grosso, M., "Toward an explanation of near-death phenomena.." *Anabiosis,* 1, 1981, pp. 3-26.
38. Becker, C.B., "The failure of Saganomics: Why birth models cannot explain near-death phenomena." *Anabiosis,* 2, 1982, pp. 102- 109.
39. Sabom, op. cit., 1982.
40. Woodhouse, M.B., " Five arguments regarding the objectivity of NDEs." *Anabiosis,* 3, 1983, pp. 63-75.
41. Gabbard, G.O. and Tremlow, S.W., "An overview of altered mind\body perception." *Bulletin of the Menninger Clinic,* 50, 1986, pp. 351-366.
42. Wade, Jenny, "Physically transcendent awareness: a comparison of the phenomenology of consciousness before birth and after death." *Journal of Near-Death Studies,* 7, 1998, pp. 269, 271.
43. Much of the material in this Section was taken from the two books: *Glimpses of Eternity,* and *Echoes From Eternity (op. cit.)* and is included by permission of Horizon Publishers and Distributors, Inc. The reader will quickly recognize that the dissertation in this Section represents an apologetic for the point of view that reincarnation is a false concept. In presenting the material I recognize that reputable and intelligent individuals have an opposite point of view. For readers interested in the evidence and arguments in favor of reincarnation I urge them to seek references by the proponents of the concept-and then form conclusions based on the pro and con arguments.
44. Wilson, Ian, *The After Death Experience—The Physical of the Non-Physical.* New York: William Morrow and Company, Inc., 1987, pp. 38-39.
45. Ring, Kenneth, *Heading Toward Omega.* New York, N.Y.: William Morrow, Inc., 1984-1985, p. 158.
46. Ludwig, Arnold M., *Principles of Clinical Psychiatry.* The Free Press, Macmillan, Inc., N.Y., 1986, pp. 626-627.

Gregory, Richard L., *The Oxford Companion to the Mind.* Oxford University Press, N.Y., 1988, pp. 328-333.

47. Moody, Raymond A. Jr., *Coming Back-A Psychiatrist Explores Past-Life Journeys.* N.Y., London: Bantam Books, 1991.

48. Moody, *op. cit.,* pp. 187-190.

49. Moody, *op. cit.,* p. 43

50. Stevenson, Ian, M.D., *Twenty Cases Suggestive of Reincarnation.* Charlottesville: University of Virginia Press, 1974 (Reprinted 1978).

51. Wilson, *op. cit.,* pp. 27-37.

52. Wilson, *op. cit.,* pp. 38-39.

53. Wilson, *op. cit.,* pp. 41-47.

54. Zilbergeld, B., "Hypnosis Questions and Answers," *The Validity of Memories Retrieved in Hypnosis.* New York, N.Y.: W. W. Norton and Co., 1986, pp. 45-46.

55. Orne, Martin T.; Whitehouse, Wayne G.; Dinges, David F.; Orne, Emily Carota. "Reconstructing Memory through Hypnosis." *University of Pennsylvania School of Medicine; from Hypnosis and Memory,* Edited by Pettinati, Helen M., New York, N.Y.: The Guilford Press, 1988, p. 47.

56. Ganaway, George K., *Historical vs. Narrative Truth. Clarifying the Role of Exogenous Trauma in the Etiology of MPD and its Variants.* December, 1989, p.209; for Reprints write George K. Ganaway, M.D., Program Director, Ridgeview Center for Dissociative Disorders, Ridgeview Institute,3995 South Cobb Drive, Smyrna, Georgia 30080.

57. Spanos, Nicholas P.; Menary, Evelyn; Gabora, Natalie J.; DuBreuil, Susan C.; and Dewhirst, Bridget; "Secondary Identity Enactments During Hypnotic Past-Life Regression: A Sociocognitive Perspective." *Journal of Personality and Social Psychology,* 1991, Vol. 61, No. 2, pp. 308-320.

Appendix B
Basic Facts About the Universe

1. Overman, Dean L., *A Case Against Accident and Self-organization.* New York, Oxford: Rowman & Littlefield, p. 112.

2. Overman, *op. cit.,* p. 112.

3. Overman, *op. cit.,* p. 112.

4. Overman, *op. cit.,* p. 113.

5. Hawking, Stephen W., *A Brief History of Time-From the Big Band to Black Holes.* New York, London, Toronto, Sydney: Bantam Books, 1988, p. 8.

6. Wilford, John Noble, "Shocked Cosmologists Find Universe Expanding Faster." New York, N.Y.: *New York Times* (web edition), March 3, 1998.
7. Ferris, Timothy, *The Whole Shebang-A State of the Universe Report.* New York, N.Y.: Simon and Schuster, 1997, p. 111.
8. Hawking, *op. cit.,* p. 41.
9. Ferris, *The Whole Shebang, op. cit.,* p. 111.
10. Hogan, Craig J., "Primordial Deuterium and the Big Bang," *Scientific American,* December 1996, web edition.
11. Musser, George, "Glow in the Dark-Science and the Citizens," *Scientific American,* March 1998, pp. 18- 19.
12. Longair, Malcolm, "The New Astrophysics," *The New Physics:* Cambridge, Melbourne, Cambridge University Press, 1989, p. 197.
13. Rees, Martin, *Before the Beginning-Our Universe and Others:* Reading, Massachusetts, Helix Books, 1997, p. 57.
14. Hogan, Craig J., "Primordial Deuterium and the Big Bang," *Scientific American,* December 1996, web edition.
15. Rees, *op. cit.,* pp. 8-9.
16. Johnson, Hollis R., "Atoms, Stars, and Us," *Of Heaven and Earth Reconciling Scientific Thought with LDS Theology,* Clark, David L., Editor. Salt Lake City, Utah: Deseret Book Co., 1998, pp.113-119.
17. Considine, Douglas, Editor, *Van Nostrand's Scientific Encyclopedia,* Fifth Edition. New York, London, Toronto, Melbourne: Van Nostrand Reinhold Company, 1976,p. 1157.
18. Nash, J. Madeleine, "When Life Exploded," *Time,* December 4, 1995, p. 70.
19. Considine, *op. cit.,* p. 1158.

Appendix C
Probability and
Other Attempts to Explain Life

1. Rozanov, Y. A., *Probability Theory: A Concise Course.* New York: Dover Publications, Inc., 1969, p. 26.
2. Ferris, *The Whole Shebang, op. cit.,* p. 207.
3. Ferris, *op. cit.,* pp. 214-215.
4. Guth, Alan and Steinhardt, Paul. "The inflationary universe," *The New Physics:* Cambridge CB2 I RP, United Kingdom, Cambridge University Press 1989, p. 42.
5. Ferris, *The Whole Shebang, op. cit.,* p. 216.
6. Leslie, John, *Universes.* London and New York: Routledge, p. 79.
7. Leslie, *op. cit.,* pp. 155, 198.

8. Schroeder, *The Science of God, op. cit.,* p p. 101 - 104.

9. Behe, Michael J., *Darwin's Black Box-The Biochemical Challenge to Evolution.* New York, London, Toronto, Sydney, Singapore: The Free Press, 1996, p. 271.

10. Behe, *op. cit.,* p. 52.

11. Behe, *op. cit.,* pp. 93-96.

12. Wilford, John Noble, *Study Backs Idea that Meteorite Hints of Life on Mars.* New York, N.Y.: The New York Times (web edition), Mar 14, 1997.

13. Gibson, Everett K., Jr., McKay, David S., Thomas-Keptra, Kathie, and Romanek, Christopher, "The Case for Relic Life on Mars," *Scientific American,* December, 1997, web edition.

14. Gribbin, John, *In the Beginning—The Birth of the Living Universe.* Boston, New York, Toronto, London: Little Brown & Co., 1993, p. 69.

15. Silver, *op. cit.,* pp. 341 -342.

16. Bernstein, Max, Sandford, Scott, and Allamandola, Louis, "Life's Far-Flung Materials," *Scientific American,* July, 1999, pp. 42-49.

17. Bernstein, Sandford, and Allamandola, *Scientific American, op. cit.,* p. 49.

18. Davies, Paul, *The Fifth Miracle-The Search for the Origin and the Meaning of Life.* New York, N.Y.: Simon & Schuster, 1999, pp. 173-186.

19. Davies, Paul, *The Fifth Miracle, op. cit.,* p. 172.

20. Davies, Paul, *The Fifth Miracle, op. cit.,* p. 174.

21. Davies, Paul, *The Fifth Miracle, op. cit.,* p. 177.

22. Davies, Paul, *The Fifth Miracle, op. cit.,* p. 184.

23. Davies, Paul, *The Fifth Miracle, op. cit.,* p. 131.

24. Davies, Paul, *The Fifth Miracle, op. cit.,* pp. 235-236.

25. Mayr, Ernst, *This is Biology-The Science of the Living World.* Cambridge, Massachusetts, London: The Belknap Press of Harvard University Press,1997, pp. 188, 191.

26. Mayr, *op. cit.,* p. 194.

27. Mayr, *op. cit.,* p. 195.

28. Schroeder, Gerald L., *The Science of God-The Convergence of Scientific and Biblical Wisdom.* New York: Broadway Books, 1998, pp. 34-37.

29. Nash, J. Madeleine, "When Life Exploded," *Time,* December 4, 1995, p. 69.

30. Schroeder, *The Science of God, op. cit.,* p. 39.

31. Schroeder, *The Science of God, op. cit.,* p. 88.

Appendix D
Cosmic Structure

1. Much of the material from this section was extracted from the paper, Near-Death Studies and Modern Physics, by Craig R. Lundahl and Arvin S. Gibson. The paper was published in the *Journal of Near-Death Studies,* New York by Human Sciences Press, and was included with their permission.

2. Lederman, Leon, with Teresi, Dick, *The God Particle.* New York, N.Y.: Bantam Doubleday Dell Publishing Group, 1993, pp. 274-341.

3. Ferris, Timothy, *The Whole Shebang-A State of the Universe Report.* New York, N.Y.: Simon and Schuster, 1997, pp. 213-214.

4. Lederman, *op, cit.,* p. 339.

5. Close, Frank, "The quark structure of matter," *The New Physics.* Cambridge, Melbourne, Cambridge University Press, 1989, pp. 398-405.

6. Hawking, *op. cit.,* p. 85.

7. Hawking, *op. cit.,* p. 54.

8. Hawking, *op. cit.,* pp. 54-55.

9. Davies, Paul, *God & The New Physics.* New York, London, Tokyo, Sydney, Toronto: Touchstone, 1984, pp. 102-106.

10. Ferris, *op. cit.,* p. 210.

11. Davies, *op. cit.,* pp. 148-149.

12. Bohm, David, *Quantum Theory.* Mineola, N.Y.: Dover Publications, 1989, p. 609.

13. Hawking, *op. cit.,* p. 161.

14. Ferris, *op. cit.,* p. 221.

15. Ferris, *op. cit.,* p. 222-223.

16. Thorne, Kip S., *Black Holes and Time Warps-Einstein's Outrageous Legacy.* New York, London: W.W. Norton & Co., 1994, pp. 164-178.

17. Thorne, *op. cit.,* pp. 187-197.

18. Thorne, *op. cit.,* pp. 197-257.

19. Hawking, *op. cit.,* pp. 99-113.

20. Ferris, *op. cit.,* p. 96.

21. Hawking, *op. cit.,* pp. 94-95.

22. Davies, *op. cit.,* pp. 171-172.

23. Davies, *op. cit.,* pp. 114-116.

24. Ferris, *op. cit.,* pp. 258-259.

25. Leslie, *op. cit.,* p. 147.

26. Thorne, *op. cit.,* pp. 483-489.

27. Thorne, *op. cit.,* pp. 492-493.

28. Thorne, *op. cit.,* pp. 498-499.
29. Ferris, *op. cit.,* p. 101.
30. Thorne, *op. cit.,* p.109.
31. Thorne, *op. cit.,* p. 521.
32. Thorne, *op. cit.,* pp.521-522.
33. Ferris, *op.cit.,* p.101.
34. Hawking, *op.cit.,* p. 40.
35. Ferris, *op.cit.,* pp. 46-48.
36. Ferris, *op.cit.,* p. 49.
37. Hawking, *op.cit.,* p. 45.
38. Ferris, *op.cit.,* p. 132.
39. Ferris, *op.cit.,* pp. 123-124.
40. Ferris, *op.cit.,* p. 127.
41. Ferris, *op.cit.,* pp. 130-131.
42. Matthews, R. (April I I, 1998). *To infinity and beyond.* New Scientist, 158. (2129) 27-30.
43. Musser, George, "The Flip Side of the Universe-Science and the Citizens," *Scientific American,* September 1998, p. 22.
44. Hogan, Craig J., Kirshner, Robert P., Suntzeff, Nicholas B., "Surveying Space-time with Supernovae," *Scientific American,* January 1999, pp. 46-51.
45. Kraus, Lawrence M., "Cosmological Antigravity," *Scientific American,* January 1999, p. 59.
46. Ferris, *op. cit.,* p. 137.
47. Ferris, *op. cit.,* pp. 167-168.
48. Sagan, Carl, *Broca's Brain.* New York, N.Y.: Random House, 1979, p. 350.
49. Longair, *op. cit.,* p. 199.
50. Ferris, *op. cit.,* p. 80.
51. Davies, *op. cit.,* p. 120.
52. Davies, *op. cit.,* p. 121.
53. Feynman, R.P., *Six Not-So-Easy Pieces.* New York, Reading, Mass., Menlo Park, CA., Ontario, Harlow, England, Amsterdam, Sydney, Bonn Paris, Milan: Addison Wesley, 1997, p. 121.
54. Ferris, *op. cit.,* p. 44.
55. Ferris, *op. cit.,* p. 277.
56. Bouwmeester, D., Pan, J-W, Mattle, K., Eibl, M., Weinfurter, H. and Zeilinger, A. "Experimental quantum teleportation." *Nature,* 390, 1997, 575-579.
57. Sudbery, T. "The fastest way from A to B." *Nature,* 390, 1997, 551-52.
58. Ferris, *op. cit.,* p. 287.

Glossary

Alga. Usually aquatic, one-celled or multi-celled plant life without stems, roots and leaves, but containing chlorophyll.

Anaerobe. A microorganism, such as a bacterium, capable of living without free oxygen.

Anthropic Universe. A universe which has laws and constants of nature uniquely tuned for the existence of life.

Antimatter. Particles with the identical mass and spin as those of normal matter, but with opposite charge—such as, antineutrinos, antiquarks and antielectrons. Matter and antimatter tend to destroy each other when in the proximity of their counterpart.

Apostle. One of the twelve governing disciples of Christ in the ancient Church and similarly in the present Church of Jesus Christ of Latter-day Saints.

Astrophysics. The physics of the cosmos.

Atom. The fundamental unit of an element made up of a nucleus of neutrons and protons, with electrons surrounding the nucleus.

Atom Smasher. A device for accelerating particles in an electromagnetic field and allowing them to collide with atoms, thus breaking the atoms apart and yielding the broken parts for study. Also known as particle accelerators and super-colliders.

Background Radiation. Microwave background radiation evenly distributed throughout the cosmos—the residual radiation from the energy released when the Universe was young.

Bacterium. A single-celled living microorganism of the class Schizomy cetes.

Baryon. The family of heavy particles—normal matter—that includes neutrons and protons. They are responsive to the strong nuclear force.

Big Bang. A cosmic explosion that marked the expansion of the universe from an initially small point of intensely dense matter and energy.

Billion. In America a billion is defined a one thousand million, or 10^9.

Biology. The science of living organisms and life processes.

Biotic. Relating to life.

Black Hole. A small celestial body with an intense gravitational field which is so strong that it exceeds the escape velocity of light. Formed by a collapsing star.

Book of Mormon. A book of some ancient inhabitants of America, led here by God from Israel, and whose history was recorded on gold plates. The writings on the plates were translated by the power of God through the prophet Joseph Smith.

Boson, Gauge. A sub-atomic particle with an integer spin which carries the force from one particle to another.

Broken Symmetry. Asymmetrical state in which earlier symmetrical characteristics are discerned. Believed to be the mechanism by which many presently observed fundamental particles were formed during the big bang.

Cambrian Period. A designation in the earth's geologic history between 510 and 540 million years ago.

Cell. The smallest unit of life capable of independent functioning. Includes a nuclei, cytoplasm, other material and a surrounding membrane.

Chiasmus. A form of ancient Hebrew poetry used in the Bible and in the Book of Mormon which employs reverse parallelisms.

The Church of Jesus Christ of Latter-day Saints. The pristine church of Christ reestablished in 1830 under the authority of Jesus Christ through the prophet Joseph Smith. Frequently referred to as the Mormon Church.

Class. A taxonomic category in the animal and plant kingdoms ranking below a phylum and above an order.

Compound, Chemical. A combination of two or more elements, usually thought of as containing multiple molecules chemically bound together.

Corroborative NDEs. Near-death experiences where the individual has an out-of-body event where he or she sees things which normally could not have been seen because of the physical state of the body, and where the things seen are later corroborated by other people viewing the events as they happened.

Cosmic Background Explorer (COBE). A satellite instrumented device for measuring the residual background radiation from the big bang.

Cosmos. The harmonious and well-ordered universe.

Cosmological Constant. A constant, initially used by Einstein and later rejected by him, which would act as some type of anti-gravity to cause accelerated expansion of the universe.

Cosmology. The astrophysical study of the universe.

Critical Density. The density of the universe in which it is defined as flat with an omega of one where it will expand forever but with an ever decreasing rate.

Dark Matter. Matter implied to exist in the universe from the observation of gravitational and other effects but not visible as stars or other bright objects. Some experiments have suggested that neutrinos may constitute much of the hypothesized dark matter.

Density. Mathematically expressed as the mass of a substance or region divided by its volume.

Deuterium or Heavy Hydrogen. An isotope of hydrogen with a nucleus of one proton and one neutron. Also has one electron.

Doctrine and Covenants. A book of revelations from God to Joseph Smith and other latter-day prophets. One of the standard-works of the LDS church.

DNA. Deoxyribose nucleic acid which is a constituent of all living matter. It is a molecule consisting of a twisted double-string of linked amino acid molecules in specific combinations which determine the genetic makeup of a single cell.

Electromagnetic Force. Fundamental force of nature between electrically charged particles. Responsible for holding electrons in fixed orbits around the nucleus of an atom.

Electron. A stable elementary particle in the lepton family with a negative electrical charge. Located at particular energy levels around the nucleus of an atom.

Element. A substance consisting of atoms, each with an identical number of protons in its nucleus. An element cannot be changed by chemical action but can be altered by radioactive processes.

Energy. The ability to do work.

Entanglement. The mysterious quantum ability to instantly sense the characteristic of two "entangled" particles over immense distances.

Entropy. A measure of the disorder of systems and of the universe. For any process, such as the expansion of steam to turn a turbine, the entropy must increase. Mathematically it is given as: $S = \int dQ/T$, where S is Entropy, $\int dQ$ is the integrated change in heat during the process, and T is the temperature.

Enzyme. A protein whose function is to act as a catalyst in accelerating the chemical action in a living cell.

Escape Velocity. The velocity required for a body to escape from the gravitational field of another larger body.

Eukaryote. An organism with one or more cells with a well defined nucleus.

Evolution. The theory that species may change over time so that descendants differ physiologically from their ancestors.

Field of Force. A region of space within which a force is produced by a single agent such as an electric current.

Force. The agency that causes change in a system, such as movement of an object.

Fossil. A remnant or trace of a living organism of a past geologic age, often in the form of imprints or calcified remains in ancient rock formations.

Fission, nuclear. A nuclear reaction where an atomic nucleus splits into fragments releasing very large quantities of energy (100 Mev or more per fission).

Flavor. Designation for the type of quark. The flavors of quarks are: up, down, strange, charmed, top and bottom.

Fusion, nuclear. A nuclear reaction where an atomic nucleus merges, or combines, with another nucleus to form a more massive nucleus and in the process emits enormous quantities of energy—much greater than from fission. This is the type of reaction that occurs in our sun and other stars.

Galaxy. A large collection of stars, gases and star-dust gathered together by gravity and having a mass roughly 100 billion times that of the sun.

Gamma Ray. Extremely short wavelength electromagnetic radiation. Given off by the sun and by nuclear reactions; highly penetrating photon.

Gene. A particular protein—created from amino acids by the DNA in a cell—which controls hereditary characteristics and is capable of undergoing mutation.

Genetic Code. The information coded within the unique DNA and RNA sequences of living creatures which determines their genetic and hereditary makeup.

Genus. A taxonomic category of living organisms ranking below a family but above a species.

Geologic Time Scale. A classification of the earth's geologic history into eras, periods, epochs and years.

Gluon. Sub-atomic particles which carry the strong nuclear force. From the boson class of particles.

Gnostic. Of or relating to spiritual or intellectual knowledge.

Gnosticism. Early Christian sects that valued inquiry into spiritual truth above faith and believed that salvation came only to those whose faith allowed them to transcend matter.

Gravity. A fundamental force of nature which expresses the attraction between two bodies which have mass. It is directly proportional to the product of the masses of the two bodies and inversely proportional to the square of the distance between them.

Hadron. Any of the class of elementary particles that are composed of quarks and are responsive to the strong nuclear force. They include baryons and mesons.

Half-Life. The time it takes for half of a given quantity of a radioactive element to decay.

Higgs Field. A theoretical field operative during early stages of the big bang which was the cause of broken symmetries and the creation of numerous fundamental particles.

Hubble Telescope. Large orbiting space telescope named after the astronomer Edwin Hubble.

Hydrogen. The lightest of elements consisting of one proton in the nucleus and one surrounding electron.

Impossibility. Defined in terms of probability to be less than or equal to one chance in 10^{50} tries.

Inflationary Period. The first few microseconds in the expansion of the universe which, for some unknown reason, proceeded at an enormously fast rate—faster than the speed of light.

Infrared Light. Electromagnetic energy with a longer wavelength than visible light.

Inorganic. Not made of organic matter.

International Association for Near-Death Studies (IANDS). The organization founded in 1977 by Kenneth Ring, Bruce Greyson, Raymond Moody, Michael Sabom and John Audette for the purpose of scientifically studying the near-death phenomenon. The first meetings were at the University of Virginia, and the headquarters were later centered at the University of Connecticut with Kenneth Ring.

Ion. An atom that has lost or added an electron and therefore has a net electrical charge of plus or minus.

Isotope. An atom that has the same number of protons in its nucleus as another atom but a different number of neutrons. It reacts chemically the same as its isotopic partner.

Karma. The total effect of an individual's actions, good or bad, in successive incarnations.

Kelvin. A measurement of temperature used by scientists. Zero degrees Kelvin equals absolute zero, the coldest value possible, and it corresponds with -273 degrees Centigrade or -460 degrees Fahrenheit. Each degree Kelvin is equal in magnitude to a degree measured in Centigrade.

Ketamine. One of the chemicals released during approaching death. Believed by some researchers to be a triggering event in the brain which causes NDEs to commence.

LDS. An abbreviation often used to designate members or to identify The Church of Jesus Christ of Latter-day Saints.

Lepton. A family of extremely small elementary particles that includes electrons, muons, taus and neutrinos. Not responsive to the strong nuclear force.

Life Review. The process in many NDEs whereby the individual, usually in the presence of other spiritually enlightened beings or being, sees, hears and feels his past life experiences played before him.

Light as Defined by Science. Electromagnetic radiation in the wavelength spectrum visible to the human eye.

Light as Seen in an NDE. An extraordinarily brilliant light which has the characteristic of invoking feelings of peace and love.

Light Speed. From relativity considerations, a constant value for any observer whether traveling or stationary relative to another observer. In a vacuum 186,000 miles per second.

Light Year. The distance light travels in a year.

Mass. The amount of matter in an object. It is a measure of the object's resistance to acceleration.

Matter. A substance that occupies space and displays inertia and gravity when at rest or in motion.

Meson. Any of a family of subatomic particles consisting of a quark and an antiquark. They are responsive to the strong nuclear force.

MeV. One million electron volts. A quantitative measure of energy and mass.

Milky Way. The spiral galaxy within which our solar system resides. Visible at night as a luminous band.

Molecule. The smallest unit of a chemical compound. A stable unit consisting of atoms bound together by electromagnetic forces.

Momentum. The product of a body's mass and linear velocity.

Mormon. An ancient American prophet who wrote a portion of the Book of Mormon. The word Mormon is often used to designate members of the Church of Jesus Christ of Latter-day Saints.

Moroni. The last of the ancient American prophets to write on the gold plates the story of his people and God's dealings with them. The angel who appeared to Joseph Smith and gave him the plates. Also the statuary shown on the spire of many LDS temples.

Multiple Universes. A theory that there are multiple universes, perhaps an infinity of them, or multiple portions of universes, ours being only one of many. The theory was developed in order to explain why ours could be anthropic and still not have the need for a Creator.

Muon. A short-lived (2.2×10^{-6} seconds) particle in the lepton family with negative electrical charge. 207 times more massive than an electron.

Mutation. An inheritable change of the genes of a living organism.

Natural Selection. The process in evolution where an advantages characteristic for continued life develops naturally over time in succeeding generations of a species.

Near-Death Experience. A spiritual epiphany brought on by imminent death, emotional trauma, prayer or other triggering event.

Neutrino. Electrically neutral, and very abundant, particle which responds to the weak nuclear force but not the strong nuclear or electromagnetic forces. Originally thought to have no mass but recent experiments have shown that it probably has a small mass.

Neutron. A subatomic particle having a neutral electrical charge which is found in the nuclei of atoms. In the heavy baryon family of particles and made up of one up quark and two down quarks. Its mass is 939.6 MeV.

Neutron Star. A collapsed star with its matter compressed into an extremely dense and small mass of neutrons.

Nirvana. A state of perfect peace or blessedness which is reached when one's karma is sufficiently good to release the individual from reincarnation's grip.

Nucleus of an Atom. The central part of an atom made up of neutrons and protons and which constitutes essentially all of the atom's mass.

Nucleus of a Cell. A complex, usually spherical, portion within an organic cell which contains the cell's hereditary material (DNA).

Olbers's Paradox. The paradox resulting from the fact that the light radiating from the billions of stars in the cosmos do not result in a bright night.

Omega (Ω). A factor which describes the density and rate of expansion of the universe. An omega less than one means that the universe is open and will expand forever. An omega more than one means that the universe is closed and will ultimately collapse on itself. Omega equal to one means that the universe is at critical density, it is flat and is slowing in its rate of expansion but will never quite reach zero.

Order. A taxonomic category of animals and plants ranking above the family and below the class.

Organic. Of, relating to, or derived from living organisms. In chemistry, compounds with the element carbon in them.

Organism. A plant or an animal.

Out-of-Body Experience. An event where the spirit leaves the physical body and the consciousness of the individual remains with the spirit.

Particle. A fundamental unit of matter or energy. In quantum mechanics particles, under certain conditions, can exhibit wave-like characteristics.

Photon. A quantum of electromagnetic force with zero rest mass, no charge and an indefinitely long lifetime. It can, therefore, travel infinitely far, as from a distant star.

Photosynthesis. The process whereby chlorophyll containing cells in green plants convert sunlight into chemical energy—as for example, carbohydrates from carbon dioxide and water and then releasing oxygen.

Phylum. A major taxonomic division in the animal and plant world, next above a class in size.

Physics. The science of matter and energy and of the interaction between them.

Plan of Salvation. A plan established by God before this world existed for the progression of premortal souls by obtaining physical bodies and being tested on earth.

Planck's Constant. A fundamental constant of quantum mechanics related to the uncertainty in the position of a particle times the uncertainty of its velocity times its mass.

Planck Time and Planck Epoch. An extremely small time period (10^{-43} seconds) at which the universe existed only as spacetime foam. After Planck time, relativity and the laws of physics applied.

Power. The time rate of doing work.

Prayer. The process by which an individual speaks to God and by which the individual may also receive revelatory answers.

Premortal Life. The belief that living beings existed as conscious individual entities before this life.

Priesthood. An ordained ecclesiastic office in the Mormon Church with the authority to act in the name of God.

Probabilistic Analysis. The use of particular mathematical equations and techniques to quantify the likelihood that certain events will occur.

Probability. A number expressing the likelihood that something will happen.

Procaryote. A cellular organism, such as bacterium or blue-green alga, with a nucleus that has no limiting membrane.

Prophet. One who speaks by revelation or acts as an interpreter for expressing the will of God, as Moses and Joseph Smith did and as living prophets do today.

Protein. Nitrogen containing molecules found in all living matter and required for growth and repair of animal tissue.

Proton. A massive particle in the baryon family with a positive electrical charge. It is 1,836 times more massive than an electron. Its mass is 938.3 MeV.

Pulsar. A rotating neutron star which gives out radio-waves in a pulsating fashion as it rotates.

Quantum. An indivisible unit of energy or matter.

Quantum Mechanics. The cumulative science which developed from quantum theory and which includes the mathematics of subatomic systems. It incorporates wave-particle duality and the uncertainty principle.

Quark. A fundamental particle from which all hadrons are made. Has an electrical charge somewhat less than an electron. Comes in a variety of types known as flavors.

Quintessence. Similar to Einstein's Cosmological Constant except that it has different values with time. In theory it acts as an anti-gravity force and accounts for the apparent observed acceleration of the universe expansion in more recent epochs of time.

Radiation. Emission and propagation of waves or particles.

Radioactivity. Emission of particles and energy from unstable elements as they decay or from nuclear reactions.

Radioactive Dating. A method of determining the age of a substance by measuring the half-life of a known radioactive material attached to the substance.

Radiocarbon Dating. A method for dating fossils based on the absorption of all living things of Carbon 14 from the atmosphere. By measuring the amount of C^{14} left in the bones of a fossil, for example, comparing it with the known residual atmospheric C^{14}, and knowing the half-life of C^{14} to be 5,568 years, the age of the bone can be determined.

Radioactive Decay. A decrease in the number of radioactive atoms in a substance as the result of spontaneous nuclear disintegration.

Radio Waves. Electromagnetic radiation with the longest wavelengths.

Red Giant. A large star that is relatively cool and is therefore redder in color than other hotter burning stars.

Reincarnation. The belief, particularly in some Eastern religions, that living beings—humans, animals, plant life—continually incarnate as different life forms.

Relativity, Special. The laws of physics developed by Einstein in 1905 which established the constancy of the speed of light and the equivalence of mass and energy. It also established the interrelationship of space and time.

Relativity, General. The laws of physics developed by Einstein in 1915 which extended the special laws to include the laws of gravity and the equivalence of gravity and inertial forces.

Resonance. An enhanced state of a system to respond to a particular set of stimuli, as in a limited range of thermal energy, where a reaction can take place.

Resurrection. The process whereby the spirit of a deceased individual is reunited with a physical body.

Revelation. A manifestation to an individual of divine will or truth.

RNA. Ribonucleic acid which functions in a cell by assisting the DNA to copy a gene which later is used to duplicate the complete DNA and thus perpetuate particular cells and life.

Second Law of Thermodynamics. The so-called heat-death law which dictates that the Universe and all that is in it must ultimately reach a state of zero energy—a state of infinite disorder. More precisely it states that in any real process the Entropy must always increase.

Singularity. A point at which the normal laws of physics do not apply, presumed to be the state of the universe before time and the universe existed as we now know them.

Solar System. The sun, nine planets and all other asteroids and celestial bodies which orbit the sun.

Spacetime. The four dimensional realm of three spatial dimensions and one time dimension within which our universe operates. The interrelationships of the various dimensions are defined by General Relativity.

Species. A fundamental taxonomic category, ranking after a genus and consisting of living organisms capable of inbreeding.

Spirit. The primary being and consciousness of the individual which survives physical death. A body of refined matter which separates from the physical body at death.

Star. A celestial body with sufficient mass to cause thermonuclear fusion reactions in its core—or did so some time in the past.

Strong Nuclear Force. A fundamental force of nature which binds quarks, neutrons and protons together in the nucleus of an atom.

Supernova. An exploding star.

Superstring Theory. A concept that all particles are made up of vibrating minute particles of space, originally in a multi-dimensional (10 or more) environment.

Symmetry. A mathematical group with a common property that unites its members in a symmetrical way. Also the quantity of a fundamental particle, such as the particle spin, which remains unchanged during a transformation of the particle.

Taxonomy. The process of classifying living organisms by category.

Teleportation. A quantum characteristic where the properties of one particle can be instantly transmitted to another over immense distances.

Thermodynamics. The physics of the interrelationships between heat and other energy forms.

Thermonuclear. The fusion of atoms at the extremely high temperatures found in stars with the release of enormous quantities of energy.

Tunnel as Seen in Some NDEs. A dark area which seems to surround the individual as he or she passes through it on the way to a bright light.

Uncertainty Principle. A part of quantum mechanics whereby the position and momentum of a particle cannot both be known accurately.

Universe. All existing things including the earth, the heavens, stars, and galaxies considered as a whole.

Uranium. A heavy metallic element. Uranium 238 is its most abundant isotope found in nature. U^{238} is not fissionable but when bombarded with neutrons will convert to Plutonium 239 which is fissionable. Uranium 235 is also found in nature in minor quantities and is fissionable.

Vendian Period. A geologic time period of about 20 million years immediately prior to the Cambrian period.

Weak Nuclear Force. A fundamental force of nature which is responsible for radioactive decay. It is weaker than the electromagnetic force.

Wave. A function expressed mathematically in quantum mechanics to describe a quantum system. In a quantum system mass and energy may be exhibited as a wave or as a particle depending upon the circumstances.

Work. Force multiplied by the distance moved in the direction of the force.

Worm Hole. An extremely speculative theory that two black holes could be connected to provide a path between different universes.

X-Ray. Electromagnetic radiation with short wavelength—between gamma rays and ultraviolet light.

Selected Bibliography
Near-Death Literature

Appleby, L., "Near-death experience: Analogous to other stress induced psychological phenomena." *British Medical Journal,* 298, 1989.

Arnette, J. Kenneth, "On the Mind/Body Problem: The Theory of Essence." *Journal of Near-Death Studies,* 11, 1992, pp. 5-18.

Arnette, J. Kenneth, "The Theory of Essence, II: An Electromagnetic-Quantum Mechanical Model of Interactionism." *Journal of Near-Death Studies,* 14, 1995.

Atwater, P. M. H., *Beyond the Light—What Isn't Being Said About Near-Death Experience.* New Jersey: A Birch Lane Press Book, 1994.

Atwater, P. M. H., *Coming Back to Life—The After-Effects of the Near-Death Experience.* New York, Toronto: Ballantine Books, 1988.

Atwater, P.M.H., "Is There a Hell? Surprising Observations About the Near-Death Experience." *Journal of Near-Death Studies,* 10, 1992.

Becker, C.B., "The failure of Saganomics: Why birth models cannot explain near-death phenomena." *Anabiosis,* 2, 1982.

Blacher, R.S., "To sleep, perchance to dream . . ." JAMA, 242,1979.

Blackmore, S., *Dying to live: Science and near-death experience.* London, England: Grafton, 1993.

Brown, J.H. *Heavenly answers for earthly challenges.* Pasadena, CA: Jemstar Press, 1997.

Carr, D.B., "Pathophysiology of stress-induced limbic lobe dysfunction: A hypothesis for near-death experiences." *Anabiosis,* 2,1982.

Cook, R.B., "Guest editorial: A theory of death." *Journal of Near-Death Studies,* 8, 1989.

Counts, D.A., "Near-death and out-of-body experiences in a Melanesian society." *Anabiosis,* 3, 1983.

Crowther, Duane S., *Life Everlasting—A Definitive Study of Life After Death.* Bountiful, Utah: Horizon Publishers & Distributors, Inc., 1997.

Durham, Elane, *I Stand All Amazed—Love and Healing from Higher Realms.* Orem, Utah: Granite Publishing, 1998.

Ehrenwald, J., *The ESP experience.* New York, NY: Basic Books, 1978.

Gabbard, G.O. and Tremlow, S.W., "An overview of altered mind\body perception." *Bulletin of the Menninger Clinic,* 50, 1986.

Ganaway, George K., *Historical vs. Narrative Truth: Clarifying the Role of Exogenous Trauma in the Etiology of MPD and its Variants.* December, 1989, p. 209; for Reprints write George K. Ganaway, M.D., Program Director, Ridgeview Center for Dissociative Disorders, Ridgeview Institute, 3995 South Cobb Drive, Smyrna, Georgia 30080.

Gibbs, J.C. , "Moody's versus Siegel's interpretation of the near-death experience: An evaluation based on recent research." *Anabiosis,* 5, 1987.

Gibson, Arvin S., *Echoes From Eternity.* Bountiful, Utah: Horizon Publishers and Distributors, Inc., 1993.

Gibson, Arvin S., *Glimpses of Eternity.* Bountiful, Utah: Horizon Publishers and Distributors, Inc., 1992.

Gibson, Arvin S. *In Search of Angels.* Bountiful, Utah: Horizon Publishers and Distributors, Inc., 1990.

Gibson, Arvin S., *Journeys Beyond Life—True Accounts of Next-world Experiences.* Bountiful, Utah: Horizon Publishers & Distributors, Inc., 1994.

Grey, M. *Return from death.* London, England: Arkana, 1987.

Grof, S. and Halifax, J., *The human encounter with death.* New York, NY: Dutton, 1977.

Grosso, M., "Toward an explanation of near-death phenomena.." *Anabiosis,* 1, 1981.

Heinerman J. *Spirit world manifestations.* Salt Lake City, UT: Magazine Printing and Publishing, 1978.

Jansen, K.L.R., "Neuroscience and the near-death experience: Roles for the NMDA-PCP receptor, the sigma receptor and the endopsychosins." *Medical Hypotheses,* 31,1990.

Jansen, K.L.R., " Response to commentaries on 'The ketamine model of the near-death experience.'" *Journal of Near-Death Studies,* 16, 1997.

Jansen, K.L.R., "The Ketamine Model of the Near-Death Experience: A Central Role for the N-Methyl-D-Aspartate Receptor." *Journal of Near-Death Studies,* 16, 1997 Journal of the American Society for Psychical Research, 72, 1978.

Krishnan, V., "Near-death experiences: Reassessment urged." *Parapsychology Review,* 12, 1981.

Kubler-Ross, Elisabeth, *On Life After Dying.* Berkeley, California: Celestial Arts, 1982, pp. 9-10.

Lowental, U., "Dying, regression, and the death instinct." *Psychoanalytic Review,* 68, 1981.

Lundahl, Craig R. & Widdison, Harold A., *The Eternal Journey—How Near-Death Experiences Illuminate Our Earthly Lives.* New York: Warner Books, Inc., 1997.

Lundahl, Craig and Widdison, Harold, "The Mormon explanation of near-death experiences." *Journal of Near-Death Studies,* 3, 1983.

Ludwig, Arnold M., *Principles of Clinical Psychiatry.* The Free Press, Macmillan, Inc., N.Y., 1986.

McHarg, J.F., "Review of At the Hour of Death," by K. Oasis and E. Haraldsson. *Journal of the Society for Psychical Research,* 49, 1978.

Menz, R.L., "The denial of death and the out-of-body experience." *Journal of Religion and Health,* 23, 1984.

Moody, Raymond A. Jr., *Coming Back—A Psychiatrist Explores Past-Life Journeys.* N.Y., London: Bantam Books, 1991.

Moody, R.. and Perry, P. *The light beyond.* New York, NY: Bantam Books, 1988.

Moody, Raymond A., Jr., *Life After Life.* New York, N.Y.: Bantam Books, 1988.

Morse, Melvin with Perry, Paul, *Closer to the Light.* New York, N.Y.: Villard Books, 1990.

Morse, M.L., Venecia, D., Jr., and Milstein, J., "Near-death experiences: A neurophysiological explanatory model." *Journal of Near-Death Studies,* 8, 1989.

Noyes, R. and Kletti, R., "Depersonalization in the face of life-threatening danger: A description." *Psychiatry,* 39, 1976.

Orne, Martin T.; Whitehouse, Wayne G.; Dinges, David F.; Orne, Emily Carota. "Reconstructing Memory through Hypnosis." *University of Pennsylvania School of Medicine; from Hypnosis and Memory,* Edited by Pettinati, Helen M., New York, N.Y.: The Guilford Press, 1988.

Osis, K. and Haraldsson, E., *At the hour of death.* New York, NY: Avon, 1977.

Palmer, J., "Correspondence: Deathbed apparitions and the survival hypothesis." *Journal of the American Society for Psychical Research,* 72, 1978.

Quimby, S.L., "The near-death experience as an event in consciousness." *Journal of Humanistic Psychology,* 29, 1989.

Rawlings, Maurice, *Beyond Death's Door.* New York, Toronto, London, Sydney, Auckland: Bantam Books, 1979.

Ring, Kenneth, *Heading Toward Omega.* New York, N.Y.: William Morrow, Inc., 1984-1985.

Ring, Kenneth, *Life at death: A scientific investigation of the near-death experience.* New York, NY: Coward, McCann and Geoghegan, 1980.

Ring, Kenneth, *Lessons from the Light—What We Can Learn from the Near-Death Experience.* New York, N.Y.: Plenum Publishing, 1998.

Ring, Kenneth, *The Omega Project,* New York: Morrow, 1992.

Ring, Kenneth and Cooper, S. "Near-death and out-of-body experiences in the blind: a study of apparent eyeless vision." *Journal of Near-Death Studies,* 16, 1997.

Ring, K. and Cooper, S., *Mindsight: Near-death and out-of-body experiences in the blind.* Palo Alto, California: William James Center for Consciousness Studies, Institute of Transpersonal Psychology, 1999.

Ritchie, George, Jr. *My life after dying: Becoming alive to universal love.* Norfolk, VA: Hampton Roads Publishing Company.

Ritchie, George G. with Sherrill, Elizabeth, *Return from Tomorrow.* Old Tappan, New Jersey: Spire Books, Fleming H. Revell Co., 1978.

Rodin. E.A., "The reality of death experiences: a personal perspective." *Journal of Nervous and Mental Disease,* 168, 1980.

Sabom, Michael. *Light & Death—One Doctor's Fascinating Account of Near-Death Experiences.* Grand Rapids, Michigan: Zondervan Publishing House, 1998.

Sabom, M.B. and Kreutziger, S.A., "Physicians evaluate the near-death experience." *Theta,* 6, 1978.

Sabom, Michael, *Recollections of Death.* New York: Harper & Row, 1982.

Saavedra-Aguilar, J.C. and Gomez-Jeria, J.S., "A neurobiological model for near-death experiences." *Journal of Near-Death Studies,* 7, 1989.

Saavedra-Aguilar, J.C. and Gomez-Jeria, J.S., "Response to commentaries on 'A neurobiological model for near-death experiences.'" *Journal of Near-Death Studies,* 7, 1989.

Schnaper, N., "Comments germane to the paper entitled 'the reality of death experiences' by Ernst Rodin." *The Journal of Nervous and Mental Disease,* 168, 1980.

Serdahely, W.J., "Similarities between near-death experiences and multiple personality disorder." *Journal of Near-Death Studies,* 11, 1992.

Sharp, Kimberly Clark, *After the Light—What I Discovered on the Other Side of Life That Can Change Your World.* New York: William Morrow and Company, Inc., 1995.

Siegel, R.K., "The psychology of life after death." *American Psychologist,* 35, 1980.

Spanos, Nicholas P.; Menary, Evelyn; Gabora, Natalie J.; DuBreuil, Susan C.; and Dewhirst, Bridget; "Secondary Identity Enactments During Hypnotic Past-Life Regression: A Sociocognitive Perspective." *Journal of Personality and Social Psychology,* 1991, Vol. 61, No. 2.

Stevenson, Ian, M.D., *Twenty Cases Suggestive of Reincarnation.* Charlottesville: University of Virginia Press, 1974 (Reprinted 1978).

Sutherland, Cherie, *Reborn in the Light—Life After Near-Death Experiences.* Australia, New Zealand: Bantam Books, 1995. (First published as *Transformed By the Light.* Australia, New Zealand: Bantam Books, 1992.)

Sutherland, Cherie, *Within the Light.* Australia, New Zealand: Bantam Books, 1993.

Swedenborg, Emanuel, *A Scientist Explores Spirit.* West Chester, Pennsylvania: Chrysalis Books, 1997.

Swedenborg, Emanuel, *Heaven & Hell—The reason we are united in spirit to both Heaven and Hell is to keep us in freedom.* West Chester, Pennsylvania: Swedenborg Foundation, Inc.

Thomas, L., "A meliorist view of disease and dying." *Journal of Medical Philosophy,* 1, 1976.

Tien, S.S., " Thanatoperience." *Journal of Near-Death Studies,* 7, 1988.

Top, Brent L. And Wendy C., *Beyond Death's Door—Understanding Near-Death Experiences in Light of the Restored Gospel.* Salt Lake City, Utah: Bookcraft, 1993.

Valarino, Evelyn Elsaesser, *On the Other Side of Life—Exploring the Phenomenon of the Near-Death Experience.* New York, London: Insight Books, 1984.

Wade, Jenny, "Physically transcendent awareness: a comparison of the phenomenology of consciousness before birth and after death." *Journal of Near-Death Studies,* 7, 1998.

Wallace, R. and Taylor, C. *The Burning Within.* Carson City, NV: Gold Leaf Press, 1994.

Wilson, Ian, *The After Death Experience—The Physical of the Non-Physical.* New York: William Morrow and Company, Inc., 1987.

Woodhouse, M.B., " Five arguments regarding the objectivity of NDEs." *Anabiosis,* 3, 1983.

Zaleski, Carol, *Otherworld Journeys—Accounts of Near-Death Experience in Medieval and Modern Times.* New York, Oxford, Toronto: Oxford University Press, 1987.

Zilbergeld, B., "Hypnosis Questions and Answers," *The Validity of Memories Retrieved in Hypnosis.* New York, N.Y.: W. W. Norton and Co., 1986.

Scientific Literature

Behe, Michael J., *Darwin's Black Box—The Biochemical Challenge to Evolution*. New York, London, Toronto, Sydney: The Free Press, 1996.

Bernstein, Max, Sandford, Scott, and Allamandola, Louis, "Life's Far-Flung Materials," *Scientific American,* July, 1999.

Bohm, David, *Quantum Theory.* Mineola, N.Y.: Dover Publications, 1989.

Bouwmeester, D., Pan, J-W, Mattle, K., Eibl, M., Weinfurter, H. and Zeilinger, A. "Experimental quantum teleportation." *Nature,* 390, 1997.

Carter, Brandon, "Large Number Coincidences and the Anthropic Principle in Cosmology." In M.S. Longair, ed., *Confrontation of Cosmological Theories with Observational Data.* Dordrecht: D. Reidel, 1974.

Close, Frank, "The quark structure of matter," *The New Physics.* Cambridge, Melbourne, Cambridge University Press, 1989.

Considine, Douglas, Editor, *Van Nostrand's Scientific Encyclopedia, Fifth Edition.* New York, London, Toronto, Melbourne: Van Nostrand Reinhold Company, 1976.

Davies, Paul, *God & The New Physics.* New York, London, Tokyo, Sydney, Toronto: Touchstone, 1984.

Davies, Paul, *The Fifth Miracle—The Search for the Origin and the Meaning of Life.* New York, N.Y.: Simon & Schuster, 1999.

Du Noüy, Lecomte, *Human Destiny.* New York, London, Toronto: Longmans, Green and Co., 1947.

Ferris, Timothy, *The Whole Shebang—A State of the Universe Report.* New York, N.Y.: Simon and Schuster, 1997.

Feynman, R.P. , *Six Not-So-Easy Pieces.* New York, Reading, Mass., Menlo Park, CA., Ontario, Harlow, England, Amsterdam, Sydney, Bonn Paris, Milan: Addison Wesley, 1997.

Gibson, Everett K., Jr., McKay, David S., Thomas-Keptra, Kathie, and Romanek, Christopher, "The Case for Relic Life on Mars," *Scientific American,* December, 1997.

Gribbin, John, *In the Beginning—The Birth of the Living Universe.* Boston, New York, Toronto, London: Little Brown & Co., 1993.

Guth, Alan and Steinhardt, Paul. "The inflationary universe," *The New Physics.* Cambridge CB2 1RP, United Kingdom, Cambridge University Press 1989.

Hogan, Craig J., "Primordial Deuterium and the Big Bang," *Scientific American,* December 1996.

Hogan, Craig J., Kirshner, Robert P., Suntzeff, Nicholas B., "Surveying Space-time with Supernovae," *Scientific American,* January 1999.

Hawking, Stephen W., *A Brief History of Time—From the Big Bang to Black Holes.* New York, London, Toronto, Sydney: Bantam Books, 1988.

Johnson, George, *Fire in the Mind—Science, Faith, and the Search for Order.* New York, N.Y.: Vintage Books, 1996.

Johnson, Hollis R., "Atoms, Stars, and Us," *Of Heaven and Earth—Reconciling Scientific Thought with LDS Theology,* Clark, David L., Editor. Salt Lake City, Utah: Deseret Book Co., 1998.

Kraus, Lawrence M., "Cosmological Antigravity," *Scientific American,* January 1999.

Lederman, Leon, with Teresi, Dick, *The God Particle—If the Universe is the Answer, What is the Question?* New York, N.Y.:Bantam Doubleday Dell Publishing Group, 1993.

Leslie, John, *Universes.* London and New York: Routledge, 1996.

Longair, Malcolm, "The New Astrophysics," *The New Physics.* Cambridge, Melbourne, Cambridge University Press, 1989.

Matthews, R. (April 11, 1998). "To infinity and beyond." *New Scientist,* 158. (2129) 27-30.

Mayr, Ernst, *This is Biology—The Science of the Living World.* Cambridge, Massachusetts, London: The Belknap Press of Harvard University Press, 1997.

Musser, George, "Glow in the Dark—Science and the Citizens," *Scientific American,* March 1998.

Musser, George, "The Flip Side of the Universe—Science and the Citizens," *Scientific American,* September 1998.

Nash, J. Madeleine, "When Life Exploded," *Time,* December 4, 1995.

Overman, Dean L., *A Case Against Accident and Self-organization.* New York, Oxford: Rowman & Littlefield, 1997.

Rees, Martin, *Before the Beginning—Our Universe and Others.* Reading, Massachusetts, Helix Books, 1997.

Rozanov, Y.A. *Probability Theory: A Concise Course.* New York: Dover Publications, Inc., 1969.

Sagan, Carl, *Broca's Brain.* New York, N.Y.: Random House, 1979.

Schroeder, Gerald L., *Genesis and the Big Bang—The Discovery of Harmony Between Modern Science and the Bible.* New York, London, Toronto: Bantam Books, 1990.

Schroeder, Gerald L., *The Science of God—The Convergence of Scientific and Biblical Wisdom.* New York: Broadway Books, 1998.

Silver, Brian L., *The Ascent of Science.* Oxford, New York:: Oxford University Press, 1998.

Sudbery, T. "The fastest way from A to B." *Nature,* 390, 1997.

Thorne, Kip S., *Black Holes and Time Warps—Einstein's Outrageous Legacy.* New York, London: W.W. Norton & Co., 1994.

Tipler, Frank J. *The Physics of Immortality.* New York, London, Toronto, Sydney, Auckland: Anchor Books-Doubleday, 1994.

Latter-day Saint Scriptures

The Book of Mormon—Another Testament of Jesus Christ. Translated by Joseph Smith, Junior. Published by The Church of Jesus Christ of Latter-day Saints, Salt Lake City, Utah, 1989.

The Doctrine and Covenants of The Church of Jesus Christ of Latter-day Saints. Published by The Church of Jesus Christ of Latter-day Saints, Salt Lake City, Utah, 1989.

The Holy Bible. Authorized King James Version. Published by The Church of Jesus Christ of Latter-day Saints, Salt Lake City, Utah, 1979.

The Pearl of Great Price. Published by The Church of Jesus Christ of Latter-day Saints, Salt Lake City, Utah, 1989.

Latter-day Saint and Other Religious Historical and Doctrinal Books

Allen, Joseph, L. *Exploring the Lands of the Book of Mormon,* Orem, Utah: S. A. Publishers, Inc., 1989.

Barrett, Ivan J., *Joseph Smith and the Restoration.* Provo, Utah: Brigham Young University Press, 1973.

Bawer, Bruce. *Stealing Jesus—How Fundamentalism Betrays Christianity.* New York: Crown Publishers, 1997.

Bloom, Harold, *The American Religion—The Emergence of the Post-Christian Nation.* New York, London, Toronto, Sydney, Tokyo, Singapore, Simon & Schuster, 1993.

Cook, Lyndon W., Editor. *David Whitmer Interviews—A Restoration Witness,* Orem, Utah: Grandin Book Co., 1991.

Crowther, Duane S., *Life Everlasting—A Definitive Study of Life After Death.* Bountiful, Utah: Horizon Publishers & Distributors, Inc., 1997.

Easterbrook, Gregg, *Beside Still Waters—Searching for Meaning in an Age of Doubt.* New York, N.Y.: William Morrow and Co., 1998.

Grant, Richard G. *Understanding These Other Christians—An LDS Introduction to Evangelical Christianity.* Sandy, Utah: Distr. By Sounds of Zion, Inc., 1998.

Hymns of the Church of Jesus Christ of Latter-day Saints. Salt Lake City, Utah: The Church of Jesus Christ of Latter-day Saints, 1985.

Johnson, Hollis R., "Atoms, Stars, and Us," *Of Heaven and Earth—Reconciling Scientific Thought with LDS Theology,* Clark, David L., Editor. Salt Lake City, Utah: Deseret Book Co., 1998.

Journal of Discourses. The Church of Jesus Christ of Latter-day Saints.

Lewis, C.S., *The Four Loves.* San Diego, New York, London: A Harvest Book, Harcourt Brace & Company, 1988.

Ludlow, Daniel H., Editor, *Encyclopedia of Mormonism.* Vols. 1-4, New York: Macmillan Publishing Company, 1992.

Madsen, Truman G., *Eternal Man.* Salt Lake City, Utah: Deseret Book Company, 1966.

Maxwell, Neal A., *All These Things Shall Give Thee Experience.* Salt Lake City, Utah: Deseret Book Company, 1979, p. 11.

Mosser, Carl and Owen, Paul. "Mormon Scholarship, Apologetics, and Evangelical Neglect: Losing the Battle and Not Knowing It?" *Trinity Journal,* 2065 Half Day Road, Deerfield, Illinois: TRINJ 19NS, 1998, pp.179-205.

Reynolds, Noel B. (Edited by), *Book of Mormon Authorship Revisited—The Evidence for Ancient Origins.* Provo, Utah: Foundation for Ancient Research and Mormon Studies, 1997.

Schroeder, Gerald L., *Genesis and the Big Bang—The Discovery of Harmony Between Modern Science and the Bible.* New York, London, Toronto: Bantam Books, 1990.

Schroeder, Gerald L., *The Science of God—The Convergence of Scientific and Biblical Wisdom.* New York: Broadway Books, 1998.

Sorenson, John L. *An Ancient American Setting for the Book of Mormon,* Salt Lake City, Utah: Deseret Book Co., 1985, 1996.

Welch, John W., "Chiasmus in the Book of Mormon," *Book of Mormon Authorship—New Light on Ancient Origins.* Reynolds, Noel B., Editor. Provo, Utah: Foundation for Ancient Research and Mormon Studies, 1982.

Wordsworth, William, *Ode, Intimations of Immortality from Recollections of Early Childhood.* 1807.

Index